STIR IT UP

Change
the way
the world
works.

Ms. Foundation for Women

THE MS. FOUNDATION FOR WOMEN

For thirty years, the Ms. Foundation for Women has been a leading advocate for women and girls, naming the issues in their lives, investing in their strengths, and helping them take crucial leadership roles in their lives and communities. Founded in 1972 by Gloria Steinem, Marlo Thomas, Letty Cottin Pogrebin, and Patricia Carbine, the Ms. Foundation was the first national, multi-issue women's fund.

Marie C. Wilson has led the foundation as our president since 1985. Under her direction, the Ms. Foundation has created groundbreaking national programs and granted millions of dollars to grassroots organizations working to move women toward economic self-sufficiency, to safeguard reproductive rights, and to support health and safety for women and girls. Executive Director Sara K. Gould joined the Ms. Foundation in 1986 and propelled the Foundation into the public eye as the recognized national leader in the field of women's microenterprise development.

The Ms. Foundation's hallmark is our support of the right idea at the right time, whether it is seen as possible or popular. Our work is guided by our vision of a just and safe world where power and possibility are not limited by gender, race, class, or sexual orientation. We believe that equity and inclusion are the cornerstones of a true democracy in which the worth and dignity of every person is valued. Our many accomplishments include:

- Creating the award-winning Take Our Daughters To Work® Day, a nationwide public education campaign that seventy-one million people have participated in since 1993. Through its new program, Take Our Daughters And Sons To Work℠ Day, the Ms. Foundation is addressing the competing challenges of work and family life.

- Receiving a Presidential Award for Excellence in Microenterprise Development for our long-standing commitment to improving economic prospects for low-income women, their families, and their communities.
- Conducting the national Raise the Floor public education campaign promoting minimum wage, child care, health-care, and tax policies that would ensure that low-income families in this country can meet their basic needs.
- Being one of the first national organizations to acknowledge that the real battleground for reproductive rights is at the state level, and supporting groups that combat the hundreds of antichoice measures introduced every year in state legislatures.
- Becoming one of the first national funders to address violence against women by funding shelters and crisis hotlines, and helping to create a movement to end all violence.
- Creating the Women and AIDS Fund, the only project in the country that identifies and supports community-based organizations run by and for women living with HIV/AIDS.

The Ms. Foundation's work is guided by our mission to support the efforts of women and girls to govern their own lives and to influence the world around them. We believe that economic security is key to women's choices and their ability to make their voices heard. Women's wages and working conditions affect not only their family's livelihood but also their access to health care and quality child care and their ability to escape abusive relationships. Since our inception, therefore, the Ms. Foundation has supported women's efforts to organize for better wages, benefits, and improved working conditions and to mobilize their collective power to influence government policy.

Women can affect crucial issues by taking charge and organizing for change. The Ms. Foundation grantees profiled in this book offer lessons and insights not only for other groups mobilizing low-income women but for any effort aimed at creating lasting social change.

Take Our Daughters To Work® and Take Our Daughters And Sons To Work℠ are registered marks of the Ms. Foundation.

STIR IT UP

Lessons in Community Organizing and Advocacy

Rinku Sen

JOSSEY-BASS
A Wiley Imprint
www.josseybass.com

Published by Jossey-Bass
A Wiley Imprint
989 Market Street, San Francisco, CA 94103-1741   www.josseybass.com

Jossey-Bass books and products are available through most bookstores. To contact Jossey-Bass
directly call our Customer Care Department within the U.S. at 800-956-7739, outside the U.S.
at 317-572-3993 or fax 317-572-4002.

Jossey-Bass also publishes its books in a variety of electronic formats. Some content that appears
in print may not be available in electronic books.

Take Our Daughters To Work® and Take Our Daughters And Sons To Work℠ are registered marks
of the Ms. Foundation.

Library of Congress Cataloging-in-Publication Data
Sen, Rinku.
  Stir it up : lessons in community organizing and advocacy / Rinku
Sen.—1st ed.
      p. cm.—(Chardon Press series)
Includes bibliographical references (p.   ) and index.
  ISBN 0-7879-6533-2 (alk. paper)
    1. Community organization—United States. 2. Social action—United
States. 3. Community development--United States. 4. Community
power—United States. I. Title. II. Series.
  HN90.C6S46 2003
  361.8'0973—dc21   2003001221

Printed in the United States of America
FIRST EDITION
PB Printing 10 9 8 7 6 5

THE CHARDON PRESS SERIES

Fundamental social change happens when people come together to organize, advo-cate, and create solutions to injustice. Chardon Press recognizes that communi-ties working for social justice need tools to create and sustain healthy organizations. In an effort to support these organizations, Chardon Press produces materials on fundraising, community organizing, and organizational development. These resources are specifically designed to meet the needs of grassroots nonprofits—organizations that face the unique challenge of promoting change with limited staff, funding, and other resources. We at Chardon Press have adapted traditional techniques to the cir-cumstances of grassroots nonprofits. Chardon Press and Jossey-Bass hope these works help people committed to social justice to build mission-driven organizations that are strong, financially secure, and effective.

Kim Klein, Series Editor

CONTENTS

EXERCISES AND EXHIBITS

Exercises

Exhibits

PREFACE

Like some young people of the mid-1980s, I experienced organizing for the first time on my college campus. In a year that included efforts to fight race discrimination, prevent violence against women, win the university's divestment from South Africa, take a stand against nuclear weapons, and expand the rights of gay and lesbian students, I got a firsthand look at a process that has obsessed me since. I watched, then participated, as people got together, analyzed their conditions, confronted an institution, and, win or lose, came back to fight another day. I didn't fall immediately—friends had to push me to move from observer to activist—but I became increasingly hooked after the first four-hour strategy meeting, the first action, the first victory. Nearly two years later, while I was working for the United States Student Association training students in the principles of community organizing, I met two African American women from a Tennessee organization called Just Organized Neighborhoods Area Headquarters who described their struggle to win running water and electricity for their community. That same weekend, I learned it was possible to make a living in organizing. I had found my sense of purpose.

What, after all, could be more important than making sure women could be safe and a community could have electricity? While there are other ways to ensure those kinds of gains, organizing appealed to me as much for the process of building a group as for the product of winning concrete changes. I remember wanting to laugh all the time, even when I was so mad I could spit, feeling energetic even on little sleep, and enjoying the freedom of preoccupation with something other than my postadolescent self. In groups I found more pleasure than frustration, and more humor than bitterness. In collective power and sharp politics, I found both identity and solution.

After graduation, I went to work at the Center for Third World Organizing (CTWO), a national network and training center for organizers of color based in Oakland, California. I stayed there twelve years, two as a staff person and ten as co-director. In that time, I worked on dozens of grassroots issue campaigns across the country, ranging from welfare rights to affordable housing, from health care to police brutality. I did all the jobs required of organizers in the United States today: recruiting members, training leaders and organizing staff, planning campaigns, conducting actions, raising money, and more. I was extremely fortunate to find a place in an organization owned and operated by economically progressive people of color and open to feminist ideas and leadership. One benefit of working in such an organization was that I learned not just the basic principles of organizing but also the many ways in which people adapt and add to those principles to suit their own situations. I got to be at the center of critical debates about organizing practice, and I met thousands of compassionate and courageous activists.

Origins and Goals

The idea for this book was generated in a conversation with the Ms. Foundation for Women, which asked me to write a best-practices manual about the fourteen economic justice grantees it funded from 1997 to 2001 under its New Voices, Proactive Strategies Initiative. Throughout its thirty-year history, the Ms. Foundation has seeded and assisted the efforts of hundreds of grassroots, local, regional, and national organizations to mobilize community residents and workers to create progressive change in economic and workplace policies. In 1995, several of these grantees were part of the Foundation's delegation to the Fourth World Conference on Women in Beijing. After the delegation returned home, the Foundation worked with these organizations to create the New Voices, Proactive Strategies Initiative in order to bring the voices of low-income women workers to bear on policies that affect their lives, their families, and their communities. The initiative aimed at shifting public and corporate policy away from a narrow "private responsibility" framework toward recognition of the need for the public and private sectors to play stronger roles in lifting women and families out of poverty. Grants supported grassroots and national organizing and coalition-building activities, such as living-wage campaigns, community/labor coalitions, regional economic networks, and efforts to organize workers in specific sectors and situations such as child care, new immigrants, and contingent workers.

The book's core is occupied by these grantees, all of which are working to reframe economic debates, win new policies, and build power for disenfranchised communities, particularly for people of color, immigrants, and women. From March 2000 to the end of 2001, I visited each organization, rifled through their documents, interviewed their staffs, and, to the extent possible, interviewed their constituents. I also reviewed the literature about organizing for social and economic justice, both contemporary and historic. The Ms. Foundation grantees provide the bulk of the book's illustrations, and the Profiles section provides a general overview of their unique and often stunning accomplishments. To the extent that I use other examples in the book, they come from organizations with which I became familiar through my past work as co-director of CTWO and my current work on the staff of the Applied Research Center. Unless otherwise credited, the quotes in the book were gathered by me through in-person or telephone interviews between March 2000 and August 2002.

The Ms. Foundation fortuitously asked me to write this book at a point in my career when I was ready to share the best practices I had seen and experienced in fifteen years in the field. History has taught me that long-lasting social change is made by large-scale movements led by the people most affected by particular systems and that movements emerge from organizations that work to build something larger than themselves. The lessons the book highlights are largely about how to build and activate a constituency, then change the dynamic of an issue by working in ways that lay the groundwork for future social movements. My experience reflects that of the Ms. Foundation: many of these lessons are drawn by women living and working in poor communities, but their experience is rarely featured in social-change literature.

The book is organized to provide an overview of organizing and then to explore specific aspects of current practice. The tools presented here can help communities transform the institutions and ideas that shape our lives. I make two essential arguments. First, I argue that today's social, political, and economic context, characterized by global capitalism, a resurgent conservative movement, and the continued role of racism and sexism in world society, requires a deeper strategic capacity than most organizations have today. Second, I argue that although organizing among the people suffering from these systems is more important than ever, the range of political skills required of us goes far beyond recruiting members and planning creative actions. Minimally, effective peoples' organizations need to have not just the people but also a system for internal leadership development and consciousness raising, strong factual research, and the ability to generate media attention. Simply put, today's movements for social and economic justice need people who are clear about the problems with the current systems, who rely on solid evidence for their critique, and who are able to reach large numbers of other people with both analysis and proposals. To help groups develop these capacities, I have included chapters on the analytic basis for our work as well as on specific arenas for building sophisticated organizations and alliances. Most chapters also include exercises designed to ease practical application of the material.

In the Introduction I review in broad strokes the history of community organizing in the United States after World War II, exploring in particular the strengths and limitations of the organizing ideas espoused by Saul Alinsky, who is acknowledged in many circles, though certainly not all, as the father of modern-day community organizing. I describe the growth of community organizing networks loosely based on the Alinsky model, their relationship to the social movements of the latter half of twentieth century, the key contemporary debates about what constitutes good organizing, critiques by feminists and people of color, and the points of inspiration that dot today's political landscape. In part, the Introduction is designed to help a group place itself in the continuum of organizing and to show how people are constantly experimenting with new and old forms of organization.

I then move into chapters that define and list the principles effective organizers use today. In Chapter One, I analyze the social and economic context in which we work—a context that includes a renewed and unprecedentedly strong right wing, a new global economy, and the continued importance of racism and sexism in defining the winners and losers in economic and social life. I argue that these shifts require new progressive responses, specifically the willingness to organize the most marginal people in our society, to choose issues that speak to those people, and to build organizations that can advance progressive ideas as well as mobilize a group. In Chapter Two, I look at the importance of recruiting people from among those most affected by social and economic problems, and I present questions that every organization needs to answer about structure, culture, outreach methods, and the dilemmas of combining organizing with service. In Chapter Three, I lay out the principles of progressive issue development, reinforcing the need to design explicit criteria to guide our issue choices. Chapter Four is about the critical role of direct action in our work and about how to design and conduct actions that further our campaign goals. Chapter Five explores the principles of leadership development, which I distinguish from leadership identification, and argues for systematic leadership programs that are rooted in popular education models and include large amounts of fieldwork. In Chapter Six, I examine the need for excellent research and ways of generating and using it. In

Chapter Seven, I consider the principles of building effective alliances and networks, ones that combine the strengths of organized constituencies rather than the weaknesses of unorganized communities. Chapter Eight helps readers design an effective media strategy, a task that is increasingly important in reframing social-policy debates and increasingly difficult to carry out in an era of media consolidation that greatly limits the dissemination of community-oriented and diverse content. Finally, Chapter Nine addresses the transformative power of internal political education and consciousness raising, an arena I consider to be one of the most important additions to community organizing practice.

Audience, or Who Should Read This Book

I have written this book for two primary audiences—people who are currently engaged in organizing and people who are thinking about getting involved. To the extent possible without making the book unwieldy or overly prescriptive, I have tried to address the different needs of both audiences. I have also written the book for progressives, people whose vision of a better world includes folks in warm homes with enough to eat, dignity and fair pay attached to every job, the freedom to express love without boundaries, resistance to war and violence at all levels—a world in which we can all be who we really are, without having punishments and rewards handed out on the basis of those identities. Certainly, many of the tools here can be and have been used to realize other visions, but I believe that the kinds of organizations committed to all the elements in this book are more likely to ascribe to the vision above.

While I present what I hope will be useful tools, I have tried also to describe the dilemmas and questions facing organizers and community leaders. In the end, readers will have to pick and choose among these tools and others to design a winning strategy that works for their communities. While all the organizations highlighted in the book do not incorporate every one of the principles I discuss, and it would be a rare organization indeed that did all these things well, I believe that these are the most promising portions of organizing practice.

The book, however, is not meant to be comprehensive; I did not have the space to explore many topics. For example, I do not address the various ways in which all these groups raise money, a subject of critical importance. Nor do I discuss in detail the principles of campaign planning. Much more can be written about outreach methods and how to design a recruitment plan. Rather than considering this book a comprehensive resource, I see it as a complement to older, still relevant texts. For a primer on the basics of organizing, there is nothing better than the Midwest Academy's *Organizing for Social Change,* by Kim Bobo, Jackie Kendall, and Steve Max (1990). Another excellent primer specifically for workplace and union activists is *The Troublemakers' Handbook* (LaBotz, 1991). Randy Shaw's *The Activists' Handbook* (1996) provides many interesting lessons from Shaw's work fighting homelessness in San Francisco. On fundraising, readers would do well to look at Andy Robinson's *Grassroots Grants: An Activist's Guide to Proposal Writing* (1996) and *Selling Social Change (Without Selling Out): Earned Income Strategies for Nonprofits* (2002), as well as Kim Klein's classic, *Fundraising for Social Change* (2000). To guide interested readers to other resources, particularly analyses of the right wing, economic globalization, and racial, gender, and sexual politics, I have included a recommended reading list in the Resources. Finally, I have not been able to include here many organizations that do excellent work. Readers will find many of them listed in the Resources.

Even as *Stir It Up* goes into production, people are in the streets all over the world disrupting the systems that cause so much division, heartache, and premature death. Although two decades have passed since my own introduction to progressive organizing, I am still moved to see that so many of us find faith, power, creativity, and humor in each other. Even as an accurate analysis of our situations threatens to paralyze us, I know that by using our own extraordinary talents and visions we will turn the tide.

Acknowledgments

Many people have assisted in the research and writing of this book since 1999. I would like to thank the Ms. Foundation staff who worked with me to conceptualize the book, manage logistics, get the research done, and improve the writing: Susan Wefald, Berta Colon, Anna Wadia, and Nora Grip. Thanks also to my current and former colleagues at the Applied Research Center who patiently reorganized their work to accommodate my research and writing schedule, especially Gary Delgado, Nicole Davis, Harvey Weinig, Kendra Field, Donna Hernandez, and Sonia Peña. People working in the grantee groups were invaluable in arranging interviews, loosening up their own time, and giving me access to materials and notes, particularly Leah Wise, Ellen Bravo, Amy Dean, Mark Toney and Dana Ginn Paredes, Bonnie Macri, Alison Bowen and Susan Winning, Tim Costello and Jason Pramas, Trinh Duong, Jennifer Brooks, Madeleine Janis-Aparicio, Sara Mersha, Judy Victor, Nadia Marin-Molina, and Jane Eeley. The organizers, trainers, and leaders I interviewed for this book are too numerous to name here, but I will never forget them. A more inspiring group of women and men is not to be found! Soyinka Rahim, Jo Su, and Chaiti Sen provided outstanding research and clerical support. The book was written in several places around the world, and I would especially like to acknowledge the care shown to me by the staff of the Blue Marlin Hotel in Scottburgh, South Africa, where I wrote and worked on the United Nations World Conference Against Racism. Dave Beckwith, Scot Nakagawa, Helen Kim, Chaiti Sen, Ellen Bravo, and Kim Fellner gave me important feedback on drafts. Special thanks to Kim Klein and Stephanie Roth for their friendship and encouragement. Without Johanna Vondeling, my editor at Jossey-Bass, the book would still be in the "nice idea" stage. Thanks also to Allison Brunner, Pamela Fischer, and Xenia Lisanevich, who worked on the manuscript. On behalf of the Ms. Foundation and the organizations profiled, I would especially like to thank the Ford Foundation—and particularly Barbara Phillips and Helen Neuborne—whose generous support underwrote the New Voices Initiative and this book. Finally, none of our successes would be possible without the work of all those who have gone before us, laughing in the face of sacrifice. I thank our ancestors and borrow their strength all the time.

New York, New York   Rinku Sen
January 2003

Dedicated to the memory of
Timothy J. Sampson.
Onward!

THE AUTHOR

RINKU SEN started her career in social-justice work as a student organizer in 1984, fighting race, gender, and class discrimination on campuses. From 1988 to 2000, she worked with the Center for Third World Organizing, a national network of organizations of color. As a staff member, then co-director, Rinku trained new organizers of color and crafted grassroots public policy campaigns around poverty, education, transportation, racial and gender equity, health care, and immigration issues. Currently she is the publisher of *ColorLines,* the national quarterly magazine on race, culture, and action, and the director of the New York office of the Applied Research Center, which conducts research on race and public policy. She has written extensively about the race and gender dimensions of community organizing and has advised many foundations and community organizations about how to support and evaluate organizing. She is a 1996 recipient of the Ms. Foundation for Women's Gloria Steinem Women of Vision award.

PROFILES

The organizations profiled here are used as the core examples in the chapters that follow. They were all Ms. Foundation for Women economic justice grantees from 1999 to 2001. This general overview of their history and accomplishments provides background information readers will find useful as they encounter the detailed descriptions of these organizations' work throughout the book.

Campaign on Contingent Work

Founded in 1996, the Campaign on Contingent Work is a Boston-based network of activists and organizations seeking to end discrimination against part-time, temporary, and contract workers in Massachusetts. CCW was founded by long-time truck driver, Teamster member, and staff person of the Service Employees International Union Tim Costello. While working at the regional organizing and training group Northeast Action, Costello traveled the state talking with activists to determine the focus of a campaign around workers' rights. "The changing nature of work came up over and over again," recalls Costello, who launched an investigation into contingent-work patterns in Massachusetts, as well as in the economy at large. CCW became an independent entity in 1998.

Although there was a great deal of pressure to build a traditional membership organization, CCW activists chose instead the innovative network form for its flexibility and ability to move quickly. Contingent workers lack characteristics that enable the organizing of traditional workers; in particular the contingent workforce is diverse, by occupation as well as by race, gender, and class, and contingent workers are not covered by many labor laws, such as the rights to be considered employees, to join unions, and to fight the employer practice of denying health benefits and pensions.

Like other parts of the country, Massachusetts has its share of contingent workers. Contingent work is a major factor in the state economy; it is prevalent in the academic and publishing industries, in human services and social work, and in health care and all kinds of assembly work, and it has a disproportionate impact on women. In its first five years, CCW contributed to the fights of tugboat workers, museum guards, and temporary workers. Although some of these workers were members of unions, their contingent status hindered their ability to use traditional union resources.

In spite of the limitations in labor law, CCW used existing legal standards to end some of the most egregious abuses at Labor Ready, a national temp agency that Gail Nicholson, former CCW administrator and current board member, says is "corporatizing day labor." CCW activists who worked for Labor Ready reported poor working conditions, discrimination in job assignments, especially against women, and lax health and safety monitoring on the job. Working with Labor Ready temps, CCW pressured the company to stop its illegal charging of ATM and other fees, and CCW combined with groups nationally to track the company's health and safety practices.

Nicholson, a former member of the flight attendants' union, notes that CCW provides everything from "first-strike media assistance, to helping [workers] strategize, to writing . . . press releases." All this assistance encourages self-organization among workers. Costello says, "We want the workers to make all the decisions on a specific battle. We bring the big frame—poor people getting abused by a wealthy institution. Now they're part of a social struggle. We're the go-to enablers."

Center for the Child Care Workforce

The Center for the Child Care Workforce was formed as a national organization to promote the interests of child care workers through research, leadership development, advocacy, and activism. The Center was started by child care workers in the San Francisco Bay Area in 1978 and has evolved into an influential voice in child care debates by bringing child care workers' needs to national attention.

Child care workers own and operate few political or workers' organizations of their own, particularly beyond the local level. There is a large, well-resourced professional organization, the National Association for Educators of Young Children (NAEYC), that is devoted to meeting the needs of kids, but draws members from many sectors and does not focus on those actually working with children. The largest portion of NAEYC's membership is center directors, academics, and for-profit administrators and other employers rather than workers. The Center was started by a small group of child care workers to address compensation issues directly.

For more than ten years, the Center has enabled workers to identify their collective issues and problems and to raise the workforce's visibility to the public and policymakers through the Worthy Wage movement. The Center has identified one day of the year during which child care workers nationwide apply their creativity to educating the public about their conditions and highlighting specific policy options. Worthy Wage Day has become the umbrella under which child care workers organize rallies, public-awareness projects, and mobilizations for specific policy and organizing goals. Through Worthy Wage Day, providers and teachers have contributed greatly to the tool kit of tactics available to child care workers who want to influence compensation and working conditions. For example, the organizing manual teaches workers how to convey policy messages by using popular theater based on familiar stories and fairy tales such as "The Teeny Tiny Teacher" and "The Child Care Provider Meets the Worthy Wage Dragon."

To support the local leaders who emerged out of the Worthy Wage campaign and to help shape the consciousness and increase the organizing skills of all child care workers, the Center created the Leadership Empowerment Action Project (LEAP). LEAP sessions reflect the Center's awareness of the diversity of the workforce; they are always conducted by a team that includes one woman of color and one white woman. The Center has adjusted the LEAP curriculum for use in college-level early-childhood-education courses; it integrates policy analysis and the economic dimensions of child care employment into what is considered basic education for the workforce. Finally, the Center prioritized a research strategy. Its first National Child Care Staffing Study led to the Worthy Wage campaign. Every year on Worthy Wage Day, the Center releases new information about the workforce, its wages, conditions, and aspirations. The Center is merging with the American Federation of Teachers Education Fund, where it will continue its commitment to improving child care jobs.

Center for Third World Organizing

The Center for Third World Organizing was founded in 1980 as a training center for organizers of color. Since then, it has evolved into a racial justice network working with a wide variety of communities of color around the country. CTWO's flagship training program, the Movement Activist Apprenticeship Program, was started to disrupt the trend of communities of color relying on white organizers to build their community organizations. In 1985, MAAP's pilot year, community organizations usually had a white, often male, college-educated organizer and a membership dominated by women of color. Since then, MAAP has trained hundreds of people of color, the vast majority women under twenty-five, who now work in community and labor organizations across the country. CTWO has since expanded its training programs to follow an organizer throughout his or her career, with three-day Community Action trainings in more than twenty cities each year, including Atlanta, Chicago, San Jose, Austin, and Providence. CTWO also helped launch the Grassroots Independence Fundraising Training, which trains people of color to conduct nonfoundation fundraising, such as major donor campaigns and earned income efforts. CTWO has also experimented with building multiracial community organizations. The oldest surviving one is People United for a Better Oakland (PUEBLO), which won measles immunization programs for thirty thousand children, the most comprehensive lead poisoning screening and treatment program west of the Mississippi, and controls on police power. PUEBLO also helped build a five-organization coalition that won more than $20 million for youth services through an Oakland ballot initiative.

CTWO has had three major, nationally coordinated campaigns. In the early 1990s, the Campaign for Community Safety and Police Accountability challenged racist law enforcement policies at a time when most community organizations were focused only on joining the War on Drugs. Involving five organizations nationwide, the Campaign piloted a new political-education process for defining key issues and framed alternative policies based on racial justice goals. From 1995 to 1999, CTWO ran Winning Action for Gender Equity, a program designed to get community organizations of color more familiar with and willing to take up feminist causes that affected women of color. Most recently, CTWO established Grassroots Organizing for Welfare Leadership (GROWL), a national movement of welfare rights and economic justice organizations. Working with the GROWL network, CTWO has been trying to shift the debate on welfare reform away from reduction of rolls to gender equity, civil rights, and poverty abatement. GROWL groups research and document people's experiences under welfare reform, advocate with members of Congress, and pursue local and state policy changes in welfare departments.

Chinese Staff & Workers Association

In 1979, a group of Chinese restaurant workers and a couple of workers from other industries came together and founded the Chinese Staff & Workers' Association (CSWA). Unlike unions, which are often single-trade or narrowly defined as "employees" organizations, CSWA started with mostly male restaurant workers but rapidly expanded to include garment and construction workers, caregivers, disabled workers, retirees, and youth. Today CSWA has a membership of over thirteen hundred workers from various trades and of various ages, and a leadership composed primarily of women. CSWA is the first contemporary workers' center bringing together workers across trades to fight for change in the workplace as well as in the community at large.

CSWA is well known for taking on tough issues. By the early 1990s, over 60 percent of New York's 7,000 to 7,500 garment factories were sweatshops. Although 80 percent of the garment factories in the Chinese community were unionized, employers freely violated labor laws and human rights standards. Union members often worked eighty hours per week, earning as little as $2 to $3 per hour. Despite this, their union diverted the public's attention to focus on sweatshops overseas. CSWA brought the issue of sweatshops in the United States into the forefront of the national agenda. CSWA's antisweatshop work was nominated as an outstanding teaching example at the 1997 Philadelphia Presidential Volunteer Summit.

CSWA is not a service organization nor does it follow an advocacy model since neither model is fundamentally concerned with developing a base. Many of the antisweatshop initiatives established by advocacy groups are consumer-driven and often male-led. CSWA believes that these campaigns fail to organize the people who produce the product itself and instead rely largely on campus activists. CSWA flips this on its head by placing workers at the center of organizing campaigns and recognizing workers as agents for change rather than treating them as victims.

At CSWA, innovative organizing strategies develop from workers themselves. For example, in 1999, CSWA spearheaded a nationwide campaign against internationally renowned designer Donna Karan (DKNY). The DKNY workers not only were standing up for unpaid wages but also were protesting in particular the inhumane treatment they endured on the job, from padlocked bathrooms to surveillance cameras to long hours spent away from their families. The DKNY campaign was led by the workers themselves, who initiated the outreach efforts, including leafleting and tabling in the heart of the midtown garment center, and who organized their own family members and other workers to picket in front of DKNY factories and retail shops. Through this outreach, the DKNY workers informed other workers about their rights and brought together garment workers who previously worked in DKNY shops. In spite of opposition from their union, the DKNY workers later initiated a class-action lawsuit against DKNY and all DKNY-contracted factories throughout New York State.

Mrs. Lai, the first DKNY worker to come forward, initially came to CSWA because the Department of Labor felt it could not address her needs and referred her to CSWA. CSWA helped Mrs. Lai to win not only her owed back pay but also reinstatement at her former job. But her fight did not stop there. Mrs. Lai continued to involve other workers to assert their rights collectively and to fight injustice in their workplace. She is now a board member of CSWA.

Since its inception, CSWA has successfully fought for increased space for day care; won a landmark case against the City of New York to stop a luxury development from being built in Chinatown that would have displaced low-income residents and at the same time put forth a new environmental perspective that includes the people as part of the environment; pushed for the passage of manufacturer-accountability legislation in 1998; and recovered over $10 million in owed back wages and overtime pay. More recently, CSWA organized to expose the federal government's willful neglect of low-income communities in the aftermath of the September 11th tragedy. CSWA successfully forced the federal government to change some of its antipoor, antiwoman relief policies. Unlike most labor groups, which focus on wages, CSWA continues to go beyond economic needs to fight for the community's health and control of time. CSWA has raised consciousness and broadened its membership especially among workers such as home health attendants and among new Chinese immigrants such as Fuzhounese workers. Most important, CSWA is able to link the individual, immediate needs of people to collective, long-term demands.

Direct Action for Rights and Equality

Direct Action for Rights and Equality is a multiracial, multi-issue community organization that has provided long-standing political leadership by poor people of color in the working-class areas of Providence, Rhode Island. Founded in 1986 by five people around the kitchen table of Mattie Smith, a prominent welfare rights leader in Providence, DARE has a multiracial membership of over eight hundred dues-paying families. DARE constantly renews its membership and ties membership development to the organization's priority issues. The struggles and concerns of its membership determine which issues and campaigns the organization takes on.

DARE's key victories include implementing a multicultural curriculum in Providence high schools, winning a groundbreaking land-reform policy, and winning wage increases and permanent hiring for city workers. DARE has also designed a unique living wage ordinance, not yet passed, which sets wages significantly higher than those in similar cities and contains antidiscrimination clauses that protect workers of color and ex-prisoners.

One of DARE's most remarkable achievements was the Home Day Care Justice Campaign, which eventually spun off to become the independent HDCJ Cooperative. In 1996, the Campaign won passage of an unprecedented state law recognizing that family day-care providers with state contracts worked mostly for the state; the sole purpose was to make the subsidized family day-care providers in Rhode Island and their families eligible for the state employees' health-insurance program. Rhode Island is now the only state in the nation that provides health insurance as part of the compensation package for family day-care providers. The Co-op continues to operate with a vision of dignity and self-sufficiency for day-care providers and all child care workers.

DARE has four campaign committees: Jobs with Dignity, Community Safety = Community Control, Behind the Walls, and Students and Parents Taking Action for a Real Tomorrow (START). Jobs with Dignity organizes low-income and unemployed families to work in coalitions with other groups to gain better jobs in the community. Community Safety = Community Control is DARE's campaign to create safe neighborhoods through police accountability. Behind the Walls engages prisoners and family members of prisoners in challenging the criminal justice system. Finally, START brings together young people and adults to fight for better schools. START focuses on defeating the criminalization of youth and parents through truancy courts, instead proposing that an improved curriculum would do more to encourage higher attendance in schools.

Justice, Economic Dignity, and Independence for Women

When Deeda Seed realized the members of the fledgling economic justice organization she had started were about to choose the name JEDI, she didn't reveal her sinking feeling that the group members would be likened to movie characters. As it turned out, calling the group JEDI was the perfect way to include many of its ambitious goals, and the name ended up symbolizing the strength and militancy this group needed to change institutions in Salt Lake City. Seed took that as a lesson that no organizer is wiser than the collective wisdom of her group. Since then, Justice, Economic Dignity and Independence for Women has become known as the premier organization of poor women in Utah. Its largely white membership base with strong rural participation mirrors the state's population, but its tactics and issues go far beyond anything Utah had seen before 1992. The group initially took up traditional issues for low-income women—access to welfare, child care, and affordable housing—but it soon expanded to related issues, including child marriage, environmental justice, and foster care.

JEDI is one of the few groups to address the custody process that can be triggered by the loss of welfare benefits. Utah, like many states, requires social services to notify the child welfare department when a woman has lost her benefits through sanctions or has reached her welfare time limits. Within one month of the loss of benefits, the Utah Division of Child and Family Services conducts a home visit and removes children, in many cases because their mothers can't afford to provide for them. Caseworkers, "young college-educated women, often mistake poverty for child abuse," says Bonnie Macri, the executive director of JEDI. When the first group of recipients hit their three-year lifetime limit for benefits, Macri says, "we [were getting] fifty calls a week from women who . . . lost their kids." JEDI has created a support group for parents faced with loss of their children and has also strengthened the legal resources available to parents who have lost their children along with their welfare benefits. Without JEDI support, parents must use public defenders with little experience and huge caseloads.

In the 2000 legislative session, JEDI was instrumental in changing the "sibling-at-risk" policy, which required that if one child was taken from a family, the rest would be removed automatically. As of July 1, 2001, each child's situation has to be considered independently. In addition, JEDI successfully changed the law that allowed the children's services department to get police support to enter a home without a court order. Today, social workers and police must go through a formal process to make such an intervention.

Los Angeles Alliance for a New Economy

Founded in 1993 as the Tourism Industry Development Council, the Los Angeles Alliance for a New Economy involves unions, community organizations, religious leaders, academics, and elected officials; it pushes for just and equitable economic-development policies and plans for the metropolitan Los Angeles area. Named by *The Nation* as one of the country's state-of-the-art economic justice organizations (Murray, 2001), LAANE has generated victories that have advanced unionization (particularly of service workers), living wage ordinances, community-benefits packages attached to new commercial developments, and accountability standards for businesses receiving public contracts and subsidies. LAANE combines groundbreaking research with organizing to design innovative policy agreements with corporations as well as with local government bodies.

LAANE is an impressive example of contemporary community-labor alliances. The group was started with the leadership of Hotel Employees, Restaurant Employees (HERE) Local 11. In 1995, that union faced a fight in which one thousand unionized food-service workers faced the threat of unemployment as existing contracts were replaced with nonunion contracts. When three hundred workers lost their jobs, LAANE saw an opportunity to help a specific set of workers and to launch its own organizing. That struggle led to the passage of the Service Contract Workers Retention Ordinance. The ordinance, passed in 1995, provided a warm-up and early track record from which the living wage campaign would be born.

In 1997, LAANE won the first living wage ordinance in Los Angeles; the law led to raises and health benefits for more than ten thousand workers. That victory built the internal capacity and coalition that would enable other successes, including working out an agreement on a major Hollywood development with living wages for all employees of the builder and subcontractors, a living wage incentive program for tenants, and seed money for a worker health care trust fund; replicating the city's living wage ordinance in Los Angeles County; passing a responsible-contractor ordinance that requires businesses seeking city contracts, leases, or financial assistance to report on their employment practices; and helping the Figueroa Corridor Coalition for Economic Justice win a landmark community-benefits agreement with developers of the Staples sports center, with living wages and resources for parks in one of the poorest neighborhoods in Los Angeles.

One of LAANE's most successful projects, Santa Monicans Allied for Responsible Tourism (SMART), won the second living wage ordinance to affect private companies not receiving public subsidies or contracts. SMART first mobilized Santa Monica voters to defeat a preemptive living wage ballot initiative, measure KK, sponsored by Santa Monica's luxury hotels. Then, after winning an ordinance improving wages for two thousand hotel workers in a 5–2 city council vote, SMART was forced to defend the ordinance against the other side's repeal efforts. In the November 2002 elections, SMART mobilized voters to support a ballot measure that was sponsored, then opposed by, business. The measure failed to pass because of the opposition's deceptive messages and unethical financial investment in the campaign's last days, according to a SMART background paper on the election (Santa Monicans About Responsible Tourism, 2002). SMART organizer Vivian Rothstein calls the election "a painful loss on a fight we won't give up."

Following mass layoffs after September 11, 2001, LAANE, HERE, and SMART provided thousands of workers with food and access to public services and helped pass the first recall-rights law in Santa Monica, which guaranteed laid-off workers the right to return to their jobs as employers rehired. The Respect at LAX campaign, which has already established union contracts with most employers at the Los Angeles airport and gotten them to pay living wages, is currently working on health, safety, and labor violations at the airport's McDonald's franchises.

9to5

When Ellen Cassidy and Karen Nussbaum called a meeting of Boston-area secretaries in November 1973, they had no idea that their ten-person study group would become the first union of clerical workers. Nussbaum, then an antiwar and women's liberation activist using her clerical job to finance her political work, recalls "walking the picket line one winter for a small group of waitresses who had spontaneously gone on strike. Walking with them I realized I should be organizing on the job too." Over the next thirty years, 9to5 evolved into two complementary organizations, a national local within the Service Employees International Union (SEIU) and the community-based National Association of Working Women. While 9to5 unionizes working women, the National Association conducts worker education, public policy campaigns, and other activities that complement worker organizing.

9to5 changed the historic trajectory of clerical workers. By the 1970s, that workforce was 99 percent women, constituted the largest sector of the labor market, and had never seen any significant union organizing, according to Nussbaum. She says, "We were surprised when we realized the clerical workforce was twenty million people; one out of three working women [was] doing clerical work. Yet we were invisible." After one year of study meetings, Nussbaum and Cassidy released a newsletter that drew 150 women to the first meeting at the Boston YWCA.

Working together, the two 9to5s became a major force, generating workplace organizing and helping to pass key pieces of legislation. In 1975, 9to5 helped women in the publishing, insurance, and banking industries win $25 million in back pay by filing class-action lawsuits for equal pay. In organizing TWA reservationists in the mid-1980s, 9to5 won an employee union, an in-house monitoring policy, and a federal law regulating employee monitoring. After the boss of a Boston clerical worker refused to give her time off after her daughter was kidnapped and raped, 9to5 won passage of the Small Necessity Act in Massachusetts. The law enables parents to take time off to help their children in emergency and nonemergency situations. Later, the organization helped win passage of a pregnancy-discrimination act, raised public awareness of the health hazards posed by computer jobs, and contributed to the fight for the federal Family and Medical Leave Act. 9to5 also operates a job-survival hotline, organizes and trains people to deal with sexual harassment in the workplace, lends its voice to the debate on welfare reform, runs the Poverty Network Initiative in Milwaukee to work on welfare issues, and works with a national network to end discrimination against part-time, temporary, and contract workers.

Southeast Regional Economic Justice Network

The Southeast Regional Economic Justice Network was initiated to strengthen organizing and cross-racial, cross-cultural relationships in the South. Leah Wise, executive director, says that the specific political and economic challenges of the

South clarified the need for a network that could avoid some of the movement-busting trends of the past. Southern groups, including the low-wage worker groups that REJN started out with, faced hostility toward unions, the lack of will among unions themselves to organize the South, and the divisiveness of racism. Wise says that she and co-founders Leroy Johnson and Bill Troy, both prominent members of national networks, "felt like what was happening in our region was so elemental compared to everybody else, it forced us into an analysis of the South. We started the network to articulate the South."

REJN not only connects groups but also advances the leadership development and renewal work critical to its members' survival. REJN's programs and activities create a laboratory in which the most effective leadership development models can be tested; these efforts in turn help the network push its member organizations to put energy into their local leadership development plans. REJN particularly emphasizes integrating youth into its leadership bodies to provide a training experience, helping leaders be allies to others, and looking after the physical and spiritual health of leaders.

REJN includes sixty-five low-wage worker groups from Tennessee, the Carolinas, Georgia, Mississippi, Florida, Arkansas, Louisiana, Virginia, and Alabama as well as eight nations in the Americas. The network functions primarily through regional gatherings and special projects and was designed to help groups develop common analyses of situations as well as relationships among themselves. Unlike many such formations, REJN rarely takes positions on issues. Wise notes that REJN groups begin working together by focusing on how to improve organizing, a process that differs from "saying here's a platform, let's launch something. [Debating resolutions] would just set people up to fight." Wise says the network wanted to avoid getting bogged down in ideological differences that would drive people away: "We constructed it as a learning space, where we all have something to learn and something to teach. It wasn't that we didn't support each other's work, but we didn't look for a single campaign to do together." For example, the contingent-work group and the poultry workers group both "figured out how to grapple with difficulties" through their exchanges. Local campaigns addressing temp services, workers' compensation, privatization, plant closings, racist immigration policies, and living wages emerged out of the common learning REJN facilitated. REJN has equipped itself to deal with international migration and free-trade issues largely by building international exchange into its agendas.

Wider Opportunities for Women

Started in 1978 as a network of organizations training women for nontraditional careers, Wider Opportunities for Women entered the welfare and jobs debate with a history of successful interventions in federal job-training and placement programs. While the original dues-paying network consisted mainly of nontraditional work groups, over time it has expanded to include other women workers, such as child care providers.

Conducting groundbreaking research and working with partner groups in six states, WOW established the Self-Sufficiency Standard, against which welfare benefit levels and job-training programs can be measured. This standard demonstrates that neither welfare benefits nor low-wage jobs provide enough income for families to meet even their most basic needs.

The Self-Sufficiency Standard is the cornerstone of WOW's Family Economic Self-Sufficiency (FESS) program and state-level organizing strategy. To bring families to self-sufficiency, WOW advocates the use of six strategies:

1. Adopting the Self-Sufficiency Standard to measure how much income is needed to make ends meet and to assess the success of employment and training programs
2. Targeting higher-wage employment in the development and design of education, employment, and training programs and in the provision of career counseling
3. Using the functional-context education model to integrate literacy and basic skills with occupational skills and family support programs to improve the efficiency and success of adult education
4. Improving the access of low-income women to nontraditional training and employment
5. Providing training and support for microenterprise development
6. Supporting the development of Individual Development Accounts (IDAs), which allow low-income families to accumulate assets

WOW chose these six strategies because they can be used in combination with each other or alone and because they provide variety: actions can be geared toward individuals, such as career counseling for one woman, or toward institutions, such as promoting the inclusion of education in welfare work requirements.

As part of the debate around the reauthorization of the 1996 welfare bill, WOW worked to institutionalize the use of the Self-Sufficiency Standard in federal policy. Joan Kuriansky, WOW's executive director, describes WOW's four primary goals in this debate as "getting education counted as work, ensuring civil rights protections in the law, targeting higher quality . . . jobs by examining the regional economy, and [gaining adoption of] the Self-Sufficiency Standard." In January 2002, Representative Lynn Woolsey of California introduced H.R. 3667, "The Self-Sufficiency Act," which would require states to calculate a measure like the Self-Sufficiency Standard and then report against it on an individual basis. States could also compete for a bonus that would reward progress in moving families toward self-sufficiency. State FESS program partners and WOW coordinated a national postcard and letter-writing campaign to support the bill. After the House passed a punitive bill, debate shifted to the Senate. WOW worked with members on both sides of the aisle to build support for its priorities and gained broad support within the key committee. At the time of this writing, however, the Senate has yet to take up the bill. Throughout the debate, those on both sides of the aisle, in both houses of Congress, and in the administration asserted that this stage of welfare reform was about helping families move to self-sufficiency. Without a measure like the Self-Sufficiency Standard, it will be impossible to determine what that might mean. As the debate goes on and other federal policies come up for consideration, WOW will continue to make the case that Congress must help families on their path to self-sufficiency.

Women's Association for Women's Alternatives

The Women's Association for Women's Alternatives was founded in 1978 in the mellow college town of Swarthmore, less than thirty minutes outside Philadelphia. The organization provides a full range of antipoverty services, including housing, job training and placement, adult literacy programs, and family advocacy. W.A.W.A. is one of the core state partners in the FESS program.

W.A.W.A.'s family advocacy program and self-sufficiency work makes the organization an important player in welfare and job-training policy. The family advocacy program serves hundreds of low-income people who are struggling with the welfare system and the labor market. Using largely an inside-track, administrative strategy, W.A.W.A. has engaged organizations and agencies from the economic-development, social welfare, job-training, and education sectors in adopting the use of the Self-Sufficiency Standard and the six strategies throughout Pennsylvania. Carol Goertzel, the executive director of W.A.W.A., involves many contacts she gained through twenty years of working in employment service agencies. The W.A.W.A. FESS program has more than eight hundred such collaborators.

W.A.W.A. has successfully used the Self-Sufficiency Standard in Pennsylvania to influence policies large and small. In Pittsburgh, the standard has been used to determine water and sewage rates. Eastern College has used the standard to lobby for raising the wages of campus housekeepers. Susquehanna County has used the standard to determine whether a low-income family is able to pay back school loans. Through the state's Community Action agencies, W.A.W.A. has trained over twelve hundred people on applying the standard, a process that proved invaluable to expanding the project into rural Pennsylvania. Goertzel says that Community

Action agencies are often "the only antipoverty network in rural areas. We were so urban; until we took on this project, we would not have known what we were doing."

W.A.W.A. provides other services to support vulnerable families who are at risk of being separated because of abuse or neglect. These services include three residential programs, as well as intensive in-home and school programs. Along with a number of employment and education programs and community-based family support programs, W.A.W.A.'s services are designed to build self-sufficiency and preserve family unity by providing counseling, mediation training, job training and placement, housing, and training in basic life skills.

The Women's Institute for Leadership Development

The Women's Institute for Leadership Development was started in Massachusetts to encourage women union members to make use of unions as "another avenue to fight for social and economic justice," according to Executive Director Alison Bowen, a former social worker who had been a shop steward in SEIU Local 668 in Pennsylvania when she got involved with WILD as a union leader. A high level of participation by women in their unions is necessary to ensure that "the real issues of women workers get dealt with," she says. WILD does its part to create that kind of responsiveness within unions by providing women leaders with access to concrete, applicable leadership training, delivered through participatory popular education methods. Diane Dujon, the director of independent learning at the University of Massachusetts, Boston, and a WILD member, says she "can't think of a woman . . . in a leadership role in unions in Massachusetts [who] isn't a part of WILD."

WILD plays four important roles. First, it challenges the all-male and all-white traditional leadership of unions. Susan Winning, former director, points out that "the structure of union activism can make it really hard for women to take leadership. The style is very male and aggressive, and tends to be based on the schedules of people who only go to work and do their activism—no cooking, cleaning, or looking after the kids." Winning points out the sexism at the steward level in unions with female-dominated membership but male-dominated leadership. She offers the example of flight attendants: they are 85 percent female, but their labor leadership is 85 percent male. Second, WILD helps women gain and hold onto official leadership positions in their unions. WILD made an explicit decision to get more women into positions of formal leadership "because that's where power really lies in labor unions," according to Winning. Third, WILD has built a tight-knit community of women labor leaders who exchange resources and support each other through the hard times. Dujon says, "Through WILD, I forged a lot of great friendships and partnerships. Walked in the door at Northeastern [University] for WILD in the Winter, felt like I had walked home. Got some new women to join, and that was the first thing they noticed: wow, this is a community." Fourth, all this work to build a leadership infrastructure has influenced the issues and organizing campaigns that unions are willing to pick up.

WILD's programs consist of two major training events and a committee structure through which members take on political projects the rest of the year. WILD's summer institute helps women leaders share activist lessons and learn about specific issues and organizing skills; it usually provides the first exposure for women who are inclined to get involved in their unions. Bowen says, "We bring women into our program, then invite them to be a part of the committee to plan next year's program [and] give [them] opportunities to plan workshops, plan meetings, work with an experienced facilitator." In addition to the week-long summer institute, WILD in the Winter runs day-long issue workshops in various regions of the state. Conference teams and caucus leaders work together to establish policy priorities for women workers for the coming year and to create ongoing projects that advance those priorities.

WILD's Women Lead project supports women as they initiate and strengthen women's caucuses in mixed-gender unions. Women Lead helped to get four women onto the executive board of the central labor council in Boston, and these women meet separately before larger meetings to strategize.

WILD leaders have influenced the issues that unions pick up, expanding them to include issues important to working women, whether in the workplace or in the community. Dujon, for example, was a welfare rights activist before she was a union member, and she has worked to educate unions about the implications of giving up the safety net.

Working Partnerships

Working Partnerships is the research and community organizing arm of the South Bay Central Labor Council in Silicon Valley. The group emerged in 1995 out of growing concern for the well-being of workers in the "new economy." By conducting original research as the basis for policy initiatives, building alliances, and promoting creative models for workforce development, Working Partnerships is committed to finding innovative solutions to the unprecedented conditions faced by low-wage workers in Silicon Valley.

In the 1990s, the underbelly of the Silicon Valley economic boom remained largely hidden until Working Partnerships intervened with research reports revealing the exploitive treatment of low-wage service and industrial workers. Working Partnerships used its living wage campaign to begin transforming the Silicon Valley economy and to deepen the alliance between community groups and labor unions in the city of San Jose. Winning a living wage ordinance in San Jose in 1998 was a major victory; the ordinance set the highest living wage in the nation at that time.

Working Partnerships works with community organizations on major issues that reach beyond the workplace, and it supports those alliances with training resources for community leaders. The most successful community campaign was a joint effort between Working Partnerships and the church-based community organization People Acting in Community Together to establish a countywide system to provide health insurance for all uninsured children, including the undocumented. That campaign led to others, such as an effort to establish an affordable-housing zone in San Jose's latest development. Working Partnerships' Labor/Community Leadership Institute, an eight-week course with follow-up networking opportunities for volunteer and staff leaders of local organizations, anchors Working Partnerships in communities by providing a constant pool of community leaders with whom Working Partnerships keeps up regular contact.

Working Partnerships also runs the Code of Conduct Campaign, which advocates for stable employment, a living wage, health benefits, and the right of temporary workers to organize. The Code of Conduct Campaign includes a membership association for temporary workers, which aims to restructure the hiring practices of the health industry. Like many organizations for low-wage workers, it has also responded to the needs of workers who have been displaced in the post–September 11th economy. Through its campaigns, Working Partnerships has helped bring together more than three hundred community leaders and activists to outline the parameters of a new economic and social development plan for the region; this plan addresses affordable health care, transportation, and education.

Workplace Project

Founded in 1992 by Jennifer Gordon, the Workplace Project set out to organize a critical mass among the 250,000 Latino immigrants living on Long Island, New York. Historically, Long Island had been both a playground of the wealthy and a settlement of World War II veterans who were rewarded for service with federally subsidized, racially segregated housing. These working-class enclaves were built near light manufacturing, the mainstay of employment for several generations of white workers.

By the 1980s, much of this manufacturing had left the area, and booming financial markets sent new numbers of young, white professionals into the suburbs. Latino immigrants took up jobs in the service industries that crop up in any community of young, affluent families. The Latino population on Long

Island jumped 80 percent between 1980 and 1990. These immigrants worked as cooks and busboys, landscapers, maids and nannies.

Local institutions colluded in an anti-immigrant backlash, and unions largely avoided organizing immigrants. The Long Island context challenged the basic industrial model of unionization. According to Gordon, "People change jobs frequently, and they also change industries. A woman might be a restaurant worker at night and a domestic worker by day. They have multiple jobs and serial jobs in different industries. There is no union that crosses industries and jobs like that." That insight shaped the Workplace Project's decision to build a community-based organization.

The Workplace Project has made significant gains in both enforcing and changing public policy affecting immigrant workers on Long Island and all over the state of New York. The legal clinic won more than $300,000 in back wages for over 250 workers and helped negotiate new severance settlements with unions and employers. In 1997, the Workplace Project won the strongest wage-enforcement law in the country, the New York Unpaid Wages Prohibition Act. The new law raised the penalty high enough to create a real deterrent to this common form of abuse.

In order to get a handle on the landscaping and domestic-work sectors, the Workplace Project developed worker-owned cooperatives. The Project got involved in these industries for three reasons: the large numbers of people employed in them, their typical structures and conditions, and the potential for building alliances with white, middle-class people. At least half the Latinos on Long Island, or almost every woman, has spent some time in domestic work. The long hours, strenuous work, low wages, difficulty in finding work, and contingent nature of the work all contribute to economic instability and make workers vulnerable to human rights violations. "The fact that domestic workers are visible to large numbers of middle-class white folks is an advantage in an alliance-building strategy," says Nadia Marin-Molina, the executive director of the Project. "The North American community doesn't necessarily see the factory workers, but they do see the domestic workers. If we can touch more people more directly, they understand [workers' needs] to some degree."

INTRODUCTION

Community Organizing—Yesterday and Today

This book is grounded in many theories and practices that have emerged mainly from community organizing. While it is certainly not necessary to have a historical knowledge of the field in order to do good organizing, sometimes it is helpful to be able to place a particular effort into the established landscape of diverse networks and models. From such an overview we can learn that there are no pure models. Developing a practice that works for us is a matter of begging and borrowing, stealing, and only occasionally having an entirely new idea. I begin with a review of the major features of contemporary community organizing, including the contributions of Saul Alinsky, the innovations created by the expanding pool of organizing networks, and the major critiques of Alinsky's rules. Then I consider the relationship of community organizing to key social movements from the 1950s to the present and discuss what community organizing can contribute to social movements and vice versa. After I review the landscape of the past, I argue that community organizing should now move into practices that support the emergence of new social movements with the potential to win large-scale progressive change. To that end, I identify what appear to me as the most encouraging trends and practices in organizing since the early 1990s. In part, this review provides a backdrop to the organizing efforts I highlight in subsequent chapters.

Establishing Principles for Community Organizing

The term *community organizing* refers to a distinct form of organization building and social activism that grew in the United States mostly after World War II. Community organizing in its most traditional form involves the building of a membership organization; such an organization sometimes comprises institutions with existing memberships, such as churches and labor unions, and other times it is made up of individuals and families. These membership organizations engage in specific campaigns to change institutional policies and practices in particular arenas, ranging from education to income to the environment. Community organizations have logged significant victories, many of which complement or enforce historic gains in federal policy, such as the programs of the Great Society, the Civil Rights Act of 1964, and the War on Poverty. There are thousands of community organizations in the United States today, even if we exclude seemingly apolitical neighborhood associations and Community Development Corporations. In these organizations, perhaps millions of regular people gather to demand accountability from city councils, public health departments, police departments, corporations, and other institutions. There are at least six major organizing networks in the United States, each with its own methods and theories. Since World War II, community organizing has grown into a profession, with its own body of literature, standards, and training institutes.

The oldest of these organizing networks is the Industrial Areas Foundation (IAF), founded by Saul Alinsky. Alinsky is widely acknowledged, especially among white, working-class community organizers, as the father of contemporary community organizing because he was the first to devise and write down a model of organizing that could be replicated. He created dozens of community organizations, all designed to test out a new portion of the theory, in addition to the IAF. Alinsky's pragmatic, nonideological approach to social change has been both emulated and challenged by organizers and groups, many of which arose to fill perceived gaps in Alinsky's work.

Alinsky was raised in Chicago during the turn of the twentieth century in a solidly middle-class, Jewish-immigrant household. He studied sociology and criminology at the University of Chicago, focusing on behavioral trends among juvenile delinquents and career criminals, before becoming a social worker just as the Great Depression hit. Radicalized by his exposure to systemic poverty and dissatisfied with the limitations of a social work approach, which he argued simply taught people to resign themselves to their lot, in the early 1940s Alinsky set about looking for a new way to make change. His search resulted in an experiment that would make him famous, the establishment of an "organization of organizations"—churches, labor unions, and service organizations in the meat-packing and stockyards section of Chicago, which was heavily populated by Polish and other southern/eastern European immigrants. To build the Back of the Yards Neighborhood Council, he recruited key actors from existing community institutions to constitute a sponsoring committee; then the committee members pressured, cajoled, and attracted other groups into the new organization. In addition, the leader of each institution contributed his own membership to the new formation. Thus, pastors brought in church members, shop stewards brought in union members, and service groups brought in clients. This incorporation of members of established institutions accounts for the reputation of institution-based groups for turning out thousands of people for local actions. The Back of the Yards Neighborhood Council quickly gained a reputation for beating city hall into submission and winning expanded social services and educational access.

These accomplishments generated media and political attention and began to put Alinsky on the map. Expanding on this model, Alinsky later created the IAF to test adaptations of the model in other cities. The IAF began to work out its theory of building organizations of organizations by establishing relationships among leaders of institutions; the IAF asserted that these organizations could revive neighborhood-based civic life and improve conditions by winning concessions from local institutions. The IAF now provides leadership training for nearly forty organizations representing over one thousand institutions and one million families, principally in New York, Texas, California, Arizona, New Mexico, Nebraska, Maryland, Tennessee, and the United Kingdom. IAF organizations are funded largely by substantial annual contributions from institutional members—churches being among the wealthiest U.S. nonprofits—and foundation grants. Over time most have become faith-based, grouping together congregations, perhaps because of the general decline of labor unions and white ethnic organizations.

In the late 1960s, the Alinsky model for unifying communities came to be embraced as an alternative to race riots and urban unrest, and communities began calling on the IAF to help them reduce racial tensions through productive organization building. The first such request came from Rochester, New York, after a series of race riots in 1964. There, Alinsky built a white solidarity organization to support black demands. The new organization, Friends of FIGHT, focused first on winning concessions to black community demands from the largest local employer, Eastman Kodak. Alinsky is famous for accusing Eastman Kodak of having contributed nothing to race relations but color film. In 1974, Ernesto Cortez went to San Antonio and started Citizens Organized for Public Service, which is now the best-known IAF group; and in 1994, an IAF organization, Baltimoreans United in Leadership Development, designed and won the first local living wage ordinance, sparking hundreds of similar campaigns nationally.

Alinsky laid out his organizing theory in two important works: *Rules for Radicals* ([1970] 1989) and *Reveille for Radicals* ([1946] 1991). The subtitle of *Rules for Radicals, A Pragmatic Primer for Realistic Radicals*, speaks to Alinsky's devotion to what works rather than to any specific theory. He had five basic premises:

1. The role of the organizer and the role of the community leader should be distinct in order to reflect an organizational model that has both local volunteer leaders and professional staff. In Alinsky-style organizations, the unpaid volunteer leader, who should be indigenous to the community in which the work is taking place, represents the organization, gets in front of the media, and negotiates with the power structure. The organizer works behind the scenes—recruiting, coordinating, doing research, taking notes, buying donuts. In *Rules for Radicals*, Alinsky also assigns leaders and organizers different motivations: "This is the basic difference between the leader and the organizer. The leader goes on to build power to fulfill his desires, to hold and wield the power for purposes both social and personal. . . . The organizer finds his goal in creation of power for others to use" (p. 79).

2. The building of the organization should be the major expression of a community's growing power in recognition of the fact that people power is mostly a matter of having overwhelming numbers. Alinsky also predicted that a shift in power relations would take place between institutions and the organization, rather than among individuals or within the community at large.

3. Issue campaigns should be focused on a specific, individual decision maker.

4. Organizing should target winning immediate, concrete changes based on the "needs, interests and issues" of local people rather than on developing an explicit ideology (Delgado, [1993] 1997, p. 11). Alinsky's main idea was that organizers were to enable the changes members wanted without imposing their own ideology on a group: the organization should be more concerned with winning concrete improvements for its members than on defending any particular ideology, such as Marxism or Communism. He seemed to believe that organizers would fall into ideology mode if they weren't vigilant about their own behavior and that organizations would be otherwise free of ideology. In *Rules for Radicals*, he wrote that an organizer must have "a free and open mind, and political relativity. The organizer in his way of life, with his curiosity, irreverence, imagination, sense of humor, distrust of dogma, his self-organization, his understanding of the irrationality of much of human behavior, becomes a flexible personality, not a rigid structure that breaks when something unexpected happens. *Having his own identity, he has no need for the security of an ideology or a panacea*" (p. 233; emphasis mine). In this framework, ideology is bad; it has the potential to become dogmatic, undemocratic, and divisive, and can deny the organization the tactical flexibility it needs to win.

5. The mode of organizing should be 24/7; the organizer needs to devote all emotional, physical, and intellectual resources to the work.

Though his prohibition on ideological line drawing made people suspicious, Alinsky is best known for helping regular people engage in campaigns that challenged the power of major corporations and unresponsive government. Stories of his organizing imply that Alinsky was opposed to at least the most obviously abusive forms of racism and rampant capitalism, though his sexual politics were rather less developed. His record also reveals that he believed generally that U.S. democracy would work if only citizens took their place in the line of protest (Horwitt, 1989; Delgado, [1993] 1997). Many people have defended Alinsky's politics, noting that what he did, though perhaps not what he said, challenged liberalism as well as conservatism.

Expanding Networks

Alinsky's ideas have been expressed again and again in the major organizing networks that have established themselves since the IAF was founded. People adapted Alinsky's basic concepts to match the changes they thought necessary for their communities and their theories of social change. Fred Ross Sr., who had been the IAF's West Coast director, was the first to make significant adjustments to the model when he developed the Community Service Organization (CSO). CSO organized Latinos in Los Angeles; it registered thousands to vote in 1948 and helped elect the first Latino city council member in 1949. Ross, reacting to the limits of the institutional model in reaching out to and finding leaders among people not already in an existing organization, developed the individual-membership model; he eventually helped Cesar Chavez start the United Farm Workers (UFW), an organization built through house meetings, which are small recruitment gatherings of people connected through a social or family network. Initially, both CSO and the UFW built their base of individuals through a *mutualista*, or mutual-aid, structure, in which members pooled their money to start purchasing cooperatives and revolving loan funds. With leadership from Chavez and Ross, the UFW organized the first national union of immigrant farmworkers, entirely outside the purview of the then exclusionary AFL-CIO, and introduced the country to an influential model of alliances through its grape boycott.

John Baumann and Dick Helfridge, priests who led the movement among Jesuits to begin new community organizations in the 1970s and 1980s, founded an organization composed largely of Christian churches and other congregations, and established a model of what is now called faith-based organizing through a new network, the People's Institute for Community Organizing (PICO) (website: www.piconetwork.org). Congregations of all denominations are the building blocks of these community organizations. PICO's emphasis on the "development of the whole person" in addition to respect for human dignity and the creation of a just society reflects in part an implicit criticism of the IAF reliance on formal leadership and its shortcomings in developing leaders among the rank and file of participating institutions.

The Association of Community Organizations for Reform Now (ACORN) is the undoubted leader among traditional community organizations based on the model of bringing individuals together into new formations that did not rely on existing institutions. Few contemporary activists, however, know that ACORN has its roots in the civil rights and welfare rights movements. In 1968, a chemistry professor and civil rights leader named George Wiley, active in the Congress of Racial Equality, implemented the idea of combining community organizing, which he saw winning significant victories, with the racial justice commitments of the civil rights movement in a new formation called the National Welfare Rights Organization (NWRO). Although it survived only six years, among its lasting legacies was the creation of ACORN, which was started by Wade Rathke, who had been sent to Little Rock, Arkansas, to build an NWRO chapter in 1970. ACORN was the first to design a replicable model for the individual-membership organization. Today, ACORN has organizations in twenty-six states and counts among its successes winning many local living wage campaigns, resisting redlining by banks and insurance companies, and reforming local public schools. ACORN's outreach to individuals and its continued commitment to organizing the very poor makes it an important supplement to the IAF and PICO, institutional models that address only marginally the question of the unorganized (Delgado, 1986).

Other IAF organizers and people trained in this thread of activism started additional networks. These include the Citizen Action network and National Peoples' Action, based in Chicago. In its heyday, Citizen Action had a tremendous base among the elderly and won many health care victories at the state level. Although Citizen Action started out largely as a set of individual-membership groups, over time it built more coalitions than membership organizations and contributed a great deal to our thinking about effective coalitions. Much of the former Citizen Action network has been reconstituted in a formation called U.S. Action, which is active in some states today. National Peoples' Action was founded by a former minister, Shel Trapp, and includes institutional- and individual-membership organizations, as well as coalitions. Trapp, in turn, was trained by Jesuit Tom Gaudette, former IAF organizer, during his effort to start regional training centers for organizers.

As the number of networks increased, so did efforts to train organizers and to professionalize the field. Every network has its own training centers. The IAF conducts ten-day trainings nationwide for its organizers, leaders, and potential members. PICO has a training institute. ACORN has its Leadership School. Citizen Action built the Chicago-based Midwest Academy, which survived the demise of the original network. The Midwest Academy established a successful and long-lasting collaboration with the United States Student Association, a national organization of progressive student associations, in the Grassroots Organizing Weekends (GROW), where student activists are exposed to the skills of community organizing. In addition to these training resources, some graduate schools of social work, such as those at Hunter College of the City University of New York and San Francisco State University, established tracks of study in community organizing. By 1980, the first masters of social work degrees were being awarded to students who had focused on community organizing.

Critiques of Alinskyist Approaches

As often as Alinsky' s ideas were taken up, they were criticized by other organizers and activists. Particularly in communities of color and among feminists, people took issue with Alinsky's rules, the issues he considered good to work on, the lack of a deeper analysis, and his reliance on formal leadership. Alinsky's rules had many implications for these populations because his principles dominated training curricula for professional organizers, foundation funding, and media attention. As the stakes became clearer with time, organizers raised important questions about Alinsky's model. These critiques led to the formation of alternative networks for people of color and for women, many of whom now dominate the National Organizers Alliance (NOA). NOA, a membership organization composed of organizers, provides practical as well as intellectual support to those working in the field.

The Antiracist Critique

The antiracist critique centers on three concerns: the domination of community organizations by white staff and white "formal" leaders such as priests and union officials; the refusal of most community organizations to incorporate issues focused on racism; and the lack of flexibility in the rules of leadership and tactical planning.

With rare exceptions, when I came into the work in the mid-1980s the staffs of most community organizations were white and male, although the membership was often mixed or even primarily people of color. In addition, the formal leadership of institution-based groups was also white and male, ranging from priests and local bishops to union officials. Many explanations have been offered for this trend. Some theorized that the low pay for organizing jobs deterred people of color, who usually entered the work with few financial assets and who were often responsible for the financial health of an extended family. Another explanation was that the networks and organizations were not yet mature enough to attract former members and children who had grown up as a part of those organizations. Finally, competing movements and organizations vied for the energy of young people of color, and many of them were more amenable than traditional organizations to the leadership of people of color. In communities of color, people were organizing in cooperatives, alternative labor structures, the civil rights struggle, anticolonialist movements, and explicitly socialist groups. Different decades offered different attractions, but these movements competed with community organizing for staff of color. By the 1990s, however, more people of color populated the staffs of community organizations than had previously.

A related critique is that community organizing's issues and rules do not match the political cultures and priorities of communities of color and antiracist activists (Delgado, 1986; Fellner, 1998; Blake, 1999). The question of appropriate issues became particularly important as a conservative backlash against the gains of the civil rights movement gathered steam in the 1980s and 1990s; this challenge from the right effectively divided communities of color through legislative campaigns that criminalized urban youth and undocumented immigrants, among others. As immigration and refugee resettlement from the Korean and Vietnam wars led to massive rises in immigration, communities struggled with the shifts and loss of traditional neighborhood boundaries; the neighborhood had always been the key site of community organizing. Shifting demographics and conservative attacks greatly challenged community organizing in the racial arena after the 1980s. Gary Delgado, founder of the Center for Third World Organizing, wrote in a monograph originally published in 1993, *Beyond the Politics of Place*, that community organizing faces the threat of becoming irrelevant if it does not keep pace with the changing identity of urban communities. He said that the development of "communities of interest" requires addressing issues that are not geographically based but are instead rooted in the identities and subsequent attacks faced by the marginal—immigrants, youth, women of color, and the very poor. If community organizing wants to survive, Delgado asserted, it has to abandon a focus on short-term, geographically based, winnable issues and move to the more complicated and controversial issues affecting new communities.

In a detailed response to Delgado's urging, Mike Miller of the Organize! Training Center agreed with the need to deal with these issues but defended the "traditional" organizing record:

> [Delgado makes] an assumption that there is a specific way in which race and gender issues must be addressed. Organizers and leaders have to have a conscious ideological construction, including notions of racism and its oppressiveness. It is their job to transmit these ideas to the membership and followers in an organization. But "traditional" community organizing has found other ways. People of diverse backgrounds are coming together on the basis of mutual respect, shared values, confidence in their own identities and self-interest issues. With the exception of independent organizations in communities of color, racial issues have been subsumed by issues of class solidarity in most community organizations. The same has been true of gender [Miller, 1996, p. 28].

Finally, people of color argue that many of the rules of community organizing run counter to the political traditions, cultures, and realities of communities of color. They point to three community organizing trends in particular: the separation of leader and organizer roles, the refusal to advance a fundamental critique of capitalism and U.S. democracy, and an overreliance on confrontational tactics as the only sign that institutional challenge is taking place. In many communities of color, organizers are a part of the community's leadership, publicly acknowledged and included in decision making. Sometimes these leaders are paid to do their organizing, and often they aren't. Examples abound, from Fannie Lou Hamer to Anna Mae Aquash. While many organizers of color see the importance of leadership that generates new leaders, they resist drawing a false line between leader and organizer.

In addition, many organizers of color share a fundamental distrust of U.S. institutions and are often excluded from the organizations meant to negotiate between them and the institutions; as a result they are critical of government and corporations and want to express that critique through organizations. They have been abandoned and abused by registrars of voters, business regulators, the school system, and so on, and they are disinclined to check fundamental criticisms of these systems. Much of the richest work in communities of color has been conducted by socialists, some raised here in the United States and others in countries from which they immigrated.

Many people of color have little faith that simply raising their voices will have a dramatic effect. Tactically, communities of color are accustomed to finding other ways to challenge institutions, including building alternatives. Some refugee and immigrant communities approach conflict cautiously, and some actions are carried out disguised as community fairs and cultural events.

Undoubtedly, some of the resentment directed toward white organizing networks has to do with the unacknowledged appropriation by white male organizers of techniques and models that have been in use in communities of color (interview with James Williams of Grassroots Leadership, 1995). Alinsky's own contributions had been used in other movements that pre-dated or ran concurrently with community organizing. In the pre–civil rights era, organizations of black people in the South, for example, relied on the alliance between existing social institutions, predominantly black churches and service societies, as the infrastructure for supporting community confrontations with local institutions. Some of these methods were replicated by the Student Nonviolent Coordinating Committee (SNCC) in its struggle for voting rights and desegregation. Building community through buying clubs and cooperatives, as Ross did in the CSO, was a common experience of Mexican and Central American immigrants, and doing so in the United States resonated with those communities.

Some of this critique stems from negative feelings about Alinsky himself, and it is irresistible to take a look at his own track record. Was Alinsky a racist, as he has been accused of being? He has been considered with great suspicion by leaders in the civil rights and antiracist movements. Organizers he trained and their organizations have been accused of ignoring the racial dimensions of neighborhood issues, refusing to take up explicitly racial issues, and undermining the leadership of local leaders of color. At the extremes in this debate, organizers of color accuse Alinsky of having been actively racist, while white organizers attempt to defend his legacy of bringing black and white communities together in common cause. Most likely, Alinsky was well-meaning but naïve in regard to matters of race. Certainly, he was easily able to condemn the racist motivations of extremist white supremacist groups like the Ku Klux Klan and of white working-class people who moved out of urban neighborhoods as blacks carried out their migration from South to North. He was hardly alone in these views.

But his efforts to disrupt that kind of thinking were frequently simplistic. Particularly after the mid-1970s, as conservatives learned that they could hide racist behavior in coded language that attacked vulnerable populations, Alinsky's definition of racism as explicit discrimination became outdated and ineffective. But even before the resurgence of conservatism, Alinsky's reputation on race was greatly damaged by the active segregationism of the Back of the Yards Neighborhood Council in the late 1960s, when it fought to keep blacks from migrating into its neighborhoods. Alinsky considered white flight a problem not just for the loss of an urban tax base but also for the loss of community power. However, the only solution he could think of at the time was a quota system limiting the number of blacks in any neighborhood to 10 percent—the amount he thought that racist whites would be willing to handle and that would also be acceptable to blacks as a better-than-nothing option (Horwitt, 1989). Alinsky's effort to have a race-relations committee in the early Back of the Yards configuration never took hold and fell apart when he left the organization. His one attempt to convince the Back of the Yards leadership to allow the 10 percent quota failed miserably. So, Alinsky knew enough about race to be embarrassed by explicit racism but not enough to embrace organizational practices that could centralize antiracist work and that could develop a sophisticated antiracist analysis that kept up with the efforts of the right wing. As years passed, the larger community organizing networks tended to follow that lead—they often included people of color and whites working on common issues that benefited both constituencies, but they rarely held explicit political discussions of race issues or waged campaigns that attacked race discrimination directly (Delgado, 1986). While whites and blacks working together on anything, as they did in Rochester, was radical in 1960, by 1990 it was no longer unusual.

The antiracist critique led directly to the formation of an additional set of networks that paid explicit attention to issues of race. The oldest of these, and the first to be founded and operated by people of color, is the Center for Third World Organizing (CTWO, pronounced C2), which was started in 1980 by Gary Delgado, a former welfare rights and ACORN organizer, and Hulbert James, a former SNCC and HumanServ organizer. In its more than twenty years of work, CTWO has become the premier network and training ground of organizers of color and the community organizations for which they work. CTWO advanced a strategy based on two notions: that people of color occupied a colonized position within the United States and could find common cause across the lines separating black, Asian, Latino, and Native American communities, and that community organizing offered potentially strong forums for such politics if it could be conducted with clear antiracist analysis and priorities. CTWO's major contributions include training thousands of organizers and volunteer leaders of color in community organizing embedded with antiracist politics, testing new forms of multiracial organizing among urban people of color, and questioning the effectiveness of organizing wisdom in achieving racial justice. Also in the early 1980s, Grassroots Leadership was founded by Si Kahn, a Jewish organizer and singer/songwriter, to be an explicitly biracial network of community organizations in the South that continued the tradition of combining art and culture with organizing practice. In the 1990s, there were further additions: the Black Radical Congress was founded in 1997 and led to the formation of groups like the Black

Autonomous Network of Community Organizers (BANCO); since 1990, the environmental justice movement has spawned a number of new local organizations and networks of color that fight on a combination of environmental and economic justice issues.

The Feminist Critique

Feminists also found plenty to critique in Alinskyist organizations. These criticisms have four targets: community organizing overemphasizes intervention in the public sphere, does not allow organizers to balance work and family, focuses on narrow self-interest as the primary motivator, and relies on conflict and militaristic tactics.

Feminists point out that Alinsky believed that organizing should take place entirely in the public sphere. Alinskyist organizations direct their energy toward reforming public institutions while ignoring the potential of using the private sphere—home and family. Because the arrangements of postindustrial capitalism created a sharp distinction between the two spheres and relegated women to the private, women's issues and contributions are easy to ignore if we focus only on behaviors and issues in the public sphere. Feminists argue that many of women's contributions to organizing have in fact taken place in the private sphere, as women turned home into community and expanded their notions of family. What Stoecker and Stall (1997) call "women-centered" organizing efforts have focused less on the policy outcome of a particular struggle and more on the process of building nurturing and compassionate relationships among participants and on offering learning opportunities. Important solutions were developed by women working together in the private sphere long before they confronted public institutions to get them to address the same problems. The domestic-violence and women's health movements provide good examples of such efforts; they led to major changes in popular opinion and behavior and only later led to institutional changes as well (Stoecker and Stall, 1997). My own experience suggests that the division of labor based on gender re-creates the public and private spheres even within community organizations as men work heavily on the external strategy questions and women work on membership recruitment and leadership development.

Alinsky's insistence on "toughening up" young organizers by holding strategic discussions late into the night excluded people, especially women, who had responsibilities in both spheres, what we now think of as the double and triple shift expected of women. In his writing about organizers, Alinsky referred only sporadically to women organizers, perhaps knowing that women's reproductive duties would be impossible to combine with the 24/7 work schedule he expected.

He wrote in 1970 about his training conversations with organizers: "Frequently domestic hang-ups were part of the conferences. An organizer's working schedule is so continuous that time is meaningless; meetings and caucuses drag endlessly into the early morning hours; any schedule is marked by constant unexpected unscheduled meetings; work pursues an organizer into his or her home, so that either he is on the phone or there are people dropping by. The marriage record of organizers is with rare exception disastrous" (Alinsky, [1970] 1989, p. 233). As a result, the majority of members in organizations were women, but they had a hard time getting staff positions until more recently.

Feminists also object to Alinsky's views on motivations and tactics. Feminists argue that women-centered organizing is not motivated primarily by self-interest, an idea that was paramount in Alinsky's theory, but by compassionate sympathy for vulnerable members of the target community and the community as a whole. Feminists also contend that Alinsky's emphasis on conflict runs counter to the many successful women's organizing efforts that emphasize cooperation and compromise to generate neighborhood improvements. In part because many women-centered organizing efforts often looked like and led to service provision, organizers in the Alinsky tradition of conflict would not recognize them as organizing, even though they also involved regular people in fighting for institutional change.

Feminist critiques of Alinskyist organizing led to the creation of new networks, such as Citizen Action, which was started by Heather Booth, as well as feminist networks that often combined social services, advocacy, and organizing around policy issues. Academic groups like the Education Center on Community Organizing at Hunter College have documented and analyzed the specific contributions to women to organizing practice. Extended networks of women working on specific issues, such as women's health and reproductive rights, domestic violence, and women in nontraditional work sectors, all have prominent national networks, with newly emerging efforts addressing the needs of women of color.

Points of Light: New Efforts at Organizing the Disenfranchised

Throughout the 1990s, activist gatherings were characterized by sometimes bitter debates based on the critiques of community organizing. In 1999, three years after the formation of NOA, the national gathering in Asheville, North Carolina, featured a series of engaging discussions, involving hundreds of organizers, about the sacred cows of organizing. NOA's members are largely identity-based activists (although many do engage in building membership-based community organizations) rather than traditional New Left, labor, or community organizers.

These discussions specifically challenged the notions that issues have to be widely and deeply felt, that democratic decision making is an appropriate reason to advance regressive politics, and that winnability is of primary importance in choosing issues. These challenges pointed to a fundamental tension between the goals embraced by traditional organizers and those of new activists.

In many ways, the lack of sophistication that traditional community organizing applies to large-scale economic, racial, and gender questions resulted in the lack of explicit ideological discussion in most traditional organizing networks. Over time, the pragmatism that Alinsky espoused came to characterize community organizations; it determined the path of internal conflicts about class, race, and gender, and eventually of those about immigration and sexuality. If a particular issue was bound to divide a community or was difficult to address entirely in the public sphere, most community organizations did not deal with it. Domestic violence and police brutality provide excellent examples of issues that could divide a community and that local institutions resisted dealing with. Only recently have some organizations modeled loosely after the traditional—that is, having a membership and engaging in direct action issue campaigns—taken on police behavior, for example. Throughout the 1980s, as the War on Drugs blew up the prison rolls, most community organizations campaigned for an increased police response to chase out drug dealers rather than for action on the larger issues surrounding the War on Drugs.

Over time, additional forces and new movements have changed community organizing by creating an imperative for different methods and politics. These forces include, but are not limited to, shifting demographics caused by migration within the United States and immigration into the country, growing inequalities in wealth and income, vast increases in private and public prison building and in incarceration, and rising expectations among people of color and women. In an increasingly conservative atmosphere, constituencies under attack have found ways to fight back. Whether these efforts take place within or outside traditional structures, they have begun to interact with community organizing in ways that shift practices. Three different kinds of efforts have been particularly critical to organizing the disfranchised. Like their forebears, they all have significant strengths and severe shortcomings. They do not constitute "the answer." Rather, they point to what needs to be done and to factors that need to be considered. First, New Labor is organizing the most marginal workers both within and outside the AFL-CIO. Second, identity-based movements among women of color, lesbians and gays, and immigrants have clarified the relationship between who people are and the issues that emerge from their experiences. Third, community organizing practice has begun to answer earlier critiques and to create new practices that enable work that is deeper and more effective than in the past.

New Labor

Many of the criticisms directed toward community organizing are somewhat milder versions of racial, economic, and gender critiques directed at the mainstream labor movement, now epitomized by the AFL-CIO. Organized labor has a long and explicit, often bloody, history of excluding blacks, immigrants, and women; it chose to protect white male workers from these constituencies rather than building an inclusive movement. For much of the twentieth century, the United Auto Workers was the only union that included black men and had a multiracial identity. Only the establishment of independent unions for workers of color, the civil rights movement, and the overall decline in union membership led eventually to some unions' embracing new constituencies. This change was a result of the work known as New Labor.

New Labor consists of both community-based worker organizing and progressive initiatives within the AFL-CIO. Since the mid-1980s, there has been a wealth of new organizing among marginalized workers, those who had been ignored or shut out by the AFL-CIO; much of this organizing is taking place in immigrant communities. These community-based worker organizations are usually known as workers' centers because they often provide services, such as job placement, cooperative development, and legal services, in addition to organizing workplaces or industries and running issue campaigns. The workers' center movement was fed and influenced by a number of political factors. First, AFL-CIO unions, with only a few exceptions, revealed a lack of interest in immigrant and low-wage workers until the mid-1980s, when many Latin American, Asian, and Caribbean refugees and immigrants gave up the notion of returning to their home countries and decided to settle in the United States. Second, even after some unions—namely the Service Employees International Union (SEIU) and the Hotel Employees, Restaurant Employees International Union (HERE)—began to organize low-wage workers and immigrants, the industry-based structure of unions and legal limitations on them made it necessary for community organizations to step into worker organizing. Currently, unions take their identity from a particular industry, and each contract struggle is based on a discrete workplace. If a worker switches from industry to industry (for example, being a hotel worker by day and a janitor at night), unions are not structured to accommodate that person's membership in more than one. In addition, labor law is supremely unfriendly to low-wage, temporary, and other contingent workers (such as those who work under contract rather than as direct employees), limiting their rights and protections, including the ability to organize a union. The situations of undocumented immigrants, who are easily exploited and controlled by employer sanctions, and welfare-to-work participants are telling examples.

Operating with a fraction of the resources available to organized labor, workers' centers represent the cutting edge in organizing marginal workers. In her book, *Sweatshop Warriors*, Miriam Ching Louie calls workers' centers "a bit like small guerilla warriors fighting a more heavily armed opponent; . . . [they] 'organize outside the box,' and utilize tactics and strategies based on their ethnic backgrounds—like the 'war of the flea,' tai chi, jujitsu, haikido and the ideas of Gandhi, Cesar Chavez and the Zapatistas—techniques that deflect and toss their opponents' weight back at them" (2001, p. 22). Workers' centers organize farmworkers, garment workers toiling in sweatshops, immigrants working in electronics factories, domestic workers, day laborers in construction and landscaping, and cafeteria workers, just to name a few of the sectors affected. They are known for winning changes where unions have been unable to by conducting extensive leadership development and expanding the definition of workers' issues. While all workers' centers focus on labor issues, many also take on social and political issues such as amnesty for undocumented immigrants, affordable housing, education, and access to health care. Many of these organizations are key to local community/labor alliances. Many are also active in issues of the immigrants' homeland.

The building of these community-based organizations to get to marginal constituencies pushed innovative organizing within the AFL-CIO; the result was the creation of an insurgent arm of organized labor that has challenged earlier political positions (Gapasin, 1999). Forced to change simply to survive, organized labor has begun to organize nontraditional workers and to take up nonworkplace issues such as child care, housing, and immigration law. In the 1980s, SEIU and HERE began organizing janitors and other service workers, many of them immigrants and people of color. In addition, the AFL-CIO has made new commitments to moving contingent and temporary workers toward the collective bargaining process. Unions have worked for the reclassification of contingent workers through creative mechanisms. In Los Angeles, seventy-four thousand home care workers classified as independent contractors joined SEIU in February 1999, after pressuring the county to set up a public agency to act as their employer in collective bargaining. And unions have used contract negotiations for standard workers to win improvements in the status of contingents. The United Parcel Service strike of 2000, for example, featured full-time workers demanding that part-time deliverers be given full-time status and accompanying benefits (Cook, 2000).

The election of John Sweeney, former international president of SEIU, as president of the AFL-CIO in 1995 raised the hopes of many labor activists that the AFL-CIO would now devote more resources to new organizing efforts and would improve some of its policy positions. Sweeney's politics are quite different from those of his conservative predecessor, Lane Kirkland, who had resisted the immigration-reform work of groups that did not do "straight organizing"; one such group was the California Immigrant Workers Association, which helped launch strikes by southern California construction workers and built resistance to anti-immigrant Proposition 187 in 1994 (Bacon, 1995). Unlike Kirkland, Sweeney began with a platform that included the legalization of undocumented immigrant workers, the repeal of employer sanctions, and the use of resources to organize new sets of workers. In addition, AFL-CIO unions, particularly SEIU and HERE, are investing increasingly in building alliances between unions and community organizations of all sorts. Both Sweeney's election and these new policy positions are in part a response to insurgent groups within the AFL-CIO, such as the A. Phillip Randolph Institute for black workers, the Labor Immigrant Organizing Network, Out at Work, and the AFL-CIO women's division.

Both workers' centers and the new progressive union initiatives have weaknesses as well as strengths. According to Jennifer Gordon (1999), founder of the Workplace Project, while workers' centers have done excellent work in enforcing existing labor regulations and developing new leaders among immigrants and people of color, they lack a broad strategy to deal with the limitations of current laws. They do not have the clarity, resources, and experience to launch and win long-term legislative campaigns. Louie (2001) notes that workers' centers have many strengths, but they have not yet been able to take on the forces of global capital in a comprehensive way by themselves; their victories are still largely at the local level. Workers' centers, unlike unions, are not allowed by the National Labor Relations Act to engage in collective bargaining, so they have had limited success in winning new comprehensive contracts. On the AFL-CIO side, progressive unions and labor councils are frequently held back by conservative unions, particularly in the building trades and manufacturing, and AFL-CIO positions on social and political issues frequently work against key constituencies. For example, the AFL-CIO took positions in line with President George Bush's war on terrorism and said little about the effects of civil liberties violations or international isolationism. While the AFL-CIO's legislative capacity is somewhat better than that of the workers' centers, most unions have concentrated on winning union-recognition elections and contract fights rather than on legislation. In addition, the basic structure of the industrial union has not changed in a century. These and other limitations will have to be dealt with if New Labor is to reach its true potential.

Identity-Based Movements

Identity politics is an overarching term for a broad set of ideas and organizations that emerged mostly after the decline of the 1960s' mass movements, partly in reaction to the contradictions apparent in the setup of the movements themselves.

The participation of specific constituencies within mass-based organizations—
for example, women in the peace and civil rights movements, people of color
in the economic justice movement, and gay and lesbian people in the New Left—
revealed contradictions that, by the mid-1970s, could no longer be ignored. In
part, identity politics started as an analytic movement, a movement of ideas,
that upheld the importance of the political experiences of marginalized constituencies and expected progressives to unify around the imperatives of attacking racism, sexism, and sexual oppression as they had around class. Identity
politics—a political vision that recognizes the problems of societies in which rewards and punishments are distributed by massive systems according to physical
attributes—led to some of the most important theoretical and political movements
of the last thirty years of the twentieth century; these movements ranged from
black feminism to the anti-AIDS campaigns to the community-based worker organizing described above, and they have, in turn, profoundly affected community
organizers and their ideas.

By the mid-1970s, feminists of color and other marginalized groups outlined
the principles of identity politics to counter the limitations of earlier "universal"
movements, which were usually oriented around class. Universal movements to
fight capital were designed around what I call the same-boat argument—that all
workers experience the same exploitation at the hands of the same bosses but do
not see their similarities because of capitalist manipulation. Three assertions presented substantial challenges to this simplistic framework for movement building
and organizing. First, activists exploring identity politics developed the idea that
identities that had been considered biological are socially constructed. Social construction is a matter of giving biological characteristics meaning by assigning values, behaviors, stereotypes, and status to meet the needs of society and its
institutions.

Second, activists developed the idea that these social constructions create vastly
different experiences among people as they relate to the institutions of private and
public life. In acknowledging this difference in life experience, activists were forced
to grapple with the reality that black autoworkers require voting reform as well as
union membership or that women might rebel against the nuclear family because
that structure burdens them a great deal more than it does men or that black
women's priority gender issue might be welfare while white women's might be
abortion.

Third, identity politics raised the idea that one solution might not fit all: controlling capital might not prevent institutional racism; third world liberation might
not address women's oppression. Activists observed that movements for one kind
of liberation might not embrace the issues that would lead to other kinds of liberation, and they urged attention to all the different systems from which people

need to be liberated. In their seminal work about the liberatory possibilities of identity politics, a group of black feminists wrote in the Combahee River Collective statement that "the major source of difficulty in our political work is that we are not just trying to fight oppression on one front or even two, but instead to address a whole range of oppressions" ("Combahee River Statement," [1983] 2000, p. 269).

The ideas behind identity politics led to new movements. The old forms of organization frequently became obsolete as particular groups of people sought places in which they could do their own political work. Women, gay/lesbian/ bisexual/transgender people, immigrants, and poor people left those organizations that could not integrate their needs and formed new organizations whose issues varied substantially from the bread-and-butter issues of the Old and New Left, the first- and second-wave women's movements, the peace movement, the civil rights movement, and the black/red/yellow power movements. In the late 1970s and early 1980s we saw remarkably innovative organizations such as ActUp and Queer Nation, which brought new attention to the structural nature of heterosexism; organizations of women of color fighting domestic violence; and immigrant-rights organizations working on amnesty and workers' issues. Often, the creation of independent identity-based organizations led to the inclusion of these constituencies in more mainstream groups—for example, in the creation of the Out at Work caucus within the AFL-CIO and of the women of color antiviolence network in the larger, white-dominated domestic violence organizations.

More important, identity-based organizations created both political and cultural change. In 2000, for the first time in U.S. history, a National Gay and Lesbian Task Force analysis of election exit polls showed that more than half of Americans support equal rights for gay and lesbian people (Yang, 2001). A range of women of color organizations, inspired by the black women's health movement and the National Black Women's Health Organization, have provided healthier environments for women and girls of color and have raised questions about women's health priorities, just as the women's health movement created a culture, followed by public programs, that encouraged women to explore rather than hate their bodies. Most recently, women of color who have been active in fighting domestic violence have initiated a new national effort to define responses to domestic violence that are more appropriate to communities of color than are traditional solutions.

Identity politics has been soundly attacked by white self-named leftists who bemoan the loss of the universal politics they believe lead to mass movements (for example, Todd Gitlin, 1995, and Michael Tomasky, 1996). They contend that progressive movements have been destroyed by the inherent narrowness of identity politics, that the privileging of individual identities is an obstacle for universal mass organization, and that U.S. activists have lost sight of the positive values of European liberalism (the Enlightenment). Some in these circles perceive the need to devise new words for identifying people (the many names for describing various peoples of color and sexual minorities stand as supremely frustrating examples) and the need to address issues that affect small numbers of people as dangerous distractions to the larger purpose of relieving poverty through attacks on capitalism. The implication here is that class war is universal, but race, gender, and sexual liberation are particular and are not appealing to all of humanity.

Their comments reflect growing resentment among white leftists (including many community organizers) toward the attention afforded identity-based movements, as well as a troubling nostalgia for universal labor and populist movements that regularly excluded people of color, encouraged nativist violence, and kept women out of the paid labor force. As Kelley (1997) writes, "They either don't understand or refuse to acknowledge that class is lived through race and gender. There is no universal class identity, just as there is no universal racial or gender or sexual identity. The idea that race, gender and sexuality are particular whereas class is universal not only presumes that class struggle is some sort of race and gender-neutral terrain but takes for granted that movements focused on race, gender and sexuality necessarily undermine class unity and, by definition, cannot be emancipatory for the whole." Researcher of conservative movements Jean Hardisty puts it more bluntly when she writes, "To the heterosexual, white, male leaders of the Old Left, class oppression (and hence the demands of the labor movement) was the movement's principal concern. The neglect of 'other' oppressions stems from their lack of relevance to that leadership" (1999, p. 197). The real challenge here, suggest Kelley and Hardisty, on behalf of activists in identity movements, is to advance ideas and policies that are truly inclusive and that are based on a complete, sophisticated analysis of the issues. It should be noted that traditional community and labor organizations also failed to build mass-based movements that speak to the broadest range of peoples' interests and achieve impact beyond the local level. Focused on bread-and-butter, motherhood-and-apple-pie issues that were easy to defend, many chose to ignore the problems their own constituencies faced daily—problems around the very issues the New Right (the conservative organizations and leaders that emerged in the late 1960s) chose as its priorities, including affirmative action, immigrants, gay rights, and reproductive choice.

Certainly, identity politics has limitations, just as community organizing does. Even in identity-based organizations, it is possible to find contradictions—for example, gay/lesbian organizations that blindly support capitalism or feminist organizations that lack an understanding of immigration. I sometimes refer to them as identity-without-the-politics organizations because they are designed to deal only with an immediate problem—let's say AIDS—and a narrow constituency—such as white, gay, upper-class men living with AIDS. Kelley (1997) makes the excellent point that white men protesting affirmative action policies are also exercising identity politics, a conservative set. In addition, identity politics arose at the same time as did therapeutic models for dealing with these structural issues, and some identity-based organizations are more therapy-oriented than political. In some cases an overemphasis on experience has acted as a barrier to the broadening of analysis and political strategies. But these limitations are no secret to activists from these communities, who consistently work to weave together the threads of different constituencies and issues and who engage in a fundamental economic analysis as well.

Identity movements and community organizing have both been growing but largely along parallel tracks; they speak little to each other and share few issues and resources. The question is how to achieve the goal of scale without leaving important nonmajority issues and constituencies by the wayside. As Hardisty writes, "In fact, people who have had trouble being heard may be the very people who hold the key to new visions, new ways of formulating solutions, or new views of equality in post-industrial capitalism" (1999, p. 233).

New Community Organizing Practices

In a significant shift in practice, community organizations are increasingly taking up the issues and constituencies mainstream groups refuse to touch. There has been significant innovation in three particular areas. First, groups have begun to organize the most marginalized people rather than those occupying the middle. The organizing of undocumented immigrants, victims of police brutality, and single mothers is indicative of this trend. Second, groups choose issues that enable the organizing of the worst-off, sometimes privileging those concerns over blander issues that might be more winnable. Third, political education has been added to organizing practice. Often, activists interpret the imperative to establish democratic organizations, in which members own the political decisions that are made, as the avoidance of ideology. But the notion of the nonideological organization has been increasingly challenged as the New Right gains power and success. That notion has led many organizations to avoid ideologically difficult issues and to suppress that kind of discussion in their organizations. Activists are beginning to recognize that the nonideological organization doesn't exist. All individuals and organizations operate from an ideology; an ideology is simply a world-view, and everybody has one, whether stated or implicit.

These developments in community organizing practice have significant implications for the organizer's role. First, the line between organizers and volunteer leaders needs to become less distinct. Innovative organizations are already blurring that line, largely out of a need for sophisticated human resources and out of the commitment to diverse leadership that arose out of the identity movements mentioned above. Second, organizers have to take their educational role more seriously; we need to become better teachers and help volunteer leaders develop that capacity as well. Third, organizers have to consider themselves learners as well as teachers. And, fourth, they have to be far more systematic about documenting and evaluating organizational activities.

Conclusion

A look at the history of community organizing reveals a number of different models, each based on a specific theory of constituency building and social change. Identifying specific models of organizing can be both liberating and limiting. If we know the model on which our tactics are based, we can follow that model to a logical conclusion, get help from others who have used it, avoid its pitfalls, and describe ourselves effectively in our attempts to raise money and train new leaders. But discussion of models can also limit our ability to innovate, which is at the heart of successful action. Pure models do not exist; every idea we have has seen the light of day somewhere in the world, sometime in history. Effective organizers mix and match, sometimes being able to identify the source of their idea, sometimes not. The history of community organizing and social movements is replete with tactics learned in one movement being applied to another. The important thing is to be able to articulate our particular theory of social change and hold on to or adjust it as we organize.

Although Alinsky is credited with having "invented" community organizing, he actually codified and developed a set of rules with roots in many other movements, including the settlement houses and the racial-liberation and labor movements of earlier decades. While he can be blamed for not acknowledging his sources, I cannot blame him for appropriating ideas that worked. Alinsky's stolen rules have been both adopted and challenged by organizers who have come after him, and both adopters and challengers have made positive contributions to struggles for economic and social justice. The potential for community organizing to remain relevant and helpful in advancing emerging justice movements is enhanced by the rise of New Labor, as epitomized in community-based workers' centers and new initiatives within the AFL-CIO, by the creation of identity-based movements, and by the development of innovations in organizing practice. If we look closely at the leaders of these efforts, we will see that people have moved from one sort of organization and movement to another, taking skills and lessons with them.

The organizations profiled in this book emerge from all the political phenomena mentioned in this Introduction. The Workplace Project and the Chinese Staff and Workers Association are among the best known and oldest workers' centers in the country. The Los Angeles Alliance for Fair Employment, Working Partnerships, the Campaign on Contingent Work, and the Women's Institute for Leadership Development represent some of the newest thinking among AFL-CIO leaders as well as that of the most effective community-labor alliances. The Center for Third World Organizing; Direct Action for Rights and Equality; Justice, Economic Dignity and Independence for Women; and the Southeast Regional Economic Justice Network have roots in traditional community organizing, welfare rights, or antiracist work. The Center for the Child Care Workforce, 9to5, Wider Opportunities for Women, and the Women's Association for Women's Alternatives come out of women-centered organizing. Whatever their origins, these organizations present hybrids that work to garner great results in the struggle for justice.

STIR IT UP

CHAPTER ONE

NEW REALITIES, INTEGRATED STRATEGIES

I f we are to shift power, our organizing has to be grounded in a clear and common understanding of how the world works. Because our world has expanded and changes at a rapid pace, we can easily become overwhelmed by the scale and character of the change taking place around us. But our analysis of the world provides more than background for our work, more than an interesting discussion every once in a while. It provides an evaluative benchmark against which to measure the effectiveness of and need for our particular organizing program.

This chapter is about what I consider the central political and economic trends we need to take into account while we do our work. In the United States today, three trends in particular are relevant to every progressive group: the resurgence of conservative movements and the power gained by such movements in the United States since the early 1970s; the character and organization of the new economy, which is distinguished by the rising use of neoliberal policies and contingent workers; and the continued, unyielding role of racism and sexism in the organization of society. The prominence and stubbornness of these three aspects of life in the United States, and globally, have many implications for our work. First, even local organizing is more likely to make a positive, long-term contribution if it addresses ideological questions while building a strong and active base among the people most affected by the trends I listed above. The most important goal is increasing our organizing to build new constituencies of progressive activists among people in the most desperate straits. Such direct action organizing needs to be accompanied by substantial research and media capacity—intellectual resources. Our daily work will be stronger if we revive the role of analysis and ideology development in our organizations. Second, our increased intellectual capacity should allow us to reframe key debates and influence public opinion. We can then take on issues that have not been traditionally popular, edgier issues that challenge the fundamental hierarchies of society. Third, we need to be able to build organizations and contribute to social movements simultaneously.

Many aspects of our current situation are not entirely new, just as many innovations in our organizing have been used before. But enough has changed in the world since the progressive mass movements of the 1960s and 1970s to warrant examination and shifts in our organizing practice. Certainly, there has always been a powerful right wing in this country, and modern capitalism was built on the backs of women, immigrants, and men of color. However, the rapid pace of technological innovation and the globalization of U.S.-style capitalism have made the world simultaneously larger and smaller. People experience the results of a shrinking safety net, religious fundamentalism, and racial supremacy regardless of where they live. Those who make decisions about our lives enjoy a further reach and more protection than they have in several generations. The New Right has influenced public opinion away from racial, gender, and economic justice; it has essentially cajoled or forced people to vote and act against their own values and self-interest. For example, legal immigrants frequently support measures limiting access to public services for undocumented immigrants, only to find themselves next in line for the chopping block. Low-wage workers might support forcing welfare recipients to work, but their working creates increased competition for low-wage jobs and drives wages down further.

Possibly, it has always been true that progressive strategies need to be as complex and far-reaching as our conditions and opposition. If so, progressives have often failed to learn from previous movements. The inability or unwillingness to address ideology and organizing simultaneously, for example, weakened a number of potentially progressive movements—labor, civil rights, community organizing, identity politics, and feminism—and undermined the possibility of sustaining power for disfranchised communities.

This chapter is organized into four sections. Initially, I explore the scope and character of the conservative resurgence, the new economy, and the centrality of race and gender in contemporary institutions. In each section, I outline the implications for our organizing. Finally, I describe the characteristics of effective organizing for economic and social liberation; these characteristics are the focus of the remaining chapters.

The New Conservative Infrastructure

With the Goldwater for President campaign in 1964, U.S. conservatives, feeling that they had been losing ground since the New Deal, launched a three-decade plan to regain control of the public imagination and institutions (Hardisty, 1999). This plan had three goals—the return to traditional family structures, the preservation of white supremacy in U.S. culture, and the reduction of government's role in redistributing wealth and controlling capital coupled with an increase in its military role around the world and at home. From the late 1960s to the mid-1980s, the New Right prepared to expand the constituency that would rebel against the gains made by liberals and progressives since the 1930s.

Building a New Infrastructure

Conservatives greatly expanded their existing institutions and built new ones, including think tanks, media outlets, philanthropic foundations, and grassroots organizations; these institutions added up to an effective new infrastructure. Think tanks form the intellectual base of this infrastructure, and they far outstrip their liberal counterparts in resources and sheer production. The Heritage Foundation, for example, was founded in 1973 with a grant of $250,000 and is now Washington's largest think tank, with an annual budget over $23 million and the ability to produce intellectual resources from books to legislative briefing packets (Heritage Foundation website: www.heritage.org/about); these publications are delivered to hundreds of policymakers and thousands of reporters nationwide and internationally. Heritage played a key role in reducing the power of federal civil rights laws and affirmative action and developed the plan that became Newt Gingrich's "Contract with America." It made stars of such people as Ward Connerly (leader of the Proposition 209 attack on affirmative action in California), Ron Unz (sponsor of California's ballot initiative outlawing bilingual education), and Charles Murray, author of *The Bell Curve*, whose pseudo-scientific theories linking race, intelligence, and poverty have been widely discredited. Heritage is joined by others, including the American Enterprise Institute, the Manhattan Institute, the Hoover Institution, and the Cato Institute, almost all of them with budgets exceeding $20 million.

Examples of conservative interconnections are numerous: trustees and advisers of think tanks are officers of the largest corporations; high-profile people go back and forth between government positions and think-tank fellowships; the networking at conferences, congressional hearings, and social events is continuous.

The Enron scandal perfectly illustrated the depth of this cross-fertilization of economic and political interests. Even the mainstream press questioned the conflict of interest implied by the fact that the chairman of the Manhattan Institute was a top executive at Alliance Capital Management, a Wall Street investment firm that repeatedly got contracts from Florida Governor Jeb Bush, despite the fact that it invested Florida's pension money in plummeting Enron stocks for eighteen months and in the process lost $300 million of pensioners' money (Lytle and Horvitz, 2002). That same Alliance executive, Roger Hertog, was also on the board of trustees of the American Enterprise Institute. Through the overarching Council for National Policy, an organization shrouded in secrecy, heads of media organizations, key congressional figures, conservative ideologues, and wealthy conservative donors craft strategy three times a year (Ambinder, 2002).

The New Right's activist groups have also built large voting constituencies and lobby operations, as well as their own research and public policy institutes. These include Concerned Women for America, the Federation for American Immigration Reform (FAIR), the Christian Coalition, the Family Research Council, and the Promise Keepers. The Christian Coalition has a huge voter base and dominates the Republican Party in at least eighteen states (Conger, 2002). Concerned Women for America, a Christian fundamentalist group, considers itself the largest public policy women's organization in the country (http://www.cwfa.org/about.asp). We cannot afford to underestimate the power and influence these institutions wield at the top levels of government and business in virtually every policy arena, domestic and foreign. Ralph Reed, former president of the Christian Coalition, said, in commenting on the Coalition's prospects at the White House after George W. Bush was declared president, "You're no longer throwing stones at the building, you're in the building" (Milbank, 2001).

Most impressive, perhaps, is the New Right's media empire. In part, empire building in this area is indicated by the consolidation of print and electronic outlets. Consolidation amounts to the erasure of the diverse points of view that are represented in a variety of outlets. Technology has enabled the right to get its message out in many ways. The Christian Coalition, for example, has access to founder Pat Robertson's *700 Club* (a television show with an estimated one million viewers) and his Christian Broadcasting Network, whose programs are distributed in ninety countries and cover a huge array of issues from the Israel/Palestine conflict to abortion to free trade. Several American Enterprise Institute fellows have regular assignments in major print and broadcast media. Each think tank has a media arm that feeds research and experts into the major outlets. The Heritage Foundation runs the Center for Media and Public Policy and the Computer Assisted Research and Reporting Database, two resources that direct journalists toward conservative research and public policy papers. Regular users include ABC

News, the *Wall Street Journal,* Scripps Howard News, the *Detroit Free Press,* the *Houston Chronicle, USA Today,* and the Associated Press. Finally, conservative recruitment and training of young journalists on college campuses provides a steady stream of writers and commentators ready to populate the newsrooms of media outlets.

Devising Policy Campaigns

The New Right built itself through a series of economic- and social-policy campaigns that it never gave up on: English only, affirmative action, welfare, multicultural education, immigration, union busting, abortion, sexuality, and crime. Each campaign resulted from years of investment in polling and focus-group research to figure out the circumstances under which Americans could be "wedged" away from liberal and progressive policies in these arenas. Conservatives have masterfully crafted language that highlights popular anxieties and values and relates them to these issues. Thus, the growing incarceration of people of color was conducted under the guise of the War on Drugs in the 1980s. Affirmative action was attacked as a system of preferences because polls showed that Americans supported affirmative action to fight discrimination but did not approve of preferences. Welfare was equated with dependence and fraud, again because Americans believe in the value of a temporary helping hand. Conservatives worked on these issues over ten to thirty years. My friends often joke about the power of the "lunatic fringe," a label that was surely applied to many conservative ideas until they gained credibility and power.

Many of these campaigns shared a central feature: reducing government's role in public life and turning over functions to the private sector. Defunding government and deregulation have been key to that agenda. Since the 1970s, conservative tax revolts effectively robbed the public coffers of the resources needed to carry out regulation. In her important work *Mobilizing Resentment,* Hardisty writes that "the trimming of the progressive income tax, the campaign to eliminate the long-term capital gains tax, and the attack on corporate taxes, federal regulations and unions—all rely on a public that identifies with free-market capitalism. The right has created such a public" (1999, p. 225).

Conservatives reduce the protective functions of government in other ways. Few are as overt as overturning specific laws. Conservative legislators and judges have gutted the power of regulatory agencies, including the Occupational Safety and Health Administration, the Legal Services Corporation, the Department of Justice, the Environmental Protection Agency, and the Department of Labor. Circuit courts and a Supreme Court peopled with conservatives have consistently ruled to undermine an agency's regulatory power or a law's coverage. For example, circuit courts decided that the millions of state employees—groups in which women and people of color are overrepresented and generally organized into unions—are exempt from the Americans with Disabilities Act and the Age Discrimination Act. And although legislation is the solution of last resort, conservatives have passed plenty of laws and have undone them when necessary.

Implications for Progressive Organizing

How does the growing power of extreme conservatives affect us? Many activists and scholars have suggested that progressives need to take a lesson from the New Right—its disciplined organizing, attention to ideas, willingness to lose battles in order to win the war, apparent unity in messages and political goals. In one of the most persuasive arguments, Hardisty points out the important lessons we can draw:

> First, dramatic social change can be achieved through the electoral system. . . . Second, moving into political dominance means recruiting new constituencies or winning to your side opposing and undecided constituencies. Third, movement building institutionalizes a social movement and prevents the movement from collapsing during periods of electoral setback. Fourth, multiple strategies—both a national and a state/local focus, both religious and secular organizing, both an electoral and a movement-building focus, both single-issue and broadly defined ideological public education—protect the movement from electoral vicissitudes. And fifth, a movement must resonate with the public mood, so that its messages can "hitchhike" on it [1999, p. 171].

But Hardisty also points out that some of the right's tactics are not options for our side: scapegoating unpopular communities and building political empires run dictatorially by powerful men do not mesh with progressive values.

Besides these lessons, the resurgence of the right has other implications for progressives. First, we cannot pin our hopes on government intervention as we have in the past. At the risk of overstating the availability of government protection—after all, it took decades before any president supported antilynching legislation—government has been the primary target of most left/liberal efforts since the 1960s. But increasing corporate control of government and the overall reduction in government itself suggest that we need a plan that allows us to take over government rather than just influence it.

Second, the right's political success, symbolized by the Republican takeover of Congress in the 1994 elections and by the election of George W. Bush in 2000, has shifted all economic and political debate rightward. The center, as defined by conservatives, is now seen as the only available space in which liberals and progressives can be taken seriously. Even progressive groups feel a strong urge to compromise for politically pragmatic reasons. Many believe that what the other side says we can win determines what we ask for. These limitations may be real, but I would argue that we have more options than to just accept these terms of debate and abandon our less "palatable" demands. By limiting ourselves in this way, we have lost valuable ground for progressive ideals. Regaining that ground requires that progressive organizers turn their attention to ideological work without delay in order to articulate a set of values that will help win back the constituencies we are rapidly losing to the right.

Third, it is important to note how interconnection affects the way in which opponents and decision makers respond to organized resistance. The average conservative officeholder's connection to the intellectual and financial resources of national organizations is much stronger than in the past. Going up against our local machine—the racist mayor and police chief working together, for example—is the least of our problems. Now that mayor and chief, along with their counterparts on the school board, in the public health department, and on the county court, communicate regularly with the Heritage Foundation, the Christian Coalition, and FAIR. Our local targets no longer even have to make decisions themselves—they are essentially told the right thing to do by the national infrastructure. Nor do they have to defend their decisions themselves—that will be done for them in newspapers and courts, again by the national infrastructure. We can point to numerous examples of such collusion: consider the cases of Rodney King and Abner Louima, those of abortion foes who kill doctors, those of undocumented immigrants picked up by the FBI, those of women who are denied welfare benefits. In every case, the national right wing has kicked in to advance the ideas that the police need to be all powerful, abortion needs to be punished, the United States is a white country, and black women need to be working rather than breeding. Given this reality, our strategy cannot stop with local targets and organizing, we have to prepare to go broader.

The New Economy

The rollback of government, the freeing of capital, and the rise of contingent work—which have resulted from a set of policies known as *neoliberalism*—have been key to the globalization of modern U.S. capitalism. These policies include allowing the free investment of capital anywhere in the world, providing tax breaks and direct subsidies to corporations for locating in a particular place, creating free-trade zones in third world countries, and enabling migration for work purposes while limiting its cultural and political effects.

Major Neoliberal Policies

We can draw parallels between neoliberal subsidy policies within the United States and those operating across national borders. A central goal of these policies is to provide public resources to draw corporate investment. National leaders like Ronald Reagan and Margaret Thatcher popularized government interventions to provide a favorable business climate through the removal of labor and environmental regulations, the provision of tax reductions and exemptions, and the privatization of publicly owned industries and services. This economic philosophy supports the structural adjustment policies forced onto developing countries by the World Bank and the International Monetary Fund, both heavily controlled by the United States, the United Kingdom, and France. Structural adjustment, which requires nations to privatize resources and functions, produce for export, and recruit foreign investment, is generally acknowledged to aggravate poverty, particularly among women in impoverished countries. In the United States, these policies find one expression in the practice of providing tax subsidies and reducing regulations to attract businesses back into urban centers after whites flee desegregation requirements.

Another important feature of the new global economy is the restructuring of the multinational firm on a scale not seen since the advent of industrialization and the merger movement that took place at the turn of the previous century. The rising use of contingent (part-time or temporary) workers signals this restructuring and offers an additional example of government's reduced role in protecting workers. Contingent work increases when companies cut back the number of workers for whom they are responsible by outsourcing as many jobs as possible. The North American Alliance for Fair Employment (2000) says this restructuring constitutes a historic shift in corporate structures; it reorganizes the workplace from the vertical/horizontal model, in which the massive firms internalize all aspects of production and marketing, to a core-ring model, in which most jobs are located outside the standard employment structure. As Working Partnerships Executive Director Amy Dean asserts, "There really is a new economy that isn't just new products and new technology; it's about the way the firm has restructured itself. Anything that is not core to innovation and product design is moved out."

Many federal laws, including those that guarantee the right to organize, do not apply to those who work fewer than thirty hours per week or who work by contract. Under the Fair Labor Standards Act, employers are not required to provide benefits such as overtime pay, protection for the right to organize, or family leave to part-time, temporary, or contract workers. In the United States, only one-fourth of contingent workers are made eligible by employers for employer pension plans, while nearly half of all permanent workers are included. Contingent work appears to contribute to the depression of wages: between 1973 and 2000, as the U.S. jobless rate fell to its lowest point in thirty years, wages rose just one cent an hour (North American Alliance for Fair Employment, 2000). While contingency has always affected women and people of color, its use has spread to transform traditionally male-dominated good jobs in manufacturing, finance, and technology.

Implications for Progressive Organizing

Neoliberal policies have effects that might not be fully apparent at first. They bankrupt government and public institutions through tax subsidies and the privatization of public holdings. They make increasing numbers of workers into contingents, with few labor rights and little job security. They force people to move to make a living, then control their movement to get the most of their labor for the least economic and social cost to the "receiving" country or city. These changes have major implications for organizing.

First, local organizing struggles cannot take place in a geographical vacuum. Whenever progressives craft an issue, more than ever before, we have to consider its relationship to other communities, some of which are far away. If Mexican and Indonesian workers can't get workplace protections and decent wages, it seems unlikely that U.S. workers will ever regain their bargaining power. Local and even national governments are often powerless to enforce labor, environmental, and other rights and protections, as they are overridden by economic policies designed to remove barriers to business and trade. For example, gay people fought for a San Francisco city resolution not to buy from businesses that discriminate on the basis of sexuality. Under the North American Free Trade Agreement (NAFTA), such a local law can be deemed an unfair trade practice and made ineffective.

Second, the rise of contingency also means that labor organizing, so basic a part of progressive infrastructure, has to undergo major changes. Labor law greatly favors employers by characterizing contingent workers as nonemployees, thereby limiting their rights to employee benefits. Contingent workers are difficult to organize because they are not a cohesive workforce with a single identity, they have few horizontal relationships with other contingent workers, and they are scattered throughout multiple workplaces. In addition, this workforce is increasingly diverse, by occupation as well as by race, gender, and class. The result is that we cannot continue to organize in neat industrial sectors—people are jumping around from job to job, wherever they can find one in the world.

Third, activists need to be aware that globalization has cultural and social as well as economic results. One cultural consequence is the violence and family disintegration endured by poor workers worldwide. One compelling example is found in the *maquiladora* zone on the Mexican side of the U.S.-Mexican border. Working for low wages in places that lack the infrastructure to sustain human life, walking several hours each day to get to and from work, far from their families, women working in the *maquilas* make easy victims for serial murderers operating along the border. Hundreds of young women's bodies have been discovered, but their murderers wander the region with impunity (Madigan, 1999). On the other side of the border, women in El Paso, Texas, scramble for a living when garment factories relocate to take advantage of the desperation of poorer countries. As a result of neoliberal policies, workers all over the world are on the move as their families disintegrate; they migrate to work zones within their countries and from poor countries to rich ones.

In addition, the exportation of culture affects the identities of the people we are organizing. Western culture can now be found almost anywhere in the world because of the movement of companies, goods, and people. Just as U.S.-style capitalism goes abroad, so does U.S. culture. The cultural shrinkage has costs that outweigh its benefits. Practices of the global corporation often lead to the death of cultural diversity, as local aesthetics slowly give way to marketing schemes that require all consumers to behave the same way. Music, film, literature, and cultural mores are increasingly subject to the commercial standards of highly consolidated media outlets and are increasingly designed for Western tastes. What Europeans and North Americans experience as cultural expansion—the integration of Eastern spirituality, ethnic food, and great previously unknown literature into Western life—masks the loss of cultural diversity worldwide. Finally, heavy migration and rapid cultural change mean that individual and group identity is extremely fluid now. Activists have to be able to keep up with the trauma and excitement of such change in order to articulate the values that allow people to be critical of the new economy and global capitalism.

The Centrality of Race and Gender

While colonialism, white supremacy, and patriarchy have been with us throughout modern times, they take on new and innovative forms today. Race and gender are social constructions: the biological and scientific differences among people are negligible and do not justify the use of these categories in discriminatory ways. Some activists conclude that we therefore should not focus on racial and gender differences in our organizing, but I would argue that the significance of these false categories makes it even more important to do so. However they were constructed, they now produce life-threatening conditions for millions worldwide. Lack of a sophisticated analysis that includes an understanding of the dynamic characteristics of racism and sexism helps conservatives split our base and stymies the search for solutions and strategies that help everyone. It is tempting to account for racial and gender divisions with economic analysis, and it is even accurate to do so to a certain extent. But race and gender systems operate independently of the economy also, and subsuming them under an economic unifier retards our efforts to strip them of their power. I would argue that economic, political, and cultural ideas and systems are intertwined and need to be addressed together. If the world became socialist today, racism would still vilify certain people, and women would still get raped.

Racism

While economic motivations seem to have led to racial categorization initially, historically white supremacy produced psychological, cultural, and political benefits for whites in addition to the material—a set of benefits I would argue few whites are ready to give up, even if the economic benefits were removed. Certainly, our current economy bears the legacy of the white supremacy that has formed the base of U.S. capitalism since the nation's earliest days. For British colonizers, a large, cheap labor force was crucial for rapid expansion of their economic and political power. The indigenous population had been decimated or alienated by war, and the availability of vast amounts of land "open" to settlement made it difficult to rely on British immigrant labor. Although indentured servitude did provide one limited source of labor, the enslavement of American Indians and Africans created a far more profitable labor force. In addition to economic enslavement, however, the pseudoscientific effort to characterize these populations as subhuman justified reproductive, cultural, and political actions such as rape, the outlawing of religious practices and native languages, forced Christianization, and the takeover of land (Davis, 1983). These cultural and political controls on people of color would continue throughout U.S. history, eventually taking on a life of their own even when they ran counter to profitable economic policy.

Although the early waves of eastern and southern European immigrants experienced substantial exploitation, they were eventually integrated into a standard white identity that brought with it educational, cultural, and political rights still often denied in practice to people of color in the United States. The industrial economy required a flexible, mobile, and efficient labor force. Eastern and southern European immigrants peopled this early industrial labor force. For the most part, they planned to return to their homelands, so they invested little into integrating with U.S. culture or organizing to improve conditions. They were noncitizens subject to deportation. They were frequently used as strikebreakers and in deskilling because they were assigned the simpler elements of complicated jobs that were redesigned by scientific management (a system of breaking down the production of an item into its smallest repetitive tasks) and the introduction of the assembly line. However, these immigrants eventually controlled the skilled-trades unions and slowly rose to economic and political power (Ignatiev, 1995). That option was unavailable to obviously nonwhite immigrants, who were welcomed for their labor but were barred from joining unions, becoming citizens, and building families because of antimiscegenation and antiwomen immigration policy. Even when the United States was flooded with European immigrants, Europe was never part of a barred zone, and, after industrialization, immigrants from Europe were never enslaved, never brought in for menial labor through guest-worker programs, and never made ineligible for citizenship.

By contrast, the United States took great pains to ensure that nonwhite immigrants would not taint the emerging white culture. Immigration law prohibited the entry and settlement of women and children in order to control the reproduction of immigrant culture, and it excluded nonwhite groups altogether when the need for their labor passed. After Asians had built railroads and staffed mining booms and the beginning of industrialization, the Chinese Exclusion Act, the first federal law prohibiting immigration from any part of the world, set the stage for limiting immigration from all of Asia. Mexican workers were brought in through the bracero program to work in agriculture but were denied the basic rights of permanent residents and citizens. When black descendants of slaves could not be controlled through immigration policy, Jim Crow, criminal justice, and welfare policies were brought to bear on them.

Even the liberalization of immigration and other economic policies came with a cultural, political, and economic price. For example, the Immigration Reform and Control Act of 1965 liberalized quota policies and led to the most significant Asian immigration of the twentieth century. In addition to removing quotas, the new law eliminated quotas imposed in earlier laws, allowed family reunification, and set preferences for recruitment of professionals and technicians. But, by allowing the entry of unprecedented numbers of professional Asian immigrants, the state, in effect, selected a group of people for success; this policy led to the creation of the stereotype of the "model minority," the assumption that all Asians were naturally inclined to intellectual and scientific pursuits. Because of this myth, later Asian immigrants, from Cambodia, Vietnam, Laos, and China, as well as South Asia, would find it difficult to get anyone, including themselves, to believe that their needs mirrored those of blacks and Latinos.

Race continues to play a role in contemporary social and political, as well as economic, policy. For example, a volley of laws since the mid-1980s has placed immigrants under economic and cultural attack. Three are particularly important: the Immigration Reform and Control Act of 1986, which imposed employer sanctions; California Proposition 187 and the Personal Responsibility Act, which made all immigrants ineligible for welfare benefits, food stamps, and Social Security; and the 1996 Anti-Terrorism and Effective Death Penalty Act, which imposed restrictions and mandatory sentencing on suspected terrorists. People of color are continually attacked through crime policy, particularly the War on Drugs, and education policy, as in the attacks on affirmative action, multicultural education, and the defunding of public schools.

Sexism

Economic and social policies have also made women second-class citizens, subservient to men. Throughout postindustrial history, women's labor has been systematically undervalued and discounted, and they have received low wages for any work resembling that which they accomplished during their unpaid time at home. For white women, changing views of their roles accompanied industrialization, as production moved from the home to the factory, where men went to work for wages. The home was stripped of its productive value and was transformed into a place of leisure and nurturing. This separation of public and private spheres controlled the aspirations and identities of white women, while it defined and devalued women's work in general.

"True womanhood" among white women was upheld by the racial order. Much of the domestic work in white upper- and middle-class households was done by servants from lower-class and nonwhite communities, and their labor maintained the myth of natural, easy domesticity among white women. Government agencies and educational institutions were specifically established to channel exslaves and their descendants into domestic work throughout the South and East. Works Progress Administration programs in the Southwest and Midwest trained young Latinas, both U.S.-born and immigrant, for domestic work, although officials already knew that such work did not allow young women to escape poverty.

Women were considered a flexible and cheap workforce, but it was the cultural and political constraints on them that allowed them to be easily pulled and pushed in and out of the paid labor force. White women entering the workforce found a gender ghetto, where jobs took on a lesser value than they had when they belonged to men. An excellent example is the transformation of clerical work, which had historically been a prestigious professional training ground for men. Labor shortages among men caused by the Civil War and expanded opportunities for men in the new giant corporations forced employers to seek clerical workers from among the increasing numbers of literate, young, white women. In an unhappy coincidence the entry of women into the clerical field was accompanied by the introduction of scientific management. Scientific management allowed the division of tasks to suit unskilled and replaceable labor, seen most prevalently in the factory assembly line, and also allowed the transformation of the secretary and clerical worker from future businessman to worker. At the same time, a new innovation, the typewriter, had not been associated with men. Rather than being seen as workers or bosses, clerical workers were considered more like office wives. They were treated according to the mores of a patriarchal family, and they did not rebel against that position for more than seventy years after the profession went female. The presence of women in clerical work introduced and made acceptable a discriminatory wage in that field. If women had not already been made culturally subservient to men, such discrimination would have been far less likely or possible.

Discriminatory wages are to be found all over our economy. For example, because U.S. society does not count child rearing as work and assigns it exclusively to women, women who are home health care and child care workers are paid low wages. A study conducted by the AFL-CIO and the Institute for Women's Policy Research shows that workers in female-dominated occupations are paid roughly 18 percent less than they would be if they worked in jobs requiring similar skills outside the "pink ghetto." If pay were raised in female-dominated jobs to levels comparable to those in the rest of the economy, the study concluded, twenty-five million women would together earn about $89 billion a year more than they do now, and four million men would gain $25 billion a year. The study estimates that pay equity would lift out of poverty more than half of poor single mothers over eighteen and three-fifths of poor, married women (Moberg, 2001).

In addition to being economically disadvantaged, women are also the targets of cultural and political attacks. The shaping of gender identity through cultural institutions such as the family, schools, religion, and the arts contributes to lower performances by girls in middle school than in elementary school and to an ongoing epidemic of sexual abuse and violence worldwide. Political attacks on reproductive freedom continue unabated. Women do not enjoy political representation nearly at parity with their numbers, and they are largely kept out of the highest levels of education and business. And one form of punishment for women's stepping outside the bounds of traditional family structures is the fact that the United States is one of only two industrialized countries that lack universal child care (Crittenden, 2001).

The Confluence of Race and Gender: Welfare Reform

Welfare reform shows us how racial, gender, and economic systems come together. The fact that the different goals of welfare reform often contradict one another points to the independence of each system as well as their interdependence. On gender, welfare policies have been designed to keep women of various racial groups in their "proper" domestic or economic roles—married to a man or working for a man, depending on who you are. Welfare programs were first started to help white women stay at home if they lost their husbands; they thereby reinforced a family ethic by replacing a male breadwinner and patriarch with the state. Since then, much of welfare policy has resulted in controlling the sexuality of poor women. Today, that control is coded into the welfare system through such policies as the family cap, abstinence-only sex education, and the prohibition on using government aid to pay for abortion, along with policies aimed at reducing out-of-wedlock births. Welfare policy has provided a window through which conservatives have been able to gain public support for reproductive controls. Once they apply to the poor and to people of color, it's only a matter of time before they affect everybody. If President George W. Bush wins the next welfare war, welfare programs will reduce funds for child care and income support and redirect them to schemes for promoting marriage.

On race, the welfare system has undergone a long transformation by which various need-based programs became racially stratified. Over the years, Social Security and unemployment insurance were separated from welfare, food stamps, and health care programs for children, the disabled, and the elderly. Programs that excluded the majority of black and women workers came to be seen as universal, while programs that served people of color and women were targeted and attacked as "special" support for the undeserving. Individual states adopted regulations and practices to curtail the number of blacks on the welfare rolls and to control black women's sexual behavior; these programs tested ideas that provide the groundwork for much of today's federal policy. Conservatives agitated public opinion through racial stereotyping and a concentrated focus on the fears of white, middle- and working-class taxpayers. The deep racialization of welfare obscures for many white people their self-interest in preserving safety nets. Sociologist Dorothy Roberts (1997) recalls the story of a white woman in Louisiana, on welfare herself, who became convinced by conservative rhetoric that black people were using welfare to avoid working for a living. As a result, the woman voted for white supremacist David Duke in his gubernatorial bid because Duke vowed to end welfare programs.

In the 1990s, scapegoating immigrants through welfare policy constituted both racial and reproductive attack. Prior to the mid-1980s, most political attacks on immigrants emphasized economic threats, with images of immigrants stealing jobs and undercutting wages. But the later political rhetoric portrayed immigrants as dependent on public benefits and a drain on the public coffer and in doing so shifted the attack from male workers to women and children. A 1986 CBS/New York Times poll found that 47 percent of Americans believed that "most immigrants wind up on welfare" (Chang, 2000, p. 201). In California, Governor Pete

Wilson made controlling public expenditures on immigrants a central feature of his administration. In a 1992 administrative report on the state's budget, Wilson called immigrants "tax receivers," referring to their supposedly disproportionate use of welfare, Medicaid, and public schools (Chang, 2000). Proposition 187–type exclusions were proposed in Washington, New York, Florida, and Oregon. At the same time as women's sexuality and family formation were being crafted through welfare policy, stringent work requirements and the privatization of welfare programs created out of poor women and their children a steady pool of low-wage workers, obviously a great boon to business, especially if hiring these women brought a cash incentive.

Implications for Progressive Organizing

The continuation of racism and sexism holds significant implications for our organizing because the ideas behind these systems split our base and prevent us from building a universal commitment to fighting all forms of oppression. The media and public policies constantly point out and reinforce our differences in status and carefully shape our impressions of "the other" so that we will support discriminatory policies. People who are normally loathe to treat anyone badly are willing to tolerate and participate in such treatment because they have become convinced that the target population deserves it or will actually benefit from it. While many of us can build organizations that are multiracial or are even composed mainly of people of color by using the argument that we're all in the same boat, most of us don't experience life that way. We are not, in fact, all in exactly the same boat—there are crucial differences in our treatment by major institutions. Black students get suspended from school for fighting, and white children don't. Women are expected to do the housework, and men are not. Legal immigrants can work and organize without fear, and undocumented immigrants cannot. A husband can go into the emergency room when his wife is ill, but a lesbian life partner cannot. These are not false differences, and people find it hard to stick to the same-boat argument when confronted with them. Thus, less marginal communities and people within these communities become reluctant to stand up and say that teenagers or the mentally ill should not receive the death penalty or that undocumented immigrants should be granted legal status. These then become the issues conservatives use to prevent coalitions among people who dislike the right. While it is certainly important for people to see their similarities—the same boat—it is equally important that when some of us are pushed up or down in the hierarchy—another boat—we do not lose our sense of community and solidarity.

Our inability to merge our understanding of the cultural and political, as well as the economic, dimensions of racism and sexism prevents us from creating a universal standard that includes the most marginalized people. Many proponents of economic justice believe that the key to racial and sexual liberation lies in eradicating or reforming the vagaries of capitalism, that racism and sexism are essentially tools of capitalist profit-mongering, and that controlling capital will remove the incentive for people to be racist or sexist. Unfortunately, hiding differences under an anticapitalist analysis often amounts to universalizing the experience of working-class white men, while leaving all others unorganized, excluded from organization, or subject only to the same tactics that worked to organize white men. In making such an economic analysis, we don't consider the social benefits of racism and sexism, which are available to whites and men who are not of the elite class. Other activists have argued that the lack of democracy unifies all our fights, but we don't all enjoy the same rights under the current definitions of democracy. Civil rights movements have failed to organize the poorest and most disfranchised—welfare recipients, undocumented immigrants, and prisoners, to name a few. Activists have turned to human rights frameworks to mine their potential, but these, too, often obscure the racial, class, and gender differences that plague communities. I am not arguing that we use race and gender as frames to replace these others. Rather I believe that whatever frames we use, we must take into account diverse experiences and the positions in which people find themselves.

Progressives need to define a new universal standard that can handle all these potential divisions—race, class, gender, sexuality, national status, and more. How do we unify all these people? Do they have to have the same experiences in order to make common cause? They do not, but they do have to have the same understanding of what causes experiences to vary so dramatically. Most "universal" ideas obscure the specific ways in which people are attacked and experience that attack; and they obscure the potentially huge tactical strengths that come from each constituency. A clear understanding of how to confront and reform capitalist structures or the institutions of democracy will emerge only from a deep understanding of all power structures and each community they affect, just as a clear effort to eradicate racial discrimination has to include an economic analysis. Increasingly, global society relies on hierarchy by race, class, and gender. If we avoid the specifics of a particular community because it does not fit the universal, we do so at our own peril.

What We Need to Do

To summarize, three trends that shape modern life hold major implications for our organizing. The growth of an extreme conservative infrastructure, the globalization of capitalism, and the continued strength of racism and sexism influence the conditions in which we live and require new strategies for reestablishing progressive values in policymaking. The vast and well-funded conservative infrastructure reduces our ability to rely on governmental institutions for protection against the worst abuses by individuals, corporations, and public agencies; presents us with a nationally connected and intellectually equipped opposition; and drives political debate rightward. The growth of global capitalism undermines the role of local and national governments, privatizes important public functions, bankrupts public agencies, and forces huge growth in migration. The central role of racism and sexism splits the progressive constituency and makes us vulnerable to conservative strategies to drive wedges that expand those splits. To analyze how these trends have affected and continue to affect your community, answer the questions in Exercise 1.1.

While these trends are huge and potentially overwhelming, they can be countered with a sophisticated, long-term strategy based on a commitment to three goals: increasing our organizing among the people affected and then addressing their issues with sustained campaigns and the addition of research and media capacity; framing campaigns on the basis of large-scale ideas and values; and supporting emerging social movements. This section explores the need for these capacities, which are described further in the remaining chapters.

Increasing Progressive Organizing

Not nearly enough progressive organizing is taking place to counter the constituency building and political action of conservatives. While it is very positive that activists are increasingly organizing among youth, ex-prisoners, low-wage workers, and welfare recipients, we don't engage in enough systematic organizing to reveal the large numbers of disaffected people and to counteract the negative media messages hitting politicians and the public about these constituencies. If we are to convince people that their tax money is best spent on improving public education or providing a safety net, we have to be able to produce human evidence of the need for and benefits of such policies. If we are to convince politicians that the general public cares about the decisions they make, we have to be able to generate enough street heat to get their attention. And if we are to make policy proposals that are grounded in reality and would make a difference either in peoples' lives or in the debate, then we have to be in touch with the people who are at the center of such policies.

Three commitments are critical here. First, we have to be willing to systematically expand our base of people who hold progressive values or have specific needs. Everyone who already agrees with us needs to have an organization to join, and everyone who isn't sure needs at least one chance to participate in a group.

Exercise 1.1. Reflection Questions: New Realities.

1. How are our local institutions connected to the New Right infrastructure? Where do our local and state decision makers get their information and policy ideas?

2. In the issues that concern us, what is the role of government now? How has that role changed or remained the same over the years? What should the role of government be?

3. How have global business practices and the rise of contingent work affected our community? Who has migrated in and who has migrated out? What are the likely future trends?

4. How does racism play out in our community? Is there a racial hierarchy? If so, what is it? Which constituencies feel they are at the bottom? Why? Who is at the top? What is the evidence for this perception?

5. How does sexism play out in our community? Which job ghettoes are assigned to women? How are women treated in schools and at home?

Many progressive organizations stop recruiting new members when they get to a certain level of stability; increasingly, groups organize among established activists rather than trying to reach new people because it is simply easier and less stressful. We rely on allies rather than on building the constituency itself.

Second, once people are relating to organizations, we need to be able to address their issues through sustained campaigns, another objective that often stumps activists. The more challenging and nonmainstream our issues are, the more systematic and detailed we have to be in designing our campaigns. While we certainly need to be able to respond to attacks and short-term issues, true social change requires long-term commitment to standing issues.

Third, given the strength of the intellectual resources on the other side, our organizing has to be accompanied by substantial research and media capacity. As people get involved, we all need to have factual as well as moral ammunition for our issues and policies, and we need to be able to articulate those facts to the media. No matter how great we are at organizing truly marginalized communities, they will never be able to make change by themselves. There has to be a larger base of elite and broad public support, and we have to be able to identify and take advantage of the support we already have. Even groups that are able to turn out hundreds of people for a particular action will find sheer turnout inadequate to challenge the reams of research findings emerging from conservative think tanks; that research often runs counter to the experience of the people affected, especially as decision makers become increasingly sophisticated at deflecting criticism and appearing to give us what we want. The media can play a critical role in defining our efforts and in protecting us from the vilifying tactics of the other side. Minimally, every organization should know in detail the institutions it is dealing with, local economic and social trends, and the effects of larger policies, and we should be able to produce at least anecdotal information about our constituencies and issues. Optimally, we should be able to produce or gain access to statistical research and alternative policies. We can begin with modest goals and projects, but we must build more capacity over time.

Addressing Core Ideas and Values

The base building, the development of sustained campaigns, and the research and media work are essentially techniques with no specific moral, economic, or political values attached to them; they are meaningless unless we also address the core ideas that shape society. Any constituency can support regressive as well as progressive ideas, as we see when people of color are recruited into conservative organizations. Just because people share with me a particular experience does not mean that they assign the same meaning to that experience as I do. If there ever was a time to lie low and not challenge the fundamental ideas of conservatives and capitalists, racists and male supremacists, it has passed. Today, we need to be clear and vocal about what we believe, about the basis on which we oppose economic and social policies, and about the kinds of systemic changes we want. While we will make many tactical decisions about where and how to reveal these ideas to the broader public, internally we need to be absolutely clear and courageous about defining what is progressive and what is not. If we do not, conservatives will continue to characterize our rather commonsense ideas as lunatic, fringy, anti-family, and dangerous.

To be more ideologically ambitious, we have to engage in analysis and political education. We have to read, share information, understand history, bring people to speak to our groups, and talk with people in other places. We have to think about our theories of how society is organized, why it is organized that way, and how change will come. We have to be willing to integrate our experiences with information because no single person can experience everything. Many organizers resist this imperative, hiding behind the notion that a lack of ideological discussion makes their organizations democratic or that attention to larger trends or theory makes organizations elitist. The further you get from peoples' daily experience, organizers have argued, the less likely it is that members will engage.

I can understand taking that position. Many of us and our members have been attacked for our lack of formal education or for not revealing our intelligence in a traditional way. Much of the analytical and theoretical writing we need is in academic and inaccessible language. I, too, have been frustrated by these roadblocks. However, these are obstacles that need to be dealt with; they are not excuses for avoiding a larger analysis. Community organizations and labor unions often have a strong streak of anti-intellectualism, which is both short-sighted and a dangerous mirror of the worst right-wing organizing strategies. The issue of language is also critical here. While it is not necessary to use a complicated word when a simple one will do, it is necessary to be accurate and comprehensive. So, those who have spent much of their life relating to prisons are usually glad to have a phrase like *prison-industrial complex* to describe the reason for their experience. Having to explain what we mean by certain words provides opportunities to engage rather than a reason to run.

Supporting Large Social Movements

We need to develop a movement orientation to our organizing. While organizations of all sorts produce incremental victories that help to prevent backsliding, shifts in the core values that shape policy take place through social movements that involve large numbers of people. For the most part, community organizations related little to the social movements of the late twentieth century, particularly those that came after the civil rights, peace, and women's movements of the 1960s. The lack of space in community organizations for the ideological debates central to radical movements prevented most community organizations from participating in the mass social movements of the 1980s, such as the antiapartheid, the Central American solidarity, the AIDS, and the sexual-liberation movements.

Aside from bad politics, the more common reason for the separation is that the process of building organizations often clashes with the process of encouraging movements. While movements grow more easily if organizations are available to help form the infrastructure, they tend to be more geographically spread out and more spontaneous than community organizations. Community organizing requires that people identify with a specific group rather than primarily with a set of ideas or principles. Building the actual organization is important for gaining a reputation, monitoring new policies, and raising money. Organizations require some centralization of decision making because they are required to be accountable to specific constituencies and memberships.

Movements, however, are generally larger than even the largest community organization or single union, and decision making in them is usually decentralized. They tend to attract people to a set of ideas or an overwhelmingly important single cause. As a movement forms, tiny local offshoots pop up as people come to know of the movement's work, and all these offshoots do not necessarily identify with an existing organization. In addition, while organizing tactics tend toward direct confrontation with individual decision makers, movement tactics can be somewhat broader, encompassing mass demonstrations and cultural activities. The spheres of influence of the two also vary. While community organizations tend to focus on specific institutions, movements have the additional goals of influencing popular culture, language, and thought. These differences can lead community organizers to build groups that are unable to see beyond themselves and can lead movement activists to design tactics that don't build permanent power.

While we can't control all the factors that enable a movement to develop, we can build our organizations in such a way as to be ready for movement work when the time is right. Most experienced activists believe that movements emerge from a specific set of conditions—rising expectations among the disenfranchised, a backlash against the status quo, or demographic shifts—in addition to explicit organizing. Being ready requires, in the first place, shifts in our work patterns and attitudes. For example, rather than figuring out how to do everything in one organization, we need to think more about how to create and support complementary organizations that work together to get the job done. Such a division of labor requires a deep understanding of and mutual respect for all the functions necessary to organize people, ideas, and money. Thus, strategists have to be able to think beyond their own organization's function. Second, much of what prevents such partnerships is the need to compete for foundation money, to defend our particular portion of the larger strategy as if we operated in a vacuum. Therefore, for example, many community organizations sell themselves to foundations as entities entirely different from research and media organizations. We would do better raising money in concert and investing in fundraising strategies that do not rely exclusively on foundation grants. Third, our attitude toward other organizations needs to be unfailingly courteous and respectful, and we need to stop making a big deal out of relatively tiny differences in approach. The larger world perceives few differences among us, so our efforts to distinguish ourselves from each other only split us—they do not convince other people that our way is the right way. If you find elements in another group's work to admire, feel free to talk about them. If you take issue with another group, the appropriate people to talk to are people in the group itself. When there are opportunities to work together, we need to take them up. All our tiny organizations can form the base of the new and emerging social movements of the twenty-first century if we build them with such goals in mind.

Local organizations may be the single most important building blocks for mass movements that can overturn the resurgence of extreme conservatism in United States, mitigate against the worst abuses of global capitalism, and eradicate racism and sexism. The stakes are high. A systematic challenge to these trends will come from people who have been exposed to a number of organizing models, who can debate the big ideas, and who can forego direct benefits to their own organization in terms of reputation and money. Not even the best community organizations, those capable of both deep analysis and great turnout, can gather the strength to make significant change by themselves. All together the forces aligned against even the mildest reform are too strong to be dislodged by organizing that remains within the confines of a neighborhood or even a single city.

As always, knowledge of the correct path is embedded in our experience. Organizers of vision have disrupted economic, racial, and sexual exploitation with a complicated analysis, innovative strategies, and inclusive ideas about the future. By necessity, much of that work has been done by people who occupy the bottom rungs of society and who have been driven by desperation and faith. In the following chapters, we consider their stories.

CHAPTER TWO

ORGANIZING NEW CONSTITUENCIES

At the base of all progressive action lies a commitment to organizing the people most affected by a particular problem. The organizing process transforms people with problems into politically active constituencies that eventually build a new collective identity and reinforce or transform the culture of their communities. Especially when a community is under attack, being organized provides a chance to counteract stereotypes and to present community members as agents of change rather than as victims of the status quo.

Of all the tasks progressives have, this kind of organizing is the hardest to do and the easiest to give up. If our notion of organizing is mostly romantic, if we are unclear about why we are organizing in a certain community, the patience and courage needed to keep a group together can be difficult to sustain. Organizing requires consistent, systematic work in the form of phone calls, reports, conversations, meetings, along with the patience to deal with the failed campaigns and incremental successes that come before mass uprisings. The romance quickly wears off, and the realities of daily organization building can depress even the most stalwart extroverts among us.

By organizing, I mean an effort to build organizations that include at least these five elements:

- A clear mission and goals
- A membership and leadership structure, with a way for people to join and take roles

- Outreach systems that concentrate on those most affected
- Issue campaigns featuring multiple tactics, including direct action
- Pursuit of changing institutions rather than individuals

These elements combine to produce power and a shift in how people are treated as a result.

Organizing differs from other forms of social-change work. It does not offer immediate relief for individuals through the provision of social services. Unlike advocacy, organizing removes the middleman. It is not collapsible with electoral work because it embraces a wider range of activities. Its goals are broader than those of economic development, which tends to focus on bricks-and-mortar projects or job training and development. I also distinguish organizing, which results in an organization, from mobilization, which involves large numbers of people expressing their resistance or support, whether through a demonstration or signing a petition, without the expectation of sustained activity. Solidarity movements can open up space for the voices of those affected, but they can never replace the clarity and power of the people who have the most to gain and the least to lose. While these are all legitimate approaches to social change, they have their own methods and rules. We need to draw distinctions to use any of them effectively.

Organizing offers important advantages for activists over these other forms of social-change work. Engaging people who experience social problems provides a barometer with which to evaluate issue and campaign choices. The people most affected are the key to uncovering patterns of institutional behavior and to determining the effects of those patterns and how much we care. The willingness among those people affected to recruit others in the same situation is a major indicator of a organization's likelihood of surviving. Even the most dedicated, insightful initial group will lose its dynamism unless members are willing to pull in others. Additionally, organizations composed of people whose lives will change when a new policy is instituted tend to set goals that are harder to reach, to compromise less, and to stick out a fight longer. Self-organization also forms the basis for mass social movements. The eight-hour day was won by people who needed it, as was access to AIDS treatment, the Civil Rights Act, and civilian police-review commissions. As one organizer put it to me, "Leadership of the real people has to be the bottom line" (Gihan Perrera, conversation with the author, October 1999).

When we start organizing, it is important to consider the constituency's strengths as well as its troubles. For example, women of all ages bring substantial strengths to organizing. Women easily constitute the vast majority of members and organizing staff of community organizations and increasingly of unions. Their diverse experiences in the private and public sphere lead to intellectual and tactical flexibility. Women appear to be both attracted to and prepared for community and political responsibilities by our life conditions, which require us to negotiate between individuals and institutions, to recruit diverse resources from an extended network that has to be maintained through regular communication, and to design creative solutions through collective problem solving.

This chapter is less about the specific techniques for building a membership than about the larger questions embedded in a strategy that emphasizes self-organization. In highlighting the key principles of good organizing, I focus on the need to pay attention to organizational structure, culture, recruitment methods, and the relationship of organizing to other approaches. I provide illustrations, mainly from four organizations. From 9to5, I draw lessons about the advantages of creating identity-based caucuses within an organization and of building a union and a community organization simultaneously (including lessons about the implications of such a structure for outreach). In the example of the Workplace Project, I demonstrate the value of building constituency-specific committees, and I track the practical shifts that strike a balance between organizing and providing services, as well as between organizing and education. In the Chinese Staff & Workers Association (CSWA), we observe how a constituency of women workers led the organization to a new set of issues, and we learn why CSWA is not a service provider. In the illustrations from Direct Action for Rights and Equality (DARE), we can see how its structure allowed it to build a democratic and multiracial culture, how it created the Home Day Care Justice (HDCJ) Cooperative, and how organizing the people most affected by a problem drives up demands.

Principles

Four major principles form the basis of our organizing efforts. First, our organizing strategy, our plan to build or expand a particular constituency, holds implications for the way we structure our organizations. Second, every organization has its own culture, which has to be shaped and refined to make room for the participation of particular groups. Third, we need to match our recruitment methods to the people we want to reach. Fourth, if we use services to attract members, we have to be extra vigilant that service provision doesn't take over the organizing.

Building Organizational Structures

Organizing requires flexible, transparent structures that have two primary functions. Structures define roles—who makes decisions, who reports to whom, who prioritizes issues and shapes campaign plans, to name a few. Structures also reflect values. For example, if we want to raise the legitimacy of particular voices, we might not choose a simple majority-rules voting structure.

Many activists come to social-change work with a justifiably negative reaction to the rigid hierarchies of dominant institutions, and they have three common ways of not reproducing that rigidity. Some build collectives. A larger number adopt modified hierarchies. Still others develop some combination of collectives and hierarchies. Whichever basic form we choose, we must define that choice. We will almost certainly adjust it as time goes on, but the organization's operating principles have to be clear to everyone involved at each stage.

Many organizations decline to define their structures at all, choosing to remain fluid and flexible, hoping to avoid rigidity and exclusion. In the beginning, a lack of formal structure works well for horizontal relationships among peers, when everyone has to be capable of doing many things. Often, start-ups are responding to a crisis that takes all their attention, and they can't spend much time developing a structure. However, the lack of structure can obscure power relationships in a group. In a still-relevant article titled "The Tyranny of Structurelessness," Jo Freeman wrote in 1973 (p. 286) about the hidden hierarchies that emerged as women's consciousness-raising groups shifted to politics. She argued that the lack of formal structures elevated the role of the informal structures—friendship networks and leadership patterns—that govern human interactions. Freeman pointed out that many past women's movements fought to formalize and reveal the structures of decision making embedded in informal old boys' networks so that they could confront the exclusion of women directly.

Freeman also worried that the lack of formal structure kept radical women's voices from shaping the larger movement and blocked accountability among feminists. "The avowedly Unstructured group . . . [has] no way of drawing upon the movement's vast resources to support its priorities; it doesn't even have a way of deciding what they are. . . . If the movement continues to keep power as diffuse as possible because it cannot demand responsibility from those who have it, it . . . ensures that the movement is as ineffective as possible. Some middle ground between domination and ineffectiveness can and must be found" (1973, p. 297).

Collectives and hierarchies each have advantages and disadvantages. In collectives people can assume great responsibility for the organization's development. When a collective makes a decision, the resistance to the option chosen has been explored and addressed so that the decision can be carried out with confidence. Collectives tend to enjoy a high level of internal trust, which helps them withstand external attacks. And, in attempting to operate in ways consistent with progressive visions of society, collectives provide an important reality check to our plan for implementing ideals. However, decision making in collectives can be slow, and such organizations can be small and cliquish. They are easiest to build among people who are alike in culture and communication style.

By contrast, hierarchies can be efficient because they create teams that are responsible for specific pieces of work. And because they do not demand the same skills and commitment from everyone, people who enjoy taking ultimate responsibility can do so, while those who don't can find another role within the same organization. Because roles are tightly defined, hierarchies can provide systematic developmental opportunities for new people. Counter to many perceptions, people in hierarchies are often able to control decisions related to their own work. However, hierarchies can isolate individual leaders, requiring them to make difficult decisions and hanging them out to dry. Leaders of hierarchical organizations have to check constantly how much everyone else espouses the direction of the organization. People who have been abused by power, whether in their families or on the job, often react badly to hierarchies.

In truth, neither model works in its pure form for progressive organizations. Some groups—the Zapatistas and the American Friends Service Committee, for example—make every decision through a complicated process of consensus building and consultation among hundreds of people. But this is a rare model, developed over a long time and grounded in the historic culture of those communities. Most contemporary organizations are collective/hierarchy hybrids, simply because that's what they have the capacity to pull off or because they are bound by the legal restrictions of 501(c)(3) status (see the discussion of this tax regulation below).

Collectives, hierarchies, and hybrids can all be manipulated and abused by powerful and unethical individuals so that they become exclusive organizations. Therefore, whatever the structure, it needs to be clear and transparent to all involved, maintained in a fair manner, and flexible enough to be changed thoughtfully according to the needs of the constituency. Minimally, groups that are new and those that are in structural transition should consider:

- Using temporary and transitional structures
- Using a variety of decision-making models at different times
- Consistently and collectively evaluating everyone's role and contributions
- Sharing leadership, so that people make at least the most important decisions together
- Instituting requirements for leadership turnover to make room for new leaders
- Delegating decision-making power to the people responsible for carrying out a particular project
- Instituting a planning system, which reduces the need for last-minute decisions by individuals

Committees can play a key role in developing a new constituency within an organization. It seems counterintuitive to build a constituency-specific committee when you are trying to integrate that group into the larger organization. But committees make it possible for a group of people to gain critical mass and experience with the organization's purpose and culture; their doing so can help old and new groups make fast progress.

Illustration: DARE Uses Committees to Become Democratic

DARE operates through what appears to be a fairly traditional hierarchy, with an executive director who is supervised by a board of directors, which is elected by the membership in an annual meeting. However, high levels of integration allow many people to help shape the organization's priorities and tactics. Board meetings are open to the rest of the staff and membership; campaign committees aren't generally required to ask the board's approval before taking action; and DARE has made a strong commitment to recruiting former members for paid staff positions.

DARE also has a long history of building committees geared toward bringing together a specific constituency that later becomes integrated into the larger organization. For example, when DARE was a largely African American organization wanting to engage Latinos in a deeper way, it built the Comite Latino, which organized around Latino education issues and operated for five years, after which it was disbanded by unanimous consent of Comite members. This process allowed Latinos to feel strong enough to hold their own in a multiracial organization.

Illustration: The Workplace Project Builds a Women's Committee for Domestic Workers

Like many mixed-gender groups, the Workplace Project has created space for its women members by building a women's committee, and it has observed practical differences in groups of women and of men. Nadia Marin-Molina, the Project's executive director, identifies the benefits: "The industries where women work are completely different, as well as the ways in which they work. Without a dedicated place to nurture women's leadership, this would be a male-dominated organization. Instead, it's a partnership." Marin-Molina points to the development of the organization's two cooperatives as an example of the difference in male and female expectations and needs. "The [domestic workers'] co-op always had issues of child care. Landscaping never had that issue. The men's co-op always had more of a dependence on me to do things, especially administrative work. The women's co-op took it for granted that women were going to participate in finances and so on." While the women's committee serves as a launching point for women-specific campaigns, it also involves women in other campaigns, such as day labor and unpaid wages.

Illustration: CSWA Builds a Women's Committee for Low-Wage Immigrants

The CSWA Women's Committee grew from the need to develop women's leadership and to challenge the super-exploitation that women workers face both in the workplace and in the home. Answering the question of whether women should retain a completely separate space in the organization, the Committee adopted the perspective that women should not limit themselves to leading other women but should lead everyone, including men. Women's leadership has grown beyond the Committee, flourishing on the board, staff, and other organizing programs.

CSWA is very critical of the mainstream feminist movement, which is dominated by middle-class women. Organizer Trinh Duong says, "We haven't seen many women's organizations address issues that affect low-income women. A lot of women's groups say we should get more women into power, or get equal pay, but for low-income women earning equal wages as a man in our community just means equal to being a slave." Duong adds that "many women, aside from working long hours outside, often must do the unpaid work at home raising children." In this way, women are bearing the brunt of the sweatshop system. When President Bill Clinton signed the Welfare Reform Bill, hundreds of thousands of single parents, the majority of whom were mothers, were further exploited and forced to work for their welfare check. To truly address the needs of women workers, CSWA asserts that the valuable work of caregiving must be recognized and paid.

Illustration: 9to5 Updates Structure and Creates Caucuses to Encourage Fair Participation

When founding executive director Karen Nussbaum left 9to5 in 1993, a strategic planning process led to some structural shifts. The staff unionized and the organization created a management team consisting of two women of color, one lesbian, and people of different ages. The membership created three caucuses: women in poverty, women of color, and bi/trans/lesbian women. The women-in-poverty caucus, for example, is composed heavily of staff who come from the 9to5 constituency—welfare recipients and temporary workers who first got involved with 9to5 before their situations changed. The caucuses allow women with particular identities to support each other in their adjustment to the organization.

When choosing a leadership structure, organizations have also to consider the legal ramifications. On the one hand, in the United States, nonprofit organizations are allowed to collect tax-deductible contributions with a 501(c)(3) tax status, but the amount of time they can devote to direct lobbying and electoral work is limited. On the other hand, organizations can do as much electoral or legislative work as they want with a 501(c)(4) designation, but they cannot receive tax-deductible donations from businesses, foundations, or individuals. Some groups of activists address this problem by forming one of each type of organization.

Likewise, unions have rights under the law that nonprofit organizations don't have, a distinction that becomes important when people organize for rights on the job. Employers are legally bound to negotiate with workers as a whole group (in other words, with unions) under the collective bargaining laws governing labor relations. Unions are allowed to have dues automatically deducted from members' paychecks, so they don't have to rely on constant fundraising from their membership or foundations. Unions are also not 501(c)(3) organizations, so they can lobby Congress to, for example, raise the minimum wage and help elect progressive candidates. However, unions also operate industry by industry and workplace by workplace and union workers are usually considered "standard" employees—full time, clearly getting their paycheck from one source, and so on. Community groups may be more effective in organizing other workers; however, when community organizations attempt to gain workplace improvements, they, unlike unions, have to contend with the lack of legal rights described above.

Illustration: 9to5 Organizes as a Union

Nussbaum says that 9to5 turned to union affiliation in 1976 out of frustration with its lack of legal power after organizing a workplace. "We'd have meetings with the boss and present a set of demands, and he'd say I'll get back to you. We had absolutely no power to enforce anything." Nussbaum recalls that the search for a union to affiliate with wasn't easy: unions were "totally male-dominated," and no union was pining for the chance to organize clerical workers. After talking with ten unions, the fledgling group decided to make a deal with the Service Employees International Union (SEIU). In 1976, 9to5 and SEIU formed Local 925, which included clerical workers in universities and nonprofits in the Boston area. Local 925 remains an independent bargaining unit affiliated with the national SEIU infrastructure. It has served as a model for the creation of other "925" locals throughout the country. Within this structure each local retains women's leadership and autonomy over its own issues and practices. Nussbaum notes proudly that Local 925, operating with a family-friendly activist structure, "ran four offices around the country, all led by mothers of young children, half of them single, yet our organizing method produced results that were as good [as] or better than those of other SEIU locals."

Even after affiliating with SEIU, 9to5 members decided to keep the National Association of Working Women (its original incarnation) going. Ellen Bravo, who started the Association's Milwaukee chapter in 1982 and is now the executive director of 9to5, notes that "someone had to continue to do worker education in places that weren't ready for a union drive. Plus, the unions weren't that focused on public policy, and

76487

someone had to fight for that." The Association was initially structured so that a national office provided funds to local chapters, but this arrangement proved financially untenable. Today, each of the twenty-three chapters is the result of self-organization by working women, and five of these raise enough money for staff. Each year, the Association holds a leadership conference in which priority issues are either confirmed or chosen for the coming period. Bravo says that the most important benefit of the national local model, which is a difficult structure to maintain in a way that meets everyone's needs, is that individuals "can work on their own thing and still be connected to a larger movement, still understand and help pass national legislation."

When neither a community organization nor a union is the right structure to build, some people look to cooperatives, particularly for "self-employed" contract workers, who are regularly hustling jobs. Co-ops use a variety of membership structures. Some are worker-owned and include a limited number of members who are employed by the cooperative. Others are associations of people who work together to train and support each other as well as to fight for new public policies. Co-ops can provide short-term advantages for small numbers of people by consolidating their labor power and forcing employers to negotiate in order to get work done. The two groups in the illustrations below were led to the co-op model by, respectively, the desire to learn more about a particular industry and the desire to get around the gatekeepers and established institutions that controlled the industry. However, co-ops also have significant disadvantages. They do not have legal collective bargaining power, and they are often slow to make a dent in the established wage rates and labor practices of an industry. By looking at cooperative models in domestic work and child care, we can learn about some of the advantages and disadvantages.

Illustration: The Workplace Project Builds a Cooperative

The housekeeping industry posed major challenges to the Workplace Project's ability to win real change for workers. The Project learned how little it could rely on government intervention during an attempt to reform the employment-agency practice of charging workers illegal fees. Marin-Molina says that employment agencies "charge $25 for the application, then the first week's salary up front. Sometimes the job may not really exist or [is] already given to someone else, or people go in and only work a couple of days so they never get paid for a whole week, [even though they] have already paid the fee." This practice is widespread among employment agencies, despite its illegality. By law, the entire application fee is supposed to be refundable, and the agency cannot charge more than 10 percent of the first month's wages.

When the Project attempted to change this practice, it found the lack of government enforcement to be the biggest hindrance to establishing a new code of conduct. The Project targeted six of the most exploitative agencies to sign a statement of principles. Marin-Molina reflects that the fear generated among agency leaders by the Workplace Project could only go so far. After some of the agencies signed the statement of principles, "we sent women in as testers to see how the agencies treated them and tried to get the Department of Labor to move, but we would have needed thousands of women organized who knew their rights every time they went in." Furthermore, the Department of Labor didn't consider the statement binding but "said they'd help with enforcement if we did everything."

Many of the other problems in domestic work arise from the tremendous control that each employer has over the worker, "whether it's because she doesn't have a bank account or believes that her immigration status depends on the employer," says Marin-Molina. The intimacy in the relationship between a woman employer and a woman domestic also aggravates the power imbalance. (For a fuller discussion of the dynamics between employers and domestics, see Chang, 2000, and Romero, 1992.) Domestic workers rarely have a job description or regular hours, and they are frequently asked to perform outrageous tasks for long hours. Unpaid wages are also a frequent problem in domestic work. Marin-Molina says, "One woman worked twelve years for an employer who said he was keeping $150 a week as savings for her. At the end of twelve years, she asked for the thousands of dollars owed her. He simply said no. People whose employers pay them less but promise to help them get a green card come in years later when they find out their employer never filed any paperwork for them."

In this context, and after a successful experience building a landscaping cooperative, the Project's women's committee decided to build a cooperative to prevent exploitation in the industry. The twelve core members of the cooperative conducted extensive one-on-one outreach at Latino churches to find interested women. They enrolled in courses covering the principles of cooperative formation, including worker control and ownership and democratic decision making. They then formed four committees: finance, marketing, rules, and education. They developed a system of equitable distribution of jobs to members. Once every member is assigned a client, the assignment cycle starts again following a sequence based on each member's level of participation in co-op activities. Clients pay $50 for the first three hours of work and $15 for each additional hour. Members pay 10 percent of what they earn in dues.

The co-op has offered some distinct advantages and benefits to the Project, and it has also revealed limitations of the co-op model. The Project built the co-op in a way that maximized the participation of all co-op members. (Maximizing participation was, incidentally, more difficult to do with the landscaping co-op, whose members were largely male and who "resisted doing a lot of the administrative work, expecting me to do it," recalls Marin-Molina.) That emphasis on participation eventually paid off. "The housecleaning co-op has emerged as one of the most stable groups we've ever had," she says. In addition, she notes that building co-ops "helps us understand the industry really really well," an invaluable boost to the base of knowledge that informs future strategy.

But obstacles have slowed down the process of building the co-op and making it profitable. Members have previously experienced the industry as workers, not as employers, so they don't know basics like how to estimate the cost of a job. In addition cooperatives have to compete within industry standards. "While you're trying to meet the goals of paying a living wage, other businesses aren't doing that, [so] you immediately run up against how come you're charging so much; even socially conscious groups don't necessarily want to pay for that. You start out with the idea that we set up this business, everybody will have a job, it will generate lots of money for the organization. Grand schemes, then the realities of running a business get in the way," Marin-Molina says.

Illustration: The HDCJ Cooperative Forms to Pursue Collective Bargaining

The HDCJ Cooperative was started as a group within DARE by four day-care providers who repeatedly received their paychecks from the state late. After the HDCJ Campaign had waged a five-year struggle to make family day-care workers in Rhode Island state employees so that they could be eligible for health insurance and after it had rejected the option of affiliating with a union so it could retain independent women's leadership, the Campaign reformulated itself as an independent cooperative hoping to pursue collective bargaining. After formalizing its structure, the HDCJ Cooperative set up services for its members. These included a substitute provider pool that could replace primary providers during vacations and when they were sick, a toy lending library, a bulk purchasing program, a parent referral program that placed fifty children in the first nine months, and a reading program through which a volunteer arrives monthly to read to children in day care and to distribute books. The Cooperative has maintained its commitment to group advocacy to resolve individual problems with state agencies, as in the case of an immigrant member with a temporary green card and working papers whom the state refused to pay after one year of service.

The biggest challenge is to translate all the energy and history of the Cooperative into a collective bargaining agreement. Collective bargaining is limited by law to official unions, so creating a collective bargaining unit out of subcontracted workers will require confronting regressive labor laws. Currently, the Cooperative is simply exploring the possibility of raising the reimbursement rates paid by the state. As the Cooperative develops, child care and other state contractors and workers will be watching to see whether this new organizational form can permanently expand the scope of public responsibility for child care working conditions.

To determine the constituencies for your organization and to ascertain which kind of organizational structure will serve them best, complete Exercise 2.1.

Actively Shaping Group Culture

Every organization has a distinct culture that is defined by a lot more than holiday events and the food eaten by its members. Organizational culture includes the

Exercise 2.1. Reflection Questions: Constituencies and Structure.

1. Who are the people around us whose political voice needs to be raised? How are they organized right now? What are the problems they face? What are their particular strengths?

2. What could be gained from organizing these folks in a new formation? How would we reach them? Who else has tried to organize them and what was their experience?

3. What is the best form of organization for our constituency? Should we put together an organization of the existing groups they belong to? Should we have individual memberships? Should we have some combination?

4. What is the best decision-making and planning structure for the members of our constituency? How do they like to communicate? What kinds of structures are they used to?

language commonly spoken, rules written and unwritten, humor, rituals, and attitudes about other communities and social change. Most organizations pay little attention to shaping their own culture, so it gets shaped haphazardly, according to the culture of whoever is around at the time. All cultures, including those of organizations, are fluid. They are never totally at a standstill, although change might take place slowly.

We usually think about the effects of the existing collective identity and culture on our organizing, but we rarely think of the opposite: how organizing affects identities and culture. Although academics have charted this process, the principle is self-evident. Any time someone tells her story of becoming an activist, we can track how the experience changed that person. But often our overly simplistic sense of community autonomy keeps us from seeing this change in identity clearly. Several years ago I had an organizing staff study the ways in which gender identities were manipulated to reinforce racial and class hierarchies. When I posed the question "If we were to organize people into a best-scenario identity, what would that identity include?" I was confronted with shocked resistance. Organizing people into an identity is something the right wing does, not our side, I was told. But it seems to me that if we don't organize people to embrace identities that enable a fight for liberation, we are lost to the other side's image of us. None of us comes into ourselves in a vacuum. We are influenced either by the Gap billboard or by the antisweatshop organizer.

For example, in Los Angeles, the Korean Immigrant Workers Advocates (KIWA) has made it clear—both within and outside the Korean community—that the vast majority of Korean immigrants are not business owners but low-wage workers in Korean businesses. That distinct identity as workers has taken shape through clashes with Korean owners and regulatory agencies. Embracing a class identity has also enabled low-wage Korean workers to clarify their self-interest in relation to other communities of color. KIWA's membership now includes Latinos who also work in Korean businesses, and KIWA was responsible for turning out the Korean vote against the anti–affirmative action Proposition 209, allying itself particularly with the black community (Toney, 2000).

Until recently, the work culture of most political organizations excluded women and those people not in a traditional family structure from employment. Certainly, organizers are required to make sacrifices to do the work. But the extreme notion of what it takes to get the work done in political organizations is profoundly discouraging to many people who have been good organizers and leaders, particularly those who lack the option to leave their children or their elderly parents with someone else for long periods of time. Working in what Bravo, of 9to5, calls a "maniacal frenzy," does not "inspire people to get involved. It inspires them to see the maniac and say, oh good, you do the work for me, and see you later."

Illustration: DARE Builds a Multiracial Culture

As described previously, when DARE was primarily an African American organization, it created the Comite Latino to more deeply engage Latinas in the organization. Over five years, key elements of the organization's culture changed to accommodate immigrants. Rather than holding membership meetings and confrontations with decision makers only in English, DARE began to use simultaneous translation machines to conduct bilingual (eventually trilingual) meetings. In addition to a program that consisted largely of externally oriented campaign activities, DARE members began to invest time in educational and community-building activities so that members could learn more about each other's roots. Two aspects of DARE's culture that did not shift were the commitment to raising money from its constituency and the notion that all leaders are responsible for helping to generate operating funds. All these elements of organizational culture allowed DARE to become a multiracial organization over time.

To determine your organization's culture and which aspects of it, if any, need to be changed, complete Exercise 2.2.

Matching Outreach to the Constituency

Outreach needs to be matched to a group's constituency, but it should be personal and systematic. Rather than using a particular form just because we've heard that it is the most disciplined or best way, it is important to test different methods and refine them over time. (Exhibit 2.1, beginning on p. 40, describes the elements of five basic outreach methods.) For example, door knocking works well to identify neighborhood and geographically defined issues but is not as useful for identifying people who are less concentrated, such as nurses or women who have been denied welfare benefits. To reach these people, it makes more sense to be outside the welfare office or at the hospital during shift changes. When trying out a new method, allow enough time before throwing it out to assess its usefulness in getting people to engage in at least one activity.

Whatever methods we choose, they must be systematic and geared toward personal contact. Contact and relationships help to motivate members to take on new responsibilities, which in turn create collective identity. For example, some organizations have hotlines people call with problems related to police violence or workplace violations. Technology has also given us new options for getting to those people who have identified their interest in a particular problem, and it has certainly given us new options for communicating with our base if it has access to technology.

We can do new outreach year-round or in cycles, but we must do it repeatedly, and we must measure it. Numbers remain important to organization building. An

Exercise 2.2. Reflection Questions: Organizational Culture.

1. What are the events, incidents, or values that indicate the culture of our organization? What was the original intent behind these elements of our culture?

2. Which elements of our current culture are we attached to? Why? Which elements do we enjoy, hate, or not care about? Why? Who else is attracted to or repelled by these elements of our culture?

3. What elements of our culture should we consider changing? What are the first three steps in doing so?

organization does not need huge numbers to be effective, but it does need a renewable leadership and a base big enough to carry out campaigns that match the group's political ambition.

Illustration: 9to5 Systematizes Outreach Strategies

Amy Stier, 9to5's organizing director, spent most of her life in unions before coming to the National Association of Working Women. Stier notes that different roles and resources force unions and community organizations to take different approaches to worker organizing. Among the differences, community organizations have a larger and more amorphous constituency than unions, whose constituencies are based in workplaces. Unions tend to focus on a narrower set of issues, and the pressure of elections and contract negotiations create stringent timelines for them. Community organizers, with far fewer resources than unions, tend to move slowly, and their fights lack the single common enemy available in the form of a boss in union struggles. Stier adds that, "in unions, we had a much more structured way of targeting, recruiting, and developing relationships, but here you have to be willing to take an approach that's not as regimented, give people more opportunity over a longer period of time to be involved."

The expansion of its constituency from clerical workers to a broader range of women workers required 9to5 to broaden not only its issues but also its organizing methods. In Milwaukee, for example, 9to5 conducts its outreach through the Milwaukee Poverty Network Initiative, whose organizers, Linda Garcia-Barnard, Mildred Naredo, and Tracy Jones, have found a variety of ways to reach nontraditional workers and poor women. They go to welfare agencies and make presentations at other organizations that serve women in economic crisis, particularly those that serve people of color and immigrants. Each organizer has developed additional turf of her own. Naredo is expert at hitting the bus stops; Jones, a former temp who worked with 9to5 to win a sex-discrimination case against a temp agency, applies for temp jobs specifically to survey and recruit temp workers.

9to5's organizing process in Milwaukee is designed to provide multiple options for involvement. The organization holds monthly women's gatherings, conducts events in partnership with a citywide jobs coalition, and helps turn out people for Keep Families First, a legislative organization. Stier notes that 9to5 tries to combine issue work with outreach as much as possible, as when it demanded that the mayor create five hundred new jobs. Through new outreach 9to5 built a list of people ready to apply for those jobs and got many to participate in the action on the mayor. Stier notes the importance of keeping good data so that people can be given several opportunities to participate. "We make sure we have a permanent contact for them [members of its constituency], usually their mother's number. We follow up within a week. We do reminders, take care of logistics. We probably keep people on our lists longer than we should, but we have experienced people showing up after three or four

Exhibit 2.1. Basic Approaches to Outreach.

	Street Outreach	Presentation	Door Knocking	Personal Visit	House Meeting
What	Meeting people where they hang out, gather, or work when the constituency is defined by issue (e.g., youth at schools, riders on the buses, welfare recipients at the welfare office)	Reaching out to people where they meet when the constituency is defined by issue (e.g., office meetings, schools, churches); needs immediate follow-up after the presentation	Doing outreach door to door in a defined community; lends itself to immediate neighborhood issues (e.g., tenant organizing, neighborhood organizing)	A one-on-one meeting with people in their home from an identified list of targeted people	A meeting at a person's home with close friends and close relatives
Role	Three-minute one-on-one; ask for a commitment	Five- to twenty-minute presentation or speech about your organization and what you do; primarily educational, usually with a broad pitch	"The rap" (ten to fifteen minutes)	A personal-visit "rap": find out more about the people, their issues, their history in the neighborhood, etc. (twenty to thirty minutes)	Help the person coordinate and host the meeting (i.e., make a list of people to invite, plan the agenda and role, role play the "ask") (forty-five minutes to one hour)

Turf	Where your targeted constituency is already gathered	Geographically defined neighborhood or community	In the person's home	In the person's home; works only across relationships—i.e., does not account for neighborhood turf, economic status, etc.
Significance	Cold contact, minimal relationship established; follow up with a phone call or personal visit	Luke-warm contact (have already established some connection), educational with broad pitch; follow up with phone call, get them to a meeting or personal visit	The most challenging cold contact; good for doing research and identifying potential leaders; follow up with getting a commitment or setting up a personal visit	The second level of contact, usually follows any of the methods previously mentioned; good for deepening a relationship and knowledge about a person; follow up with a commitment, house meeting, or get them to do outreach with you!	Good way to test leadership and commitment to the organization, good way to fundraise, good way to recruit more people into the organization

Source: Reprinted with permission from the Center for Third World Organizing.

attempt[s]." The organizer's skill plays a key role in providing multiple opportunities for involvement. Stier says, "Insincerity can be spotted miles away, especially in populations with radar fine-tuned to that. You have to have a patient willingness to talk through the obstacles and be able to articulate why the issues are important enough and how winning will ultimately remove the obstacles. A good organizer has to be able to tell whether she's spending time with people [she] should be spending time with. And, of course, be tenacious."

At the national level 9to5 identifies organizing opportunities through the national hotline that operates out of its Atlanta office. Bravo notes that the hotline is one way in which the organization tracks "the realities of women dealing with sexual harassment, workplace health hazards, problems with getting family and maternity leave." Each caller is encouraged to join the Association. Enthusiastic callers are encouraged to become activists with access to broader sets of materials and organizing advice; they then form local clusters with other workers, respond to policy proposals, and speak to the media. If callers are driven by workplace issues that lend themselves to unionization, 9to5 refers them to the AFL-CIO in their area.

Illustration: DARE Finds That Organizing the People Most Affected Drives Up the Stakes

When DARE started working on its Jobs with Dignity living wage campaign, the organization set out to ensure that the people who would be directly affected by passage of the city ordinance developed solutions because it knew that workers would have the most at stake and would fight hardest to win. Unsurprisingly, the campaign attracted lots of women and men of color, who had the hardest time finding permanent, good jobs in Providence and who had been excluded or underserved by some local unions. To flex the campaign's political muscles, DARE took on fights to improve the lives and working conditions of members; at the same time, starting with teaching assistants, it developed leadership skills in its members and provided them with experience that would strengthen the campaign as a whole.

Janet Santos Bonilla, a long-time DARE member and city worker, recruited her friend Sara Gonzalez, who had been unjustly fired from her job as a temporary teaching assistant for the Providence public schools. Three days, one direct action, and a meeting with the superintendent later, Sara had her job back. But the campaign realized that being reinstated into her minimum-wage, no-benefits, "temporary" job, in which she had worked for nearly three years, was simply not enough. Bonilla hosted a house meeting with others in the same situation, and the teaching assistants formed a subcommittee of Jobs with Dignity. Their "Teacher's Assistant Bill of Rights," outlined clear demands to improve working conditions, such as procedures for performance evaluations and inclusion in trainings and, most important, permanent hiring.

That spring, DARE recruited Gonzalez into the organizer-in-training internship, during which she recruited more teaching assistants to testify and conduct actions at school board meetings. This activity got the attention of the press and of the teachers' union. Once the union started working with DARE, the school department agreed to hire teaching assistants permanently for all vacant positions in the fall. A year after they began their struggle, eighty teaching assistants were making double the wages they had before, with full health coverage, vacation and sick pay, pensions, and union membership.

Inspired by the victory of the teaching assistants, bus monitors began organizing their own subcommittee, winning a similar commitment in writing: after working sixty consecutive days, they would receive "long-term" status (with higher wages and benefits) and would be made permanent after another sixty consecutive days. Being able to win union support, higher wages, and permanent employee status fuels the commitment of these constituencies to hold out for the best possible living wage policy.

Completing Exercise 2.3 allows you to plan your organization's outreach strategies. The example shows how the form might be filled out for an outreach program designed to recruit tenants in low-income neighborhoods.

Limiting Service Provision

If service provision is a part of your organization, think carefully about its relationship to your organizing efforts and be vigilant that it does not overshadow them. Many organizations have used services to build a group and to provide desperately needed resources. There are increasing examples, too, of direct action membership organizations integrating other approaches into their work. ACORN, for example, runs mortgage services that help people get house loans and avoid redlining. Centers for immigrant workers provide job training and placement services.

Some organizers, including myself, fantasize that running services will bring the people most affected right to our doorstep, identified and available to be organized. There are three problems with this fantasy. First, people go to service providers for different reasons than they go to a political organization. This is not to say that none of the people in a soup line or waiting for legal services are interested in organizing, but they might not be acting on that interest at that moment. Second, service provision is easier to conduct than organizing; organizing is more demanding because you have to get people to do something. As a result, if different pieces of work are competing for attention, the services usually win. In addition, when one constituency resists the entry of another into the organization, the often overwhelming demands of providing services can be a convenient excuse to stop organizing. Even unions, which we perceive to have enough money to do both, gave up their organizing for decades in order to service their existing members. Third, service provision is far easier to fund than organizing, so some activists

Exercise 2.3. Outreach-Planning Worksheet.

Constituency (describe conditions in detail):
Example: Tenants in low-income neighborhoods, majority of color, lots of monolingual immigrants

Activity	Turf	Role of Organizer	Ask for	Follow-up	Potential Pitfalls	Dealing with Pitfalls	Timeline
Door knocking	Neighborhood	Knock, talk on established rap, and track information	Feelings about just-cause eviction	Twenty-minute visit	Can't get in	Ask to speak to people outside the building or get someone in the building to door-knock with you	June 6–August 1
			Contact information		Bad info		
			Yes to community meeting		Tip off landlord	Verify information afterward	
			$5 contribution		Language needs	Assume landlord will know, watch for retaliation	
						Carry translated materials and get agreement to send back someone who speaks that language	

try to use the same people for both service provision and organizing only to find that the tasks require different skills.

Although it is difficult to integrate organizing into a service organization, it can be and has been done. Occasionally, as in the case of Seattle's El Centro de la Raza, service providers and organizers work side by side; in this case, their co-ordination grew organically out of the community's organizing efforts. Some service organizations incubate political organizations effectively. For example, Mothers on the Move, an education-reform organization in the South Bronx, developed out of an adult literacy class that focused its learning on the educational system affecting participants' children. Eventually, Mothers on the Move left the literacy group and became independent. The Central American Refugee Center, which provides immigration and other services to Central American immigrants and refugees, builds into its service budgets a portion of the salary of an organizer working on community education and organizing.

The key to combining service and organizing is a thoughtful plan that takes into account the differences between the two strategies. Often, the leaders of a service organization have not considered all the implications of creating a whole new constituency-owned structure within the organization. When the people you have thought of as "clients" suddenly make decisions, that can be destabilizing. Sometimes the service organization's funding or reputation is threatened by the actions of the organizing group. When service and organizing are combined in one group, each needs to keep its autonomy and identity.

Illustration: The Workplace Project Rethinks How to Use Legal Services

A lawyer who had worked on both individual cases and organizing campaigns resisting employer sanctions, Workplace Project founder Jennifer Gordon believed that "legal advice would draw in people who might otherwise not come to the organization, at a time when they're strongly experiencing the problems that I wanted to take on as an organizer." Gordon had in mind a new way of providing services that would build a relationship of trust and respect between the advocate and the person; she saw "the legal case as a road that I would travel with the worker. When we reached a road block, that would be an opportunity for us to talk about why legal services won't solve the problem in a bigger way." Gordon began talking to immigrants every morning about their workplace problems (especially the issue of back wages), drawing them into the legal clinic, and from there seeking out those who expressed an interest in organizing to participate in a workers' organizing course.

Initially, in exchange for the services they received, people were asked to sign a contract agreeing to attend the workers' course and to commit time to ongoing organizing. Later, this system was adjusted. The clinic's individual in-take system was replaced by ongoing Friday workshops, in which people shared their problems and solutions. As a result, all people with individual problems could immediately join an industry team through the Friday afternoon workshops. That got them straight into organizing mode, without a stop at the advocate's office. The coordinator of the legal clinic now provides research support to the industry teams. Monthly membership meetings reinforce this process: the first hour people meet in their industry teams; the second hour focuses on a multi-industry campaign.

Workplace Project leaders pledged to evaluate the new system according to the amount of back wages won, the number of industrial teams, and the number of people who remained involved through the whole process. Marin-Molina says that the Project has tripled the number of people who are active in the organization since the system was changed. She attributes this growth to the fact that, from the first interaction, activities are carried out by a group rather than individually. She says, "Before, we talked about organizing, but we were giving individual consultation. With [the] previous workers' course, people might have missed a cycle and not be[en] able to sign up for a class for three months; they could have gotten bored or gotten their problem solved. Now, people are immediately channeled into organizing." From August 2000 to July 2001, the Project had 270 people come to the group workshops, and 60 of them participated on an industry team; 40 of those graduated and became members of the Workplace Project; and about 30 of those have stayed active on the teams. In the previous year, out of sixty who graduated from the workers' course, only ten remained active for six months or more.

Illustration: CSWA Provides No Services

Staff Member Wah Lee says, "When someone comes into CSWA, we tell them very clearly who we are. We are not a service or advocacy organization. We ask them to stand up for themselves and encourage them to bring other workers to get involved." Since many people come in to inquire about a specific issue, membership is not usually an immediate option. Instead, people are invited to participate in committee activities. In 1991, garment worker Fun Mae Eng came to CSWA when her employer withheld her wages. She soon discovered that the prospect of recovering her back wages through the legal system was dim. With support of the garment committee at CSWA, Mrs. Eng decided to organize her co-workers to picket against their employer, who later ran away. Undaunted, Mrs. Eng and her co-workers took their case to the next level and aggressively pursued the manufacturer. Their organizing efforts, combined with legal action, led Mrs. Eng and her co-workers to successfully win their back pay from the manufacturer in 1992. The first such effort to pursue a manufacturer, Mrs. Eng's case inspired other garment workers in New York to stand up for their rights and also sparked a movement across the country to hold manufacturers accountable for sweatshop conditions. A couple of years after being involved in CSWA, Mrs. Eng and other co-workers paid membership dues ($30 a year per person) and became members. In 1999, Mrs. Eng became chair of the Health and Safety Committee.

Conclusion

Organizing is essentially the process of creating politically active constituencies out of people with problems by focusing on their strengths and the solutions embedded in their experience. It is the basic work of progressive social change. For groups that are new to organizing, it is most important to define a clear constituency and a systematic plan for involving people. Having a clear but flexible structure, in which people can become leaders but not get permanently attached to a position, will help make the effort inclusive. For groups that have already been organizing for a long time, it is important to review the organization's constituency, structure, and culture during all strategic planning processes, so the group can be deliberate about expanding or deepening its work. Experienced groups tend to become complacent about and limited in their outreach; they work mainly among already established leaders and activists rather than continuing to expand their base. Groups that combine organizing with services need to be completely clear about the differences between their various strategies, what they are trying to get out of each, and how they will deal with potential conflicts between the two. The illustrations in this chapter show that organizational forms must be crafted creatively, with transparent structures and cultures that are actively shaped by members. Today's organizations, built through systematic outreach, will form the backbone of the next mass movements, which are already emerging to deal with issues like abuses by global capitalism, the prison industry, war, attacks on civil liberties, and environmental degradation.

CHAPTER THREE

PICKING THE GOOD FIGHT

One of the most difficult and hotly contested organizing tasks is to help members decide which issues to take up and how—a process known as issue development. Issues are the most public expression of an organization's values and world-view. Like all the other parts of organizing, issue development is a craft, both science and art. As such, it has rules and logic, a language and systems. These can always be improved and adapted for your particular organization, but the need to develop issues can never be denied. Each organization and coalition has to decide, therefore, what will guide its issue choices, how to frame those issues, and how to educate its community about the issue and the frame.

Webster's dictionary defines *issue* as a conflict between two parties. Organizers distinguish issues from problems. Problems refer to large-scale systems that are too large and vague to help us focus on real changes worth fighting for. Identifying specific issues within large-scale problems helps us define clear conflicts to which our group can propose a resolution. Issues always have at least three elements: a constituency with a grievance, a set of demands that address that grievance, and an institutional target at whom the grievance is directed. If a group cannot identify these three elements with specificity, then it is probably still dealing at the level of problems rather than carving out issues.

We have to craft issues carefully because they have long-lasting implications for the people who lead our organizations, the ideas we advance in the larger society, and the kinds of institutional changes we are able to gain. For example, women's membership in and leadership of unions has affected the kinds of issues taken up at the bargaining table. Women have traditionally been more concerned than men about child care, paid family leave, flexible work hours, and paid sick days. "These things can fall off the bargaining table to make room for other critical improvements," says Netsy Firestein, director of the Berkeley, California–based Labor Project for Working Families. "It makes a huge difference if women are there to articulate their needs directly" (interview with author, October 2002). But whether an issue is named explicitly and immediately by our constituency is not necessarily the best way to judge its value. Groups sometimes find themselves attracted to an issue that seems to offer strong potential but is one for which an insignificant constituency exists in the organization or one that evokes fear in its constituency. In these cases, organizations sometimes take on community education in an effort to build a constituency.

In this chapter I begin with the importance of having clear criteria, then move to how to craft demands, identify targets, and frame our issues. The illustrations come from the Los Angeles Alliance for a New Economy (LAANE), from which we learn how it makes detailed demands and how it targeted billionaire developers; the Center for Third World Organizing (CTWO), from which we learn that the criteria for choosing issues sometimes must be changed; Working Partnerships, from which we learn the importance of prioritizing criteria and also how to align criteria, demands, and targets; the Campaign on Contingent Work (CCW), from which we learn the importance of devising multipronged demands; Wider Opportunities for Women (WOW), from which we learn about the importance of language in framing issues; and the Chinese Staff & Workers Association (CSWA), from which we can see the clear relationship between a particular constituency and its priorities and demands.

Principles

There are four principles to crafting good issues. First, we must have clear criteria that guide our issue choices. Second, demands define the conflict and provide negotiating points, so they must be ambitious and specific. Third, demands should always be directed toward the individual decision makers who constitute our targets. All these add up to the fourth principle: we must pay attention to the frame we put an issue in as well as the issue itself.

Defining Clear Criteria

Many activists resist the requirement to apply criteria when they are deciding on issues. When I was a nineteen-year-old student organizer training other students around the country through the Grassroots Organizing Weekends, we taught the Midwest Academy's session called "Choosing Issues." In the session, we asked participants to review a set of criteria for good issues, apply them to four campaign options, and rank the options to determine the best issue. Students of color, women, and lesbian/gay/bi/trans (LGBT) students, arguably the most explicitly marginalized constituencies on their campuses, frequently resisted our characterization of "good" issues. They asserted, quite correctly, that they rarely had the luxury to choose issues. Issues were thrust on them by oppressive institutional policies and practices that forced them into a survival mode. Furthermore, they said, choosing issues creates a hierarchy among oppressions: groups have to make implicit, if not explicit, judgments about which issues are important enough to work on and which are not, who deserves liberation and who does not. Years later, I was able to acknowledge that these students had good reason to resist this framework. The criteria we were using and the notion of prioritizing issues had been used against these groups by less marginal groups to justify avoiding their controversial issues.

Today, I would suggest that those students create their own criteria for prioritizing issues. While it is true that some attacks must be answered, having clear criteria can help you respond effectively, as well as move beyond defense posture to victories that improve the quality of life. Without a set of clear criteria to guide them, organizations tend to jump from issue to issue, and thus they have difficulty applying the successes and capacity built during one campaign to the next. As Marion Steeg, the former staff director of Working Partnerships, says, "Some issues you choose, some issues choose you. Even when they choose you, you still have to decide whether or not to act like the chosen people." When our opponents pick a fight that agitates everyone and has major implications, we risk becoming irrelevant if we don't respond. However, strong organizations cannot be driven entirely by the crises created by their opposition. A completely reactive stance produces stagnant organizations that can never get ahead of their opposition and that are always running to shift a debate whose parameters have already been set.

The Midwest Academy's criteria for issues are still the best known. These emerged from the organizing theories of Saul Alinsky and the practices honed by the previous Citizen Action network. The central point made by former and current Midwest Academy staff members Kim Bobo, Jackie Kendall, and Steve Max in their book, *Organizing for Social Change*, is that problems are too huge for community organizations to grapple with through the format of the issue campaign. But even going into specific issues can reveal hundreds of options. For example, to take on the problem of women's poverty, how does a group choose between working on welfare benefits or demanding a new jobs program? The Midwest

Academy coded key principles for choosing among issues into these criteria (Bobo, Kendall, and Max, 1990, p. 28):

1. The issue meets the principles of direct action organizing—that is, it leads to a real difference in people's everyday lives, it gives people a sense of their own power, and it changes the relations of power.
2. The issue is worthwhile, widely and deeply felt, nondivisive, and consistent with the organization's values and vision. Many people in your constituency must find it important enough to take some action on it.
3. The issue suggests clear demands. The changes you propose address the negative conditions you've identified.
4. The issue is winnable. You have determined the likelihood of getting your solutions adopted by a particular agency or institution; precedents in other places, the affordability of your plan, the strength of your legal arguments, a clear strategy, or some other advantage raises your chances of winning.
5. The issue is easy to understand. The common rule is that you should be able to explain it in one paragraph on a flyer.
6. The issue has a clear target. In organizing, the target is always an individual who can agree to meet your demands.
7. The issue has a clear time frame that works for you. Issue campaigns, like good novels or movies, should have a beginning, middle, and end, and you should know roughly how long each of those phases will last.
8. The issue gives you opportunities to build leadership. An issue campaign should have many roles for people to play because the issue itself lends itself to many different creative tactics. For example, an issue that can be won only through a lawsuit is not the kind that builds leadership, as the key decision-making and negotiation roles tend to be limited to lawyers and judges.
9. The issue sets up your organization to tackle additional and related issues. The issue should help build a track record, a base of people and knowledge that the organization can easily transfer to other arenas.

Few issues perfectly meet all these criteria every time, so we have to negotiate to find the most promising ones. A group might prioritize criteria differently at different phases of the organization's life. Winnability, for example, might be more important to a newer organization that is trying to establish a track record, so it will choose smaller, less controversial issues. Because all organizations cannot be all things to all people at all times, most of us have to find compromises among choosing ideal criteria to guide our issue work, the need to react to our opposition, the limits of our organizational resources, and the requirements of our organizational mission.

Illustration: CTWO Chooses New Criteria for Issue Development

Sometimes the traditional criteria clash with the need to take up issues that are breaking down a community, and a group has to develop new criteria that more accurately reflect its interests. CTWO had successfully used the traditional criteria for fifteen years to win victories on substantial issues like preventing lead poisoning in children, winning new monies for youth services, and preventing racist labor practices. By the mid-1990s, however, CTWO had turned its attention to building organizations not just owned and operated by people of color but also with explicitly antiracist and feminist as well as progressive class politics. To do so, CTWO had to develop criteria that would guide organizations in their issue research and their development process.

CTWO learned about the need to be explicit about racial justice criteria from its experiences organizing the Campaign for Community Safety and Police Accountability in the early 1990s. CTWO started the Campaign without broad criteria to help guide all the issue choices that would have to be made. As a result, the Campaign was guided largely by the traditional criteria. It was designed to challenge the power of police departments while upholding concerns about safety. This divisive issue wasn't easy to understand, wasn't widely supported, and wasn't particularly winnable in the short run. Rather than understanding that there were nevertheless good reasons to take on police accountability, the Campaign began to look for the portions of the problem that lent themselves to the traditional criteria.

One choice of a smaller issue undermined the racial justice goal of adding police accountability to the notion of community safety. For a time, the participating organizations ran local campaigns demanding that the assets seized by the police in drug raids be returned to the community in the form of grants to local nonprofits. This demand had been tested by groups in the National Peoples' Action network, which had won thousands of dollars from such grants, thereby preventing local police departments from simply using the assets for their own ends. CTWO's groups also succeeded. It was a winnable demand that, on the surface, doesn't appear to have a downside. However, assets were frequently seized before a person was convicted of a crime; in effect, police departments were stealing cars and houses from suspected drug dealers. The position of the American Civil Liberties Union that asset forfeiture constituted a civil rights violation stood as a glaring criticism of CTWO's attempt to get that money given back to the community. Former Co-Director Francis Calpotura reflects that "we sacrificed our interest in moving a racial justice frame to the need to win something—anything—now. Really, we should have been demanding an end to asset forfeiture instead of a redistribution of that money."

The contradiction that emerged between the need to win and the need to advance an unpopular idea greatly influenced the Campaign's next national effort to shape an issue. When CTWO launched the Winning Action for Gender Equity (WAGE) program, staff member Sandra Davis recalls seeing the limitations of the traditional criteria in a project that was meant to challenge the gender and racial organization of society. Davis says, "We realized that the issues we were working on were not sharp enough to make a significant shift in the institutions and in the way people think about these problems." Early in the process of recruiting community groups to participate in WAGE, CTWO staff designed a set of issue criteria that would direct groups to identify and take up specific campaigns at the intersection of race, class, and gender. These criteria included the following (adapted from the 1999 CTWO training handout on issue development):

1. The issue surfaces a clearly discriminatory or oppressive practice or policy directing the treatment of women/girls or people of color; it reveals a clear conflict between the constituency and an institution. The issue can be crafted to show explicitly how an institution keeps certain groups in an assigned place in relation to the dominant group. For example, in looking at welfare policy for potential good issues, a group might talk explicitly about the ways in which removing the safety net forces women to stay in subordinate, abusive relationships with men, both at home and at work.

2. The issue offers the possibility of using good gendered or racial data. Data collection disaggregated by race and gender faces attack by conservative forces, so the generation and use of such data constitute an important intervention in themselves. In Los Angeles, when the Bus Riders Union, a project of the Labor/Community Strategy Center, effectively used data to show that cutbacks in bus service would constitute transportation discrimination against all kinds of women and men of color, it brought the reduction plans of the Metropolitan Transit Association to a halt.

3. The issue expands the rights of people of color or women electorally, legally, economically, or otherwise. For example, because Supreme Court decisions on racial discrimination lawsuits have placed the burden on the victim to prove that an institution engaged in intentional discrimination, many antidiscrimination struggles are greatly limited. It is nearly impossible to establish intent, as few institutions will state that goal explicitly. Therefore, any issue that wins on the basis of discriminatory effect would constitute an expansion of rights at this point.

4. The issue has race and gender antidiscrimination handles—laws, data, anecdotes, and precedents that a group uses to build support for its proposals beyond its moral position.

5. Solutions offer new ways of organizing society and go beyond the framework of "disproportionate impact" or simple representation to challenge the traditional gender or racial division of labor and benefits. These are often solutions geared not just toward lifting up the situations of the oppressed but toward undoing the privileges that accompany whiteness and maleness in this society.

6. The issue introduces new or stronger language, such as white privilege/supremacy, patriarchy, feminism. Issue campaigns should enable the organization, over time, to call social phenomena by their proper names or by new names

that the organization assigns so that it is not always running to correct right-wing language attacking its communities.

7. Tactics can be designed to challenge cultural domination and disrupt "proper channels," which are largely the product of European social bureaucracies. Whenever possible, tactics should be within the cultural experience of members and outside that of targets.

These criteria led the WAGE organizations to prioritize winning sexual-harassment policies in junior high and high schools, organizing home day-care workers, improving the translation system in family courts, and expanding the availability of public transportation for workers and students.

These criteria also led CTWO into its next national campaign, the effort to build a national network of welfare rights groups and community organizations that would shift the debate surrounding reauthorization of welfare reform and generate new organizing of poor women, especially women of color. Working with more than sixty groups nationwide, many of them newly formed to deal specifically with the effects of welfare reform, Grassroots Organizing for Welfare Leadership (GROWL) used the frames of "Supporting All Families" and "Fair Treatment" to define welfare as an issue of race and gender discrimination and of economic exploitation. CTWO and GROWL have challenged the ideas and values embedded in welfare reform by documenting harm (to counteract mainstream research), educating policymakers, developing new policies, and taking direct action. The project to document harm, a necessary step in reshaping the debate, built common purpose, as well as advancing the intellectual and tactical capacity of GROWL members.

Working with the Applied Research Center, which designed a racial-equity bill for inclusion in reauthorization, and the NOW Legal Defense and Education Fund, which analyzed implications of the Bush Administration's marriage proposal, GROWL took its message to the public and to policymakers. GROWL'S postcard campaigns and town meetings posed a significant challenge to both liberals and conservatives who insisted on narrowing the welfare debate. Armed with evidence of systemic discrimination, GROWL crafted activities designed to firm up the support of sympathetic legislators, to prevent their "making a deal too early and cutting off the debate," says Dan HoSang, former organizing and network director of CTWO. Organizers avoided moving aggressively on a specific piece of policy quickly because "we're trying to establish some basic education for decision makers that will influence them in more than one area of the debate."

The racial-equity bill, which includes money to enforce civil rights laws and restores benefits to legal immigrants, was adopted into the Democratic version of the Senate's reauthorization bill. GROWL resists the marriage proposals within the policy frame of supporting all families, which includes a set of fifteen criteria against which to measure welfare policy. Even if these ideas do not make it into federal reauthorization, they form the basis of continued organizing at the state level.

Illustration: Working Partnerships Prioritizes Its Criteria

Working Partnerships has clear priorities that allow it to jump on opportunities to craft and win good policy. Steeg says, "You can manufacture an issue, but if it isn't taken up in the heart of your membership, it won't last very long as a priority for the organization." Executive Director Amy Dean notes that crafting good issues involves a process of research, education, testing, and evaluation that reveals which issues to prioritize because they are going to be worth long-term organizational investment. First, the issue has to be of real benefit and fit into the equity frame—that is, it has to shrink the gap between rich and poor in Silicon Valley. Second, it has to help build the alliance between unions and community groups and must strengthen community groups and their leadership. Third, the demands have to be focused and possible to implement.

For Working Partnerships, taking up children's health insurance involved placing a lower priority on leadership development than did passing a living wage ordinance for the city of San Jose a few years earlier. Steeg compares the two issues:

> Living wage was a much longer, more organic process, involving . . . community meetings, union meetings, and consensus around what should be in living wage. All of that developed more ownership and leadership than children's health. The timing around children's health prevented that. The heat of organizing had to take place in one month to six weeks max. After that the City Council would have decided how to spend its money and our opportunity to win a major benefit would have been gone. The enemies were also different. In living wage, it was the council and employers. We didn't have six votes on the council, and we had all kinds of opposition to be overcome, from small businesses, the Chamber of Commerce, and the press. In children's health there was one enemy, the Mayor; there was no business interest against it. We got less leadership development out of that, but great victories.

Working Partnerships has also found that prioritizing criteria in coalitions can be difficult. In such formations, the temptation to include all the policy changes required by all the groups often wars with the desire to win a significant change for a smaller group. Steeg says that unions, which tend to be among the stronger partners in coalitions, have a particular responsibility to help pass policies that are less politically palatable. She notes that "once you've come together, you have to make a fascinating decision about whether to prioritize the base building and the coalition building, which often gets expressed in a policy platform that includes everything, versus something realistic that you can win." Most often, this decision requires all the major players to pull back from the external strategies they had been ready to pursue in order to come to an internal agreement about how to prioritize the issues. "It's worth doing that," says Steeg, "if you get to a strategy that is able to produce one win after another."

Steeg also notes that good community education is key to taking on ambitious issues and complicated policy challenges; many issues are not easy to understand, and solutions are more complicated than can be explained in one paragraph. As Working Partnerships moved into a struggle to win affordable housing in San Jose's latest development, Steeg reflected, "Who the hell knows what inclusionary zoning is? But if you craft it so people understand what it means, the precedent it sets, what it will do for diversity in [a] community to keep an inclusive population, they come to own it. It's not a heart stopper, but you can craft a solution and educate people."

Before you start to pick your issues, complete Exercise 3.1 to be sure you have thought through your criteria clearly.

Crafting Ambitious and Specific Demands

Because demands define the conflict, they must be ambitious and specific. Demands provide your major negotiating points; they help determine the ebb and flow of a campaign. In this section, I cover the difference between substantive and procedural demands and also the common challenges groups face in crafting demands.

Strong campaigns have multiple demands, which give a group the chance to fight for incremental victories. If you enter an issue arena with only one demand, which is refused, you have no chance either to debate the merits of your demands or to build the constituency that can come together during an extended campaign. Incremental victories, although they may not cause systemic collapse, can motivate your membership to stay together, put cracks in the system that can be widened with additional campaigns, attract allies who can collaborate on more ambitious efforts, and raise your level of knowledge about a specific institution and arena. I would argue that multiple, incremental demands are more important, not less, when we are taking on a fundamental change.

In addition, it is important to recognize the difference between substantive and procedural demands. Substantive demands are the changes that will make a difference, and procedural demands are those that enable making that difference but don't constitute a change in and of themselves. Examples of procedural demands include getting a meeting with your target or getting that person to meet you on your home turf rather than at his or her office; getting a decision maker to commission a study about the conditions you want addressed; getting one of your leaders on an institutional planning committee; making the institution run a new policy by your group for feedback before implementation; forcing a politician to host a public hearing. Substantive demands have more of a policy character: winning a moratorium on death-penalty sentencing in your state; getting $5 billion dollars redirected from highway construction to public transportation; forcing the family court to hire five new translators to aid women in domestic violence and custody cases.

Exercise 3.1. Reflection Questions:
Criteria for Issue Development.

1. What criteria have guided our issue choices so far? Does everyone in the organization operate from the same criteria? Which issues meet which criteria? For new groups: What criteria should guide our issue choices? Do we have priorities? If we are forming around an issue, why did we choose it? What criteria will we use to craft the incremental issues in this area?

2. If we stick to these criteria or to traditional criteria, what opportunities do we lose or gain?

3. Do our current criteria reflect the values and conditions of our constituency? Why or why not?

4. What changes do we need to consider in revising our issue criteria? Deletions, additions, reprioritizing?

Groups face some common challenges in crafting demands. They ask for too little, abandon demands that are deemed unwinnable, and make vague demands. When a community is accustomed to rough conditions, its expectations are sometimes low. When groups ask for too little, they can make demands that make no difference in daily life, creating a fake issue. In situations like this, it is important to go through a vigorous research process that involves and educates the community before making a final decision.

Illustration: Residents of City Center Hotel Expand Their Demands

I first experienced this dynamic while organizing sixty-five homeless families living in a transitional welfare hotel in San Francisco. These families usually consisted of a woman of color and her children; they had lived on the streets until the city gave them a spot in the transitional hotel. The hotel was meant to provide families with one month's housing until they were assigned permanent subsidized housing, but most families had been there at least six months, and one family had been there for three full years. The building was totally uninhabitable: the children had skin fungus conditions, the bathrooms did not work, and no one had kitchen facilities—people hung their groceries out the window to prevent them from spoiling. At first, the tenants wanted to demand that the landlord fix up the building so they could be more comfortable while enduring the long wait for permanent housing. Research revealed that the landlord made $600–$800 monthly for each "suite," that the city was subsidizing the rent at a rate of $400–$600 each month, that there were ten thousand units of abandoned housing in San Francisco, and that the building would not pass an inspection that wasn't influenced by bribes and limited to two clean hallways. We discussed the real danger that a demand on the slumlord would simply lead him to suspend his contract with the city rather than making costly improvements; all our people would then be back out on the street. After they became aware of these facts, the tenants began to feel righteous in demanding that the city provide the same level of subsidy for apartments they found themselves, and, after two months of campaigning, they settled for permanent section 8 apartments.

Some groups abandon their demands if they are deemed unwinnable. Particularly when our constituencies are under attack, criteria other than winnability become more important. Perhaps we need an opportunity to advance our ideas, consolidate or increase our leadership, or frame the issue in ways that lead us to additional issues. Steeg of Working Partnerships bluntly says, "It's OK to lose if your goal is to organize and come back after the loss." Coming back after a loss requires leaders who are more politically sophisticated and experienced than they were before the fight and a membership that is more educated and committed to standing up for the original and similar issues.

On occasion, the excessive winnability of an issue can work against the larger goals of progressive organizing. Since the notion of the living wage has gained support nationally, some municipalities have initiated their own policies without waiting for a community coalition to come together. LAANE director Madeleine Janis-Aparicio sees these efforts as feeding the justified skepticism that many activists have about the potential value of living wage ordinances. She says:

> People who are rightly cynical about living wage say that if you raise wages automatically the workers will not want to organize. Raising wages is a helpful framing device, but really the important thing is the whole program around it. We probably get a call every couple of weeks from a group around the country that has an opportunity to support legislation that some public official wants to move. For whatever reason the opportunity is time-limited, groups don't have the chance to envision the ordinance or shape it. If they do go ahead, they'll get something passed that doesn't have all the components built in; they don't take the time to build the organizing, infrastructure, and research capacity. The infrastructure is the most important thing.

Illustration: CSWA Shows Concern for the Well-Being of the People Through Its Health and Safety Campaign

As the hours worked in factories lengthen, more and more women are citing severe injuries and occupational diseases from toiling long hours at a breakneck pace, often performing endless repetitive motions or standing on their feet for over twelve hours at a stretch while operating dangerous machinery. Over 50 percent of women garment workers in factories are injured. The most common health problems include carpal tunnel syndrome; chronic back, neck, and leg injuries; vision impairment; and asthma. Some workers are even maimed to the point of permanent disfiguration.

After sustaining an injury, workers face another nightmare: a Workers' Compensation system not designed to compensate. The New York State Workers' Compensation system provides some of the lowest benefits in the country; the minimum weekly benefit rate is a paltry $40. Cases are often dragged out for over ten years before an injured worker receives even a single penny. This "starving out" process often places injured workers in a precarious and desperate state, and eventually workers are frustrated into accepting a ridiculously insignificant settlement, often exclusive of any ongoing medical treatment. Meanwhile, injured workers' families face serious hardship and are torn apart. Other workers become homeless or even suicidal.

CSWA began organizing injured women workers into the Health and Safety Committee. At first, Committee members provided services to other injured workers, such as filling out forms, translating, and assisting them to navigate the system. Quickly, injured workers saw through the corrupt system and developed an education plan to reach out to injured workers of other nationalities. Although most Chinese injured workers speak virtually no English, they worked alongside young people to communicate with African American, Polish, South Asian, Latino, and Caribbean injured workers entering the Workers' Compensation Board office. To organize and develop this new base of emerging leaders, the CSWA Health and Safety Committee worked closely with National Mobilization Against SweatShops (NMASS), which started as a Project of CSWA prior to becoming independent. CSWA and NMASS linked together with the New York University Immigrant Rights Clinic and Workers Awaaz, a workers' center for South Asians, to launch the It's About TIME! Campaign for Workers' Health & Safety.

Through It's About TIME!, injured workers themselves have emerged as leaders, calling for immediate changes in the Workers' Compensation Board as well as leading other not-yet-injured workers to call for preventive measures to protect all working people from long hours, the leading cause of occupational injury. Their demands became further concretized when It's About TIME! introduced the Workers' Health and Safety Bill in the New York State Assembly; the bill calls for a complete overhaul of the Workers' Compensation Board, specifically: (1) provision of immediate interim living and medical benefits within one week of filing a claim; (2) resolution of an injured workers' case within three months; and (3) an increase in the minimum benefit to a rate consistent with minimum wage standards. To prevent future injuries, the bill calls for an end to mandatory overtime so that working people will have the right to say no to long hours.

The Workers' Compensation Board has functioned without anyone to monitor its abuses. Insurance companies, which are connected to the compensation process, are extremely powerful and exert tremendous influence to protect their profits. Furthermore, CSWA members note that most unions do not prioritize injured workers. Once workers get hurt on the job, they are unable to make money for their employers, are unable to pay union dues, and thus are out of the union. Legal avenues for addressing government abuse are also limited since many law firms with the capacity to handle class actions run into conflicts of interest with insurance company clients.

In October 2001, the It's About TIME! Campaign went to Mexico to file an unprecedented international lawsuit using the Labor-Side Agreement of the North American Free Trade Agreement (NAFTA); it charged the United States, New York State, New York Governor George Pataki, and the New York State Workers' Compensation Board with violations of international labor and human rights standards. The lawsuit sparked a flurry of media attention worldwide by spotlighting human rights abuses of working people on U.S. soil. Both the Workers' Health and Safety Bill and the NAFTA lawsuit have galvanized injured workers from around the state to come together as leaders, educators, and fighters and to thereby pave the way to a healthier, just society for us all.

Many groups craft demands that are not specific enough. Some adopt the attitude that we simply need to make the demand, then let the institution figure out how to meet it. This is understandable—after all, the institutions have the resources and public charge to meet the needs of our communities. However, the danger is that the institution will meet our demands in ways that are ultimately harmful to our constituents and allies. For example, in many state budget fights the demand for an increased appropriation for child care is met by moving money from some other critical need, such as public transportation. An unspecific demand may also be used by an institution to justify other negative policies. Conservatives used the demands for more responsive policing that came out of so many communities during the 1980s and 1990s to initiate "crime-fighting" programs without accompanying guidelines about how the police were to act and to build up both the power and the budgets of police departments. Crafting our demands with specificity helps to ensure that they are not ultimately used against us or against some other impoverished community. Our demands should minimally include a specific timeline, a clear institutional home for implementation, a source of funding, a monitoring system that involves our members and allies, and a clear geographical scope.

Illustration: LAANE Develops Specific Demands

LAANE crafts living wage policies very carefully. For LAANE, living wage fights provide a winnable policy goal that fuels the organizing of specific sets of workers, allows it to frame a region's economic needs from the perspective of workers, and serves as the launching point for campaigns on a variety of other issues that affect the quality of life, such as transportation, housing, child care, and recreation. "Living wage is a really powerful concept; it's a great way to frame the issue, and it helps bring a denunciation of the trend of working poverty together with a hopeful vision for the future," says Janis-Aparicio.

Most ordinances crafted by LAANE require every company receiving public contracts above a certain level to pay its employees a wage higher than the minimum or the prevailing wage for that industry. Ordinances usually have additional features as well. The wage is set at one amount if the employer is providing health benefits and at a higher amount if not. Ordinances include protections for workers currently in low-wage jobs, so they cannot be replaced by other workers after the higher wage kicks in, and protections from employer retaliation against workers leading organizing efforts. Unions that are in collective bargaining are also permitted to use "supercession" (partial or full exemption from the ordinance) as a point of negotiation with specific companies. Some ordinances explicitly name the monitoring methodology. Innovations in living wage ordinances apply them to businesses that do not hold contracts but receive direct public subsidies or occupy a geographical zone in which a city has invested broadly.

We sometimes settle for the handles we have rather than the ones that need to be built. Sometimes the law isn't enough or isn't on our side, as in the situations of undocumented immigrants or contingent workers. Groups must fight simultaneously to apply existing laws, generate new ones, and get voluntary agreements.

Illustration: CCW Covers All Bases

Although legal options have produced very little for contingent workers, CCW finds it important to organize contingents around their rights when existing laws are being broken, as in organizing day laborers to resist illegal fees charged by temp agencies. But where legislation doesn't provide coverage, CCW has tried to win voluntary changes through workplace codes of conduct. Organizers are also committed to continuing to fight for legislation, as agency by agency organizing is virtually impossible. Tim Costello of CCW argues that any victories that are won at individual workplaces should be leveraged to produce legislation: "The more ability you have to force whatever it is that you agree on, the better off you are. We need either legislation or a union contract, some kind of legal obligation."

Identifying Targets

Targeting individuals prevents the real decision makers from hiding behind the protective walls of institutions. Any campaign can have multiple targets, and it is a sign of sophistication if we can manage such a scene. If a group is looking for a vote from its city council, for example, it should target each individual member. We would not treat the entire city council as a single target because each person has different attitudes, constituencies, and interests that we need to take into account in designing tactics. In addition, targets should not be confused with the opposition or with allies. What makes people targets is not whether they like or dislike our group but whether they can give us what we want. If we spend a lot of time going after people whom we don't like because they have bad politics but who can't meet our demands, we will be frustrated and unsuccessful.

Just as there are two kinds of demands, there are primary and secondary targets. Primary targets are the individual decision makers within institutions who have the power to concede our demands, even though such targets always try to say they can't make a decision alone. We should know as much about our primary targets as possible: their work history, their voting records, their legal history, their family structure, their immigration history, how they act under pressure, their regular lunching places, where they attend religious services, where they went to school, and just about everything else we can think of. We can never know what piece of information will become central to our strategy. There are many ways to get such research done. These days, a great deal is revealed by doing a simple Internet search on Google.com or findarticles.com. We can also follow someone around for a time. We can hire a private investigator. We can search out legal histories on Nexus-Lexus. But one of the best ways to find out about people is to ask other activists, former employees, reporters, lawyers, and political opponents.

There is an ongoing debate about whether using certain pieces of information constitutes a violation of a target's privacy. Perhaps the most contentious issue arises in the fight for sexual liberation. On occasion, someone with a secret history of homosexuality or cross-dressing, for example, emerges as an important target or as opposition in a sexual-rights campaign. Is it acceptable to out that person to expose his or her hypocrisy? Or to threaten exposure as a tactic? There is a wide range of thought on this question. Certainly, the guarantee of privacy around nonabusive sexual behavior should be the cornerstone of a free society and not given up lightly. And exposing someone's sexual behavior might reinforce the message that it is immoral. However, if such people have the power to deny rights to others while protecting themselves, what of the rights of that larger group? Ultimately, an organization has to make such decisions on a case-by-case basis. My only caution is that revelation has far-reaching consequences and should not be done without wide agreement among members.

Secondary targets are individuals to whom our primary target feels some sense of accountability and to whom we can also get access. The relationship between the two might be formal or informal, direct or indirect. Secondary targets can be used to pressure or persuade our primary. The rare target may be persuaded by the morality or logic of our arguments, but most will just want us to stop ruining their weekly bowling date. When the City Center Hotel families finally decided to demand that the Department of Social Services let them move into permanent housing, our target was the director of the department. However, we also targeted the director of public health with a demand for a new building inspection led by the tenants. He was a secondary target because he could not meet our most important substantive demand for new housing assignments and because the new inspection would put additional legal and peer pressure on the Department of Social Services director. Researching a target's informal relationships also leads groups to great secondary targets. In the 1980s SEIU made an art out of chasing down the business partners, wives, children, pastors, charity co-chairs, and squash partners of building owners who used nonunion janitors. Boycotts essentially treat customers of a company as secondary targets; they send messages to the primary target through their consumption choices.

In addition, it is important to decide whether we want to target individuals within private or public institutions. Whom we target points to who is responsible for a problem. Often, we target government agencies and legislative bodies because we have leverage there that we lack in relation to private employers, religious institutions, newspapers, and so on. Without doubt, public institutions are easier to target, and they do deserve our wrath for not doing their job. At least there we have the language of democracy and accountability on our side, and we have a history of responsiveness especially from the federal government and some state governments. For certain groups of workers, like child care workers and family day-care providers, who are often subcontractors not working for large corporate employers, many groups have gotten the best mileage from treating government as their employer to create a collective bargaining unit.

But there are downsides to targeting public institutions. First, an exclusive focus on government targets can dangerously feed into the right-wing strategy of generating disgust with government and slowly dismantling its progressive functions. Campaigns that attack only the government don't help our own people, the press, or the larger public understand the positive roles that government can play if we own it. Second, targeting government is like talking to the wizard's image rather than the guy who runs the light show behind the curtain. The presence of big money in election campaigns ensures that, in many ways, government is controlled by business rather than the other way around. For these reasons, Karen Nussbaum, former executive director of 9to5 and current director of the AFL-CIO's Working Women Division, stresses that groups should take up issues that point to corporate culpability as much as possible. She says, "At this stage, my preference is to choose issues that employers are responsible for. That's who we want to be identifying as the source of the problem. We may need to force government action to force employer accountability, but that's where we need to be directing our attention."

Illustration: LAANE Gets Concessions Out of Corporate Targets

Over time, LAANE has framed its work as a community-benefits package that encompasses the full range of worker and community issues, from living wage ordinances to social services. In one of its victories, five industrial unions and twenty-nine community groups banded together into the Figueroa Corridor Coalition for Economic Justice to demand union contracts and additional benefits for the community surrounding the Staples sports complex. They quickly formulated a list of demands around housing, environmental issues, living wage, and union recognition. Such a coalition was clearly necessary to challenge the big developers of the complex, including billionaires like Phillip Anshutz and Rupert Murdoch. LAANE's landmark agreement with the developers stipulated that 70 percent of the jobs created by the planned development would pay a living wage of $7.72 per hour with benefits or $8.97 without benefits and that local residents would get first notices of jobs. The developers agreed to set a goal of filling 50 percent of the jobs with local residents and pledged $1 million for the creation or upgrades of parks within a mile of the project, which encompasses some of the poorest neighborhoods in Los Angeles. LAANE's work on attaching benefits to government subsidies and contracts helped build the power that allowed victory in a project that had few subsidies and contracts but needed to be accountable to the surrounding communities.

One of LAANE's most successful projects, SMART, supports hotel workers who work in luxury oceanside hotels and restaurants. These workers were members of a moribund HERE local that was so ineffective it became vulnerable when management initiated a decertification campaign in 1997. Decertification efforts nullify an employer's recognition of the union as a collective bargaining unit, and since the 1980s union-busting firms have made a profitable industry of decertification campaigns. Vivian Rothstein was a Santa Monica resident and longtime community organizer and social service worker when LAANE organizer Stephanie Monroe got her involved in the decertification fight. "We got to see what conditions were like at the hotel [the Miramar], got to know the workers and their lives. The decertification campaign developed the first bond between community members and the workers." The decertification effort went on for so long that the coalition had many opportunities to deepen that bond. SMART organized a mock election in which the workers were able to cast their votes about the union without fear of retaliation; in this election decertification was soundly defeated. Employer pressure, however, led to the opposite result in the formal NLRB election, to which the union responded with multiple charges and complaints against the company. As the NLRB forced a new election, the hotel's ownership changed, and SMART and HERE were able to persuade the new owners to remain neutral in the follow-up election. By 1999, Miramar workers had saved their union and negotiated a dignified contract for themselves.

The following illustration shows how the first three principles—having clear criteria for choosing an issue, crafting ambitious and specific demands, and directing those demands at individual targets—were combined in a campaign to expand health-insurance coverage for children.

Illustration: Working Partnerships Aligns Criteria, Demands, and Targets

Working Partnerships and the church-based community organization People Acting in Community Together (PACT) got the idea of appropriating tobacco-settlement money to fund health insurance for all children, regardless of their immigration status. The two organizations were driven almost entirely by opportunity. They had not been working together, but when they learned about tobacco money being available, they developed a proposal to create a children's health-insurance plan. This issue had some great advantages. First, Working Partnerships recognized the issue's importance to low-wage workers and immigrants, both legal and undocumented, which far offset its lack of relevance to union members, who tend to enjoy full coverage under their contracts. Immigrants face significant barriers to full health coverage because they are afraid to expose their immigration status to public institutions. Second, the issue played to the strengths of both organizations: Working Partnerships' research capacity and ability to turn out union members, PACT's experienced leadership and mobilization capacity, and the credibility of each. Third, the issue offered multiple primary and secondary targets, attracted local allies and national media, and was highly fundable.

Campaign leaders crafted a multilevel policy proposal. It focused on getting children's health insurance for those families in San Jose and Santa Clara County who had the hardest time accessing existing public health programs, especially the state's Healthy Families program, because they were afraid or because their income exceeded the eligibility guidelines. The proposal also included a viable medical plan and outreach plan, a specific allocation from the tobacco money, and additional funding streams for which the city would have to apply. Steeg recalls that the proposal was especially exciting because "it had 100 percent of kids in San Jose, was measurable, doable, supportable, and had a formula for how to make the money work." Steeg notes that it was a real challenge to develop a viable health-insurance program "with a rating system and complicated forms. We weren't going to administer the program; we had to find a provider. We lost some momentum; as we had to shift to [a] technical approach, it became harder to keep supporters involved in it."

But even before the alliance could begin talking about the specifics of their plan, they had to engage in a procedural fight. The mayor "tried to sneak through 100 percent of [the] funds to his after-school programs," recalls Steeg. Working Partnerships and PACT had to organize city council resistance to defeat the mayor's proposal, then win an agreement to hold public hearings to determine priorities for that money, and then "compete with hundreds of people who swooped in with millions of proposals." Much to the mayor's shocked dismay, the city council voted 6–5 against his proposal, inspired by the alliance's "lobbying of city council members, bringing out community [and] health care providers, and arguing children's health had to be a part of this." Rather than targeting the mayor to get him to withdraw or adjust his plan, the alliance simply treated him as opposition while focusing on the city council members as primary targets. A decision to target the county board of supervisors led to a unanimous vote for the proposal there, which further isolated the mayor; but that victory had costs. Steeg says, "In order for the county to commit, they wouldn't do only San Jose; they had to cover the whole county. Then it became very expensive. Then it wasn't [the] same kind of story anymore, just a huge project."

The mayor remained in oppositional mode; he campaigned to ensure that the children's health-insurance proposal would not pass, "strong-arming, threatening, and punishing folks for supporting it," according to Steeg. But the alliance's organizing created too much public pressure. PACT was holding church-based community meetings, inviting members of the city council and the board of supervisors. Steeg describes the final hearing on the issue: "It was a beautiful thing; we had three hundred to four hundred people in a rally, the hard-hat trades guys, service workers, janitors— [the] whole array of labor was there, though it had little benefit to them directly. Church folks, community folks packed city hall with over a hundred well-prepped, practiced speakers." The overflow crowd forced the city council to open up additional space where the proceedings were broadcast on television. In the end, the alliance won not just the largest single allocation of the available tobacco money but also a rearrangement of the relations of power. Steeg says, "This was the first fight anyone had ever taken [on] against the mayor; we recruited [the city council president], who is not a friend of labor, and we got a unanimous yes vote at the county board of supervisors." In the process, the Working Partnerships/PACT alliance became very tight. The new program was kicked off with a huge enrollment fair in which thousands of children were signed up.

By filling in the worksheet in Exercise 3.2 with the criteria you have chosen and how they relate to issues you are considering, you can determine how well you have aligned your criteria, demands, and targets for each issue. By rating issues on the worksheet, you also will be able to prioritize them. The example in Exercise 3.2 shows how one organization's criteria matched their plans for a living wage campaign.

Framing Issues Creatively

Once an organization has decided on an issue to work on, it still has to determine how to frame that issue in the course of a campaign. A good frame has two important characteristics. First, it operates even as we move from issue to issue because it speaks to the shared values of our constituency and allies and, as much as possible, to the values of the larger public. Strong frames have to have multiple applications, and they have to be flexible enough to be applied from one campaign to the next, partly by shaping the membership's expectations about what kinds of issues fall within the organization's mission. For example, We Make the Road by Walking's language-rights campaign, which was targeted at welfare offices, was easily transferable to other arenas. As Make the Road prepared to wrap up a legal settlement with the City of New York after several years of campaigning on welfare access, the membership turned its attention to the treatment of immigrants in hospitals. Hospitals, like welfare offices, often have too few translators, and their written materials, such as bills and instructions, are usually only in English.

Good frames are critical to unions that are trying to make a transition into taking the leadership on issues that can't be narrowly defined as workers' issues. Steeg expresses great pride in the way that Working Partnerships has been able to "build from labor issues to real social justice issues like transportation, housing, and health." That success is a direct outgrowth of the way Working Partnerships shaped a community blueprint, which frames living wage and traditionally union issues as only one portion of the larger conditions that workers and their families encounter.

Exercise 3.2. Issue-Development Worksheet.

List your criteria for a good issue in order of priority with the most important at the top. Describe how well each issue meets each criterion by giving it a rating from 1 to 5 (with 5 the highest). After comparing the total rankings for the issues, consider the rankings going down the chart. Are the rankings high on your high-priority criteria? If not, you may not want to pick an issue even though its total ranking is high.

Example Criteria	Example Issue: Living Wage	Your Criteria	Issue 1:	Issue 2:
1. Gives sense of power, changes conditions, and shifts power relations	Wage hike, right to organize and new constituency of low-wage workers, 5			
2. Worthwhile	Deeply felt, 5, but not widely felt, 1 (small impact) Average: 3			
3. Nondivisive	Small businesspeople in our cross-class organization don't like it but everyone else does, 4			
4. Clear demands	Model already written but lots of detail to fight for, 4			
5. Clear target, challenges corporations	City council members, 5 All public-sector targets, 2 Average: 3.5			
6. Easy to understand clauses, no, 3	Basic idea, yes; complicated			
7. Winnable	Not in current city council, 2			

8. Attracts allies	Unions, 5
9. Reveals race, gender, and economic inequity	Subsidy handle, 5
10. Clear time frame	Before city council runs again, six months; clear but short time, 3
11. Leads to other issues	Health care, child care, affordable housing, environmental protection, 5
12. Creates new handles	Makes it easier to organize workers, 5
13. Surfaces discrimination, good data	Requires research to compare, data not easily available, 2
14. Uses race- and gender-discrimination handles	No, 1
15. Introduces new or stronger language	Living wage is better wage, but doesn't meet the Self-Sufficiency Standard, 2
16. Variety of tactics	Research, press, direct action, 4
Total rankings	54.5
Criteria placement considerations	Most important criteria are 1–10. Rankings there are between 3 and 5 (except for 7); rankings for 13–16 are generally lower. Do it.

Second, because framing is a matter largely of working with language, a good frame will shape your media messages to your greatest advantage. Frames can be expressed in various ways—through campaign slogans and names, the headlines of press releases, or simply the repetition of particular words and phrases. The New Right has successfully framed its issues in part by investing resources in testing and evaluation to see what kinds of frames provide the most fuel for the issues on its agenda. For example, in fighting abortion rights, the Christian Coalition used popular language and shared values to frame many of its specific campaigns as being based in "family values" and as "pro-life." Other examples of effective framing by the right wing abound: the attack on welfare was framed as reducing "dependency"; affirmative action was reframed as "special preferences"; the estate tax was renamed the "death tax"; and union busting became the "right to work."

Among progressives, many of the most effective living wage campaigns stress the need for corporate accountability in exchange for tax subsidies, or subsidy accountability. Struggles to win higher wages and benefits for child care workers have been attached to the goal of raising the quality of child care by reducing the turnover that plagues the industry. Campaigns designed to increase access to welfare are framed as "fighting discrimination." The need for higher baseline wages is framed as "self-sufficiency."

Our frames are certainly influenced by the political and social contexts in which we find ourselves. A phrase that makes a good frame at one point may not work so well ten years later as the culture changes. One way we can measure progress is by noting the extent to which we can use more radical frames over time.

Illustration: Framing of Wages Issue Leads to Debate in Child Care Community

Marci Whitebook of the Center for the Child Care Workforce reflects that "we were somewhat forced into the 'quality' frame by the nature of the child care debate in the 1970s and 1980s. Because of both the political climate and the ethos among teachers, it was hard to talk about equity without making the link to quality of care." In such a climate, the Center decided to concentrate on the ways in which low wages pushed experienced and committed providers out of the field; the resulting instability caused trauma to small children and thereby lowered the quality of care.

The framing of this issue has now moved to another level, which is the cause of current debate. Studies have linked higher levels of education, as well as higher pay, to a higher quality of care. Currently, most public policies related to wage rates for child care workers tie financial incentives and rewards to specialized training and education in early childhood education. Although these policies get some providers more money, the Common Sense Foundation (2000) points out that workers of color and low-income workers face distinct disadvantages: they can't afford the tuition or the time to attend school without evening child care and transportation in addition to partial financial support. The Foundation supports separating the basic wage from additional educational requirements and urges lawmakers to cut corporate tax breaks to fund the wage increase.

Many providers, such as the HDCJ Cooperative, also resist linking compensation and training. While they used arguments about quality improvement to win health insurance, they combined them with strong moral arguments about the value of child care and a worker's right not to live in poverty. Judy Victor, executive director of the Cooperative, offers just such a moral argument when she says, "To offer people the opportunity to become more professional in what they do is excellent, but I think that that is a free choice. When we begin to take peoples' free choice and use it as leverage for a basic right, it becomes immoral." Victor questions raising academic standards for child care at the same time as there is a rising need for both child care and jobs for poor women. "First," she says, "all you needed to be was someone who liked children and was willing to follow rules and be licensed. Then you had to have a high school diploma; then you had to have additional hours. Now you must be accredited and move toward child assessment. Now they want you to go to college. They put all these barriers in the way of people of color and poor people to discourage us." Shannah Kurland, the HDCJ Campaign's first organizer, favors framing the issue in a way that focuses almost exclusively on compensation rather than training, stating that "there is no way to go down a professional track without replicating the racism and sexism of the institutional players who control the debate right now."

Illustration: WOW Uses Self-Sufficiency Language

WOW developed the Self-Sufficiency Standard as a measure of the income necessary to meet basic needs. It used the term *self-sufficiency* to refer to a situation in which a family would be able to cover its basic necessities without relying on public assistance in the form of government programs or on private subsidies in the form of unpaid child care by relatives, meals skipped by parents, or doubling up in a friend's apartment. WOW encountered resistance from both antipoverty activists and advocates who thought that the term *self-sufficiency* was too limiting and implied that people could and should get along without help from others, whether they be friends, family, community, or government. Other activists argued that the definition did not allow people to accumulate important poverty preventers such as savings for a college education or retirement. Diana Pearce, creator of the standard, recognizes the limitations inherent in any definition of basic needs but argues that advocating for economic policies that enable families not to have to choose between basics such as food and transportation constitutes significant improvement over earlier measurements of poverty (Brooks and Pearce).

Potential allies expressed concern about the political marginality of high-wage policies. In most cases, the self-sufficiency wage for adults with even one preschooler outstrips local living wage proposals, and thus proposals for a self-sufficiency wage raise concerns that the standard will undermine local living wage demands. For example, the Los Angeles self-sufficiency wage for such a family is $13.06, while the living wage is $8.50; the Alexandria, Virginia, self-sufficiency wage is $15.l6, while the living wage ordinance calls for $9.84. Cindy Marano, WOW senior organizer, reflects, "It was so difficult for people to look at how high the wages were and not completely dismiss the whole thing. Advocates would say this is just too high, you can't use this."

To counter these arguments, WOW focused on the question of how to achieve the support necessary for families to live at a dignified level rather than on the seemingly unwinnable goal of getting businesses to pay such high wage rates. Joan Kuriansky, executive director of WOW, notes that the standard makes clear that the whole community must come together to help families meet their basic needs. Individuals have the responsibility to seek out education and training opportunities; employers have the responsibility to pay good wages with adequate benefits; and government has a responsibility to make publicly funded supports available to help families fill the gap between self-sufficient wages and their current wages. Many of these concerns were overcome simply by the practice of implementing the Self-Sufficiency Standard. For example, although living wage advocates were initially concerned about the high standard, today the standard is used in living wage campaigns across the country.

Illustration: Living Wage Frames Resonate with the Public

Living wage campaigns reframe conventional economic wisdoms. The first reframing asserts that not every job is a good job: good jobs provide decent wages, benefits, and the right to organize. Second, these campaigns assert that U.S. residents expect some level of corporate accountability; they challenge the ideas that corporations should be allowed unregulated freedom to operate and that deregulation that results in higher profits will somehow trickle down to produce benefits for workers and communities. Third, living wage campaigns maintain that public contracts and subsidies require that corporate beneficiaries be accountable to the surrounding community. These frames are expressed in living wage ordinances themselves through their stipulations and through the kinds of businesses that are affected. By the middle of 2001, more than fifty municipalities, ranging from Lexington, Kentucky, to Los Angeles, had passed living wage ordinances.

ACORN's Living Wage Resource Center provides research and tactical support for emerging campaigns, and ACORN is currently running campaigns in seventeen states as well. In New Orleans, a coalition led by the Greater New Orleans AFL-CIO, ACORN, and SEIU Local 100 won a ballot measure establishing a wage floor of a dollar above the minimum wage throughout the city; this measure covers approximately fifty thousand employees, many of them tourism workers, in a state that has the second highest proportion of people working for minimum wage in the country. Jen Kern, director of the Center, discusses some of the reasons living wage policies are so attractive. "It is such an issue of basic fairness that it resonates with a lot of people along the political spectrum. If you work, you shouldn't be poor. It helps organizers get to a whole bunch of connected issues: privatization, child care, health care, and quality of services, increasing the accountability of government and corporations." Kern notes that living wage organizers have been able to use the language of business investment and that the requirement to pass a piece of legislation gives the issue an urgency that is frequently missing in other campaigns for economic justice.

Exercise 3.3 provides practice in articulating problems, demands, and frames. The questions to ask are: What is the problem? How does the opposition assign blame? What do we think causes the problem? Consequently, what are the opposition's demands and what are ours?

Before making final decisions on the issues you choose to work on, read the essay in Exhibit 3.1 to see how issues are sometimes picked in practice.

Exercise 3.3. Framing Worksheet.

Problem	As Framed by Opponents	Their Demands	As Framed by Us	Our Demands
Rising incarceration of African Americans for drug offenses	Poor parenting and unstable families lead African Americans to drugs and crime	Tougher sentencing and more police to prevent African Americans from drug dealing	Racist sentencing guidelines punish crack possession much more seriously than cocaine possession; crack is cheap and available to African Americans; cocaine is expensive and available to whites	Revise drug sentencing laws

Source: Adapted with permission from the Center for Third World Organizing.

Exhibit 3.1. A Practical Look at Issue Development.

MORE THAN THE SUM OF OUR PARTS

By Shannah Kurland

When I first started learning how to organize, one of my few formal trainings dealt with the rules for selecting a good issue. That list is like the pledge of allegiance, or the mysteries of the rosary—information you may not consciously draw on too frequently, but you never expect to forget.

The official list was part of the orthodoxy, handed down from organizer to apprentice, and occasionally analyzed but never questioned. "A good issue is widely felt." Check. Who wants to work on something that only a few people care about? "A good issue is deeply felt." Sure, I can get with that. But there were contradictions to these and other rules. When we started organizing with family child care providers, a campaign that went on to define the organization and make national history, it only directly affected about 250 women in the whole state. And let's take the school system. You can't get much more anger than what parents of color feel at the way their children are disrespected and discarded. But, in the twelve years I spent at DARE, we never managed to convert that anger into parent or student power over the school system. OK then, "a good issue brings people together, and doesn't divide them." Yet our work on police violence brought DARE (and eventually the city of Providence) to a new level in our racial politics, even as it sparked intense internal debate and drove many allies and funders to maintain a polite distance for years to come. Were these issues not worth taking on because they didn't meet the traditional criteria?

No magic formula can predict what will or won't be a good issue for an organization. Very often the conflicts between obviously good organizing issues and not-so-good ones are crystallized in the individual needs of our constituency. A good issue depends on having clear political and organizational goals, on framing those goals in ways that speak to the experiences of people, and on identifying a spark that will ignite people's hearts and minds. Live organizations jump on new opportunities to build their base and address negative trends affecting their communities. Just as armies voluntarily send scouts to test the enemy, our organizations can rely on individuals who have small confrontations with the enemy. We can convert those individual skirmishes into the birth of a new organizing campaign.

DARE is often called on to intervene when a member or even a stranger walks in needing help with a problem. We help to navigate a hostile bureaucracy with a phone call to a supervisor, use of the English language, or a tag team visit complete with good cop–bad cop theater and not-so-vague references to storming offices with crowds and media. Done without principle or thought, individual support work can reinforce all the worst tendencies of bad organizing, like the supposed helplessness of oppressed people, the need for intermediaries to orchestrate confrontations, and hero worship of the organizer. But when we play out these scenes with a commitment to building leadership and reaching for justice, they can serve as training ground, taste of victory, and a window on the battle yet to come.

For instance, one woman complained in 1990 that the state was three months late sending her meager paycheck for the backbreaking work of caring for children. Collectivizing that problem was as easy as a door-knocking role play: "Is this happening to anyone else?" Within six weeks, a list of names, a form letter, and a spot on the membership meeting agenda transformed Miss Pearl's problem into a community problem. Six months later, a few dozen black and Latina women making less than minimum wage had forced the state to revamp its dysfunctional administrative apparatus for a major social program. As the campaign developed into a six-year battle for health-insurance coverage, it built on the obvious racial and gender exploitation of the child care economy to change the consciousness of the entire organization.

To sustain this struggle for six years required providers to redefine their relationship with the state. The regular exercise of the power to "fix" the state's dysfunction helped providers speak collectively to key legislators as if they were correcting wayward children. In the end, this experience of organizing within such a clearly abusive economic structure inspired providers to create the Home Day Care Justice Co-op, an organization that would combine efforts for greater institutional changes with member-driven services.

But sometimes you can address a problem only through individual work. Maybe the injustice is so heavily entrenched or so removed from the organization's capacity that effective collective work cannot happen at that point. Yet in a movement that is about advancing human dignity, how can you hear of the abuse of one person without responding? At DARE, we wrestled with that question and came up with some general guidelines, but even those were frustrating and fluid. We decided that if a situation related to one of the larger issue areas of our organizing campaigns or if one of our members was being attacked, we would jump in and do everything we could. But those guidelines weren't always sufficient.

There is a serious lack of support systems in our community that work with individuals respectfully and from a social-justice perspective. There is no place that gives you a list of sources for money to pay gas bills without demanding to know your financial history or telling you how to budget what you don't have. There is no place that will help you figure out how the rules on reporting income can be utilized so that you can "maximize your earning potential" without losing your SSI check. And there is no other place that will cuss out police officers when you file a complaint about how your son was beaten.

So while there are rich and valuable ways that individual struggles can get translated into campaigns, it's not just about that. It's about standing up for human dignity and putting cracks in the system wherever you can. It's about creating an experience of successful defiance. And it's about constantly learning about how the machinery of oppression takes its toll on people in our communities every single day, even as we try to lessen its effects, because that knowledge will ultimately help teach us to defeat it. These same values ought to influence our decisions to take on organizing campaigns.

I had several occasions to work one-on-one with women who were being attacked by the child welfare system. An aunt who had devoted her life to her sister's kids, with no help or even basic medical information from the state agency, saw her family ripped apart when a child needing a lot of help made up an accusation that she beat him. We never managed to defeat that machine, but she (and I) learned everything we could about how they function. Meanwhile her belief in herself was constantly bolstered as people talked about how the Department of Children, Youth and Families (DCYF) was as racist as the police and as they sold raffle tickets to raise money for her legal defense. We always thought we would turn that issue into a campaign eventually, but when we started to push, we just couldn't figure out how to find enough people to form a critical mass that would hang in through the hard work of creating demands. Even so, every one of those exchanges mattered. A year later, DCYF had learned something: when a mother appealed a decision that found her guilty of neglect because her daughter had grown too big for her car seat, they were embarrassed enough to drop the charges.

Sometimes these women stuck around and got involved with the organization, and sometimes they didn't. What was exciting was that when one did, it wasn't out of some sense of debt; in fact the ones who expressed that guilty

"Oh I need to get to the meetings 'cause I really owe you folks" sentiment never stuck around. Those who stayed did so out of the joy that developed from fighting back and winning, from being around other people who respect your anger. As they fought their individual fights, they began to realize their potential as soldiers in a larger struggle.

We can get so effective in supporting individuals, however, that we forget to look for opportunities to do the heavier lifting of campaigns. For years, DARE leaders had talked about the need to address the way people in our community were affected by the prison system. When one member, whose daughter was a star youth volunteer, asked for help with the way her son was being held in lockdown twenty-three hours a day because of his political affiliations, my individual advocacy kicked in. Even as a seasoned organizer, I certainly couldn't take it on myself to launch a new campaign, or so I reassured myself. After one meeting with the Department of Corrections director, it was clear that his view of the 5% Nation as a "terrorist" threat and of her son as a "predator" was not going to change. Ironically, a contact in the governor's office pointed out that prisoners were such a hated group in society that the governor would never give the issue the time of day until there was a group of family members ready to show a pattern and exert some pressure. Never too proud to accept good advice, we brought a request to the membership to make this campaign a priority for the coming year. As important as the campaign was to DARE's political vision and as much as it could push the organization beyond where many other groups were prepared to go, it took one family's story to personify the outrage, to provide the spark, to move forward on the issue.

So maybe the only victories we can sustain are the ones where collective power is felt within each individual consciousness, much the way a computer network exists only virtually and depends on the hard drives of its "member" computers. But like the infinite difference between a bunch of individual computers doing their thing and the dizzying exchange of ones and zeros that make up the Internet, we can barely imagine the results if the souped-up power of individuals with victories under their belts transforms into true shared struggle.

Shannah Kurland is the former executive director
of Direct Action for Rights and Equality.

Conclusion

Issue development is a task that encompasses all aspects of organizing practice—outreach, research, ideology, and strategy. Requiring that any new issue meet every single one of our criteria greatly limits our choices. However, having a clear set of criteria and being flexible about which of the criteria is most important at a particular stage in the organization's history can help us make more ambitious issue choices. If we involve the community in researching issues and designing the solutions, our organizations are more likely to be able to sustain longer and more ambitious struggles.

CHAPTER FOUR

READY, SET, ACTION!

Direct action is a critical tool for organizations that are serious about making change. However, direct actions are effective only in the context of a sustained campaign that involves several direct actions interspersed with other tactics. By direct action, I am referring to the face-to-face confrontation between your constituency and an individual target over a specific demand. Direct actions can include storming the target's office, leafleting the neighbors (as secondary targets), haunting the target's public appearances, testifying at hearings, or conducting a mass meeting with a target at your own community center. The key elements are a cohesive group, a target, and a demand. An activity that does not include those three elements generally counts as something else—demonstrations and news conferences come to mind. These activities can incorporate some of the elements of direct actions, such as an escalated tone, and they can help to apply pressure on a target, but they are not especially direct. By contrast, activities that we aren't used to thinking of as confrontational count as direct action simply because the constituency, target, and demand are there. These include tea parties, cultural gatherings, and Christmas caroling.

While the idea of direct action is often scary, using it can provide important benefits. First, direct action can clarify the stakes, presenting our take on an issue in sharp contrast to other proposals or the status quo. This kind of clarification makes it less likely that the interests of our constituency will be negotiated away by people who are not affected—a distinct possibility when liberal policy, research, and lobbying groups are deeply involved in a controversial issue, whether it be welfare or immigration. As one organizer put it to me, "If the people who are supposed to be on our side won't ask for what we need and want when they compromise with the conservatives, we have to show that there is a constituency willing to turn up the street heat" (Lee Ann Hall, executive director of the Northwest Federation of Community Organizations, interview by the author, November 2001). When your issue has been watered down or the debate has been captured by the other side, you can regain some of that ground with the militancy of a direct action. Second, nothing is better than a well-timed confrontation to help targets feel the pressure, which leads to victories that weren't forthcoming without the action. Third, direct action demystifies the halls of power for a constituency, and the people occupying those halls start to realize it and treat us with more respect.

Fourth, face-to-face conflict can sometimes help protect the members of a group when they are under attack. The mere process of taking risks together, which direct action requires, helps to build the group's sense of itself as a group. Actions can also help protect individuals who are having problems with the system by making it clear that they are surrounded by a whole group. The fact that a target knows a group is willing to go direct can help prevent retaliations, and actions are certainly useful in exposing and resisting retaliation should it occur. Fifth, direct action offers fun, creative, and effective ways to get your message out.

This is not to say that people's fears and attitudes about direct action should not be discussed and addressed. The first job is to identify the sources of reluctance to engage in actions. Most people dislike conflict. Others are intimidated by people in power. Still others fear retaliation, imprisonment, or deportation. These are all legitimate feelings that need to be honored and then tested against experience. An organization unaccustomed to doing such actions should build up the capacity slowly. I have found it useful to validate that people have a right to be angry and that anger can be a positive emotion to drive us out of the status quo. Author Audre Lorde wrote in *Sister Outsider,* "Anger, used, does not destroy. Hatred does" (quoted in Maggio, 1998, p. 30). I find this distinction most useful. Most of us have been taught to respect authority and power, but have those who are vested with authority been doing their jobs? Do they deserve our unblinking obedience? During these discussions, and over time, people begin to question the sources and validity of their fearful feelings.

The retaliation fears are harder to deal with because they are real. Several efforts to organize workers, including the undocumented, went bust when employers anonymously called the Immigration and Naturalization Service (INS) to investigate immigration violations, and as a result the strongest workplace leaders were deported (Bacon, 1998). Right now, the Patriot Act enables many of our targets to label our direct actions as terrorism. U.S. AIDS groups conducted a demonstration against Tommy Thompson, the Secretary of Health and Human Services, during an international AIDS conference in Barcelona. When the members of the groups got home, they all found themselves targets of Congressional audits challenging their federal funding (Brown, 2002). And we have to fear not just government institutions but also private citizens, such as those who think killing abortion providers is God's work. Listing these possibilities is scaring even me as I write, but the truth is that the more despised your constituency is by the mainstream and by the right wing, the more real the danger.

If we don't want to let the threat of danger stop us from doing what needs to be done, we can take several steps. First, we have to determine how real the threat is. Our targets and opposition make frequent threats they have no intention of carrying out. What has happened to other groups in the same struggle? What are all the factors in those fights, and how are they similar or different from yours? Physical threats are always the most important and should be distinguished from the threat of a lawsuit or smear campaign. Second, you have to make contingency plans in case the threat is carried out. What will you do if the INS conducts a raid? Who will post bail or defend those who have been arrested? Who are the people whose conviction records make them vulnerable to police action, and what should their roles be? What kind of protection measures can we take for individuals? Third, the group, knowing all the potential consequences, must agree on whether to take the action. Unfortunately, there is no single comforting response to retaliation, except to expose it and look for recourse. But in my experience people on the outskirts of polite society are accustomed to a high degree of danger. Battered women live with it at home, refugees survived war, urban youth have learned to fear the police. If we have a choice between continuing to bear those threats or generating some new ones from a place of power and vision, we will often choose to instigate new ones.

Still, no matter how successful any individual direct action is, it is meaningless outside of a campaign. Campaigns indicate sustained intervention on a specific issue; they have clear short- and long-term goals, a timeline, creative incremental demands, targets who can meet those demands, and an organizing plan to build a constituency and build internal capacity. Within campaigns, different tactics accomplish different goals. There are tactics for building a base, recruiting allies, educating the larger public, and proving a point, in addition to those that pressure targets. Campaigns require planning and discipline, the ability to think about life in six-month, one-year, or multiyear terms. Many organizations do great actions but cannot sustain a defined campaign that pursues a specific set of demands that fit into their larger vision.

This chapter is designed to help the reader understand the implications of direct actions and to execute them effectively within campaigns. I present several case studies of organizations that rely heavily on direct action. The illustrations from Justice, Economic Dignity and Independence for Women (JEDI) show us how direct action works in a conservative political and social climate and how to plan appropriate visual effects. The illustrations from the Home Day Care Justice (HDCJ) Campaign reveal how it uses successive actions against multiple targets and how direct action fits into its larger set of tactics. The illustration from the Center from Third World Organizing (CTWO) and Grassroots Organizing for Welfare Leadership (GROWL) indicates how these groups increased leaders' and members' comfort with and enthusiasm for direct action. The DARE illustration details the planning process for an action. The illustration from Santa Monicans Allied for Responsible Tourism (SMART) presents ideas for using multiple tactics, including direct actions.

Principles

There are three important principles in using direct action effectively. First, each action has to have a clear purpose grounded in an irrefutable need and expressed in the action's specific target and demand. Second, the best actions are heavily choreographed. Third, direct actions are always part of a larger campaign.

Clarifying the Purpose

Clarity is the key to success. Focused on one demand and one target, each direct action has to make sense in the larger scheme of the campaign. Actions work best when our take on the issue is irrefutable, so they challenge us to figure out what is most clear and appealing in our campaign. The tighter the agenda of an action, the more pressure a target will feel. Deeda Seed, founding organizer of JEDI, warns that direct action should not be overused, that "it's a tool, not a magic solution. Use it when it makes sense, if your message is going to be communicated effectively."

We should not do a direct action if we are uncertain about what we want and who we want it from. A common mistake is to pile all our demands into one action. Even if a campaign includes multiple targets and multiple demands, as sophisticated campaigns do, advancing on each target through separate actions delivers incremental victories and begins to shift the attitudes of decision makers. The only exception to this rule is that we can add a fall-back to our main demand, which gives the target a way to save face and do something to move the cause forward. Completing Exercise 4.1 will give you practice in identifying the target, demand, and fall-back for each of your direct actions.

Exercise 4.1. Direct Action Worksheet.

Target	Demand	Fall-Back	Direct Action

Remember that these kinds of actions are quick hits, involving relatively small numbers of people, twenty to three hundred for the most part. Most actions don't go on for days at a time. They last thirty minutes to an hour when it's a surprise for the target, perhaps three hours if the target has come to you in response to an "invitation." If an action takes an hour, we may get only ten or fifteen minutes with our target, so the demand has to be clear and defensible enough for the target to respond to quickly. This does not mean that a demand has to be procedural or meaningless. Organizations have won many substantive things from targets during actions, including health inspections, turnover of information, undoing of retaliatory evictions, and an outreach plan to prevent lead poisoning.

Illustration: The HDJC Campaign Wins Paycheck Reforms

When Providence home day-care providers wanted to get a guarantee that their paychecks would arrive on time, they confronted the people who ran the Rhode Island

Department of Human Services Child Care Division. In each successive action, the Campaign worked its way up the ladder of child care administrators. The actions pointed out the unfairness of the state's refusing to pay low-income women for work they had already done. Each action focused on a different demand: first, to get late paychecks issued immediately; second, to get an explanation of how the payment system worked; third, to get the department to prioritize the addition of children to a provider's roster; fourth, to have the entire payment system redesigned. The focus on individuals isolated and pressured administrators to take steps. Some of these administrators later became the Campaign's best allies in the health-insurance fight. Barbara Gianola, the acting director of the Child Care Division, recalls one such accountability session: "I was sitting on this chair with no arms, and I felt like there was a naked light bulb swinging over my head. We felt like we had to tell the higher-ups that these people could do some disruption" (interview by Darlene Lombos, September 1998). After several months of militant actions interspersed with phone conversations and negotiation meetings, officials standardized the pay system, put new children on providers' rosters the same month they started day care, and began to issue paychecks on time.

Illustration: JEDI Defends Child Care

Although organizer Seed had experienced the advantages of using direct action in Chicago, she knew when she started JEDI in Salt Lake City that "Utah is not a place that has a reputation for boat rocking of any sort. The concept of direct action was very foreign to everyone here." Ironically, the new group found its first strengths in the local culture. Although the Church of Latter Day Saints doesn't give women a significant role in its otherwise strong lay ministry, all members from birth to death are expected to participate in a process called bearing testimony. Seed says, "Everyone in a ward has this experience of standing in front of the whole congregation and talking about something important in their lives, so what I got was women who were really good public speakers. For direct action that was a huge advantage." The group's first major tactic was not all that direct—a news conference about the lack of affordable housing—but this first news conference in the region by women who were directly affected by and passionately committed to the issue of affordable housing "just blew the press away," according to Seed.

From there, the group eased into using direct action as a strategic component of its work, being careful "not to be considered frivolous," Seed recalls. As an organizer, she had to "not push too hard and make sure that [the goal was] held out foremost." JEDI generally started out in advocacy mode, always first trying to work with the institutions to resolve a particular problem. However, when those steps proved futile, JEDI women learned to get over their fear and face the decision makers. Over time, this capacity led to the group's biggest victories.

The most dramatic example came in 1994, when the state legislature threatened to end full funding for the child care subsidy program in Utah, just as the welfare-reform debate was moving toward pushing women off the rolls and into jobs. The lack of funding would have required the state to create a waiting list for these services, but a mere $500,000 would allow all women to have the child care they needed. JEDI's initial strategy, according to Seed, included packing to overflow "the tiniest room in the world" during a state interim session about the waiting-list system, getting a huge front-page article in the *Salt Lake Tribune,* lobbying individual legislators, presenting lawmakers with a giant key ("the key to getting off welfare is child care"), getting a positive editorial in the *Deseret News,* sending cards from children and letters from low-income moms. Finally, JEDI got verbal agreement from key legislators, including the senate president, but could not get around the governor's resistance, which gave other legislators an out. Having tried repeatedly to get a meeting with the governor with no response, JEDI was "at the end of the line in terms of our options. We'd been organizing some kind of action-oriented thing every weekend for two months, we were exhausted, the legislative session was almost over, and we were losing big time. Finally we said we'd go to [the] governor's office and just sit there and wait. It would be the first time we were prepared to be arrested," says Seed.

The governor was there but refused to come out of his office and talk to the group; his aides "spent the whole day trying to decide whether to arrest us or not," says Seed. The top news story of the evening showed JEDI mothers and children spending the night in the governor's office, and the governor looking "like an absurd idiot." The next morning, JEDI members greeted the governor's chief of staff as he stepped over sleeping bags and bodies to offer a meeting four days later. The *Salt Lake Tribune,* which had not taken an editorial position earlier, strongly favored the women in the days preceding their scheduled meeting. Seed outlines the outcome: "The legislature found the money, no one went to a waiting list, and they didn't touch that program again for a long time."

Seed says that, after two years of organizing, this was the action that "got us recognized as trouble—don't mess with those women!" Bonnie Macri, the executive director of JEDI, says the group's willingness to take action has gained it a reputation as the go-to organization on controversial issues: "People say that's one for JEDI because we take no government money and can get away with things that other groups can't."

Illustration: CTWO and GROWL Democratize the Welfare Debate

Former GROWL coordinator Dana Ginn Paredes recalls that many welfare rights groups turned to or were founded to provide services after reform kicked in, so they were not comfortable with direct action tactics. She says, "The first thing they say is that people in their base need direct services, otherwise they're not going to make it to next week, [they'll be] forced to live without food or stay in an abusive situation. Most organizations have few resources, so if they have to choose, they choose the service and advocacy route because that best meets the immediate needs of their constituency."

Quite often, the way that GROWL members defined direct action was more like "occasional advocacy, a day at the statehouse," says Paredes. However, she also notes that these welfare rights groups have many assets that lend themselves to effective direct action—namely great people, great stories, and media relationships.

In November 2000, CTWO and its research partner, the Applied Research Center, learned that the Gerald R. Ford School of Public Policy at the University of Michigan was going to conduct the New World of Welfare conference in Washington, D.C., in February 2001. Conference planners aimed to assess the body of information and analysis that had been produced in the aftermath of welfare reform. But the program ignored substantial research on discrimination and continued poverty and included not one group representing welfare recipients, even while it gave time to right-wing extremist Charles Murray. This conference was the first major national forum for the reauthorization debate.

Efforts to get recipient voices and progressive research inserted into conference presentations netted one eight-minute slot during the closing panel, granted to Mark Toney, CTWO's executive director. To protest the measly accommodation and get more space, GROWL conducted three actions over the course of the two days. During the opening remarks, GROWL members tied gags around their mouths and handed out alternative research packets to the seven hundred conference attendees. At the beginning of Murray's speech, they initiated a picket line that circled the audience. Although Murray is well known for simply speaking over frequent protests at his speeches, this time he held his speech while the group silently picketed the room with signs refuting his theories of intelligence and single motherhood. "For about five minutes, there was total silence in the room, except for our feet going around. You could hear seven hundred people breathing," recalls Paredes. The following day, Community Voices Heard, the Fifth Avenue Committee, and We Make the Road by Walking, all New York groups, confronted the New York director of human resources, demanding a meeting they had been trying to get for months. The conference ended with talks by three GROWL members who spoke during the time assigned to Toney in the closing panel.

Taking action together in Washington, D.C., helped advance the network's comfort with direct action tactics. For many GROWL leaders, the conference provided their first experiences with direct action. One participant says, "I was really afraid before the first one, and I wanted it to be totally silent so we wouldn't get in trouble. By the third one, I was hollering." For others, the conference put them face-to-face with the people who make the decisions that control their lives. Brenda Stewart, a former Work Experience Program (WEP) worker and now an organizer with WEP Workers Together, says, "I had heard of Charles Murray from the organizers, but I couldn't believe he was actually saying the things he was saying." "The experience of directly confronting the people we are most afraid of, the ones we don't want to hear, consolidated our group a lot, and made people realize they could count on each other," reflects Paredes.

Sometimes direct action is not the best option. Macri of JEDI believes that child welfare is one of the most complicated implications of welfare reform and therefore is not the best kind of issue on which to use direct action. "It's really difficult; there's a lot of aberrant behavior in families. The public believes that children should be taken away from situations of real abuse, but often they are taken because the mother doesn't have food or the utilities are turned off or the house is not clean." These competing moral imperatives undermine one of Seed's most important criteria for doing direct action, that "your issue has to be absolutely clear." On foster-care issues, JEDI spends its energy organizing group advocacy (in which parents accompany each other to hearings), providing legal advice, and working with legislators to change policy.

Choreographing the Action

Actions are heavily choreographed and rehearsed, like a play. When we do an action, we bring our situations into a new venue, and the interaction in that venue has to read like a drama. A good action has stages; people play roles, and everyone prepares and practices. Actions start with an opening, an announcement of the group's presence; the opening might be a silent march, a scheduled appointment, or a loud chant. The announcement gives way to the setup, in which we describe the problem through testimony or a statement. That leads to the confrontation, the presentation of a demand to a target. Then we have an outcome and a conclusion. A successful group knows before going into the action what is supposed to happen at every stage.

We generally spend a great deal more time preparing for an action than actually doing it. Preparation includes plotting the entry and exit, checking out the security, making sure the target is going to be there, talking through demands, preparing testimony, alerting the press, and making contingency plans. A group defines the tone of the action in the preparation stage, not in the target's office. All actions imply firm resolve, but there is gentle firmness and there is angry firmness. Macri says, "This is about making the most of the positive elements you have put into an action, the real people, good stories, and good visuals."

A group needs to think about how to use all the emotions present, certainly anger and sorrow, but also humor and fun. Various factors raise the voice of an action. These factors include the personalities of the spokespeople, the presence of the press, simultaneous leafleting, and a clear threat about the next step.

Actions always have a limited number of spokespeople—usually one to run the action and negotiate over the demands and one or two to make the case. The rest of the people are there to make noise and provide support, and their role also has to be choreographed and directed. A team member can undermine an action, either deliberately or unknowingly, in many ways. Someone might lead a chant just when your spokesperson is about to push for the target's answer; another person might go into a long diatribe about her own case; or someone who knows your target personally might start reminiscing about last week's golf game. During the action itself, two people need to act as directors, one standing next to the spokesperson to back her up and another standing toward the back of the group to lead chanting and deal with disruptions. These people need to have a good sense of the timing of actions, and they need to be good at listening and paying attention so they can identify the proper intervention.

I can hear now a little voice saying, "All that is going to take the fun and spontaneity out of our actions!" My response is this: while actions can be fun, fun is not their main objective—getting something out of a target is. Additionally, people tend to have more fun at an action that goes well than one that falls apart because no one knows what the plan is.

Illustration: DARE Members Prepare for an Action

DARE members put in at least ten hours of collective planning time for an action. This planning includes recruiting people to come out for the action, talking with specific people in one-on-ones to get them to take particular roles, meeting to discuss the target, crafting the demands and establishing the timing of them, scoping out the physical layout of the site, figuring out the media message, writing songs and chants, practicing, and getting props and visuals together such as flyers and signs. Often these planning sessions are led by experienced members, and the spokespeople roles are rotated. Each action has a list of props, like a play. When the HDCJ Campaign transferred a family day-care group to the governor's office, they made sure to carry grape juice so that administrators would be nervous about the pristine carpet. When they did an Easter bunny action on the director of human services, they had beautiful colored eggs with messages attached. When they wrote chants, they used children's nursery rhymes and songs so the children could sing along. They made sure the words were available to all on a song sheet. These touches made the actions fun, tapped into the group's creativity and the target's vulnerabilities (fear of carpet stains!), and enabled many people to participate.

Illustration: JEDI Uses Visual Effects to Advantage

After two years of unsuccessful fighting to get the legal marriage age in Utah changed from fourteen to sixteen in order to deal with the problem of girls being married off to adult men as polygamous wives, JEDI decided to pull out all the stops. The organization staged a marriage ceremony between a very old man and twelve-year-old girls in the state capitol rotunda, to the dismay of legislators who had voted against the previous bills. JEDI took special care over the visual effects. The girls wore frilly white wedding gowns at least one size too large and stuffed with a pregnancy pillow to play up their childishness, and the old man in a tuxedo could have passed for the oldest man in the West. The "minister" read a traditional text, and rice was thrown at the happy new family. During the ceremony, JEDI passed out flyers asking legislators to change the law to prevent the sexual exploitation of children. News coverage followed. The law was changed within a week.

Sometimes, things happen during an action that we can't predict and plan for, and we just have to stay on our toes. In those cases, it helps to stick to the plan. According to Seed, during JEDI's child care action at the governor's office, described earlier, just as the group of twenty moms and "herd of little kids" finished their pre-action news conference to march into the governor's office, their presence was bolstered by a hundred schoolchildren on a tour of the capital who joined the protest. "All of a sudden, instead of twenty women with kids, we were twenty women with 120 kids. The kids yelled to activate the echo, literally stampeded their way into the governor's office, and threw open the boardroom door," recalls Seed. JEDI took some criticism later for "inciting children to riot," but the children eventually left with their teachers, and the small JEDI group settled down to wait.

Taking the time to do Exercise 4.2 will help ensure that your direct actions are impeccably thought through, with all the details thoroughly planned and contingencies anticipated.

Integrating Actions with the Overall Campaign

Direct actions are always part of a larger campaign in which other tactics are also being used. In the campaign context, direct actions apply the extra pressure your target needs to make the next commitment. Within a specific campaign there is a proper place for direct actions. Before we use direct action, we have to prove, to our own group and the outside world, that the proper channels have not brought satisfaction. We define what counts as satisfaction, so we can move on to the next step.

Campaigns have a natural flow—the initiation, the struggle, the negotiation, and the aftermath. One direct action never constitutes your entire campaign. Direct actions represent peaks in the conflict, and other tactics represent plateaus, valleys, or slower escalations, all indicating the level of heat or cooperation your group is trying to generate at the time. If we turn people out to a rally after police officers kill a neighbor, we can't expect an immediate, affirmative response from the chief. Sometimes there are spontaneous shows of solidarity or outrage after a volatile incident, and those are often positive. But after they end, a group still has to go back to the butcher paper and chart out a course of action.

Exercise 4.2. Planning Worksheet.

QUESTIONS TO THINK ABOUT WHEN PLANNING A DIRECT ACTION

• What is the issue?

Do we have members who can testify?

• What are the demands?

Do we have someone who can speak about our demands?

• Who is the target?

Where can we find the target?
Why are we holding this target responsible?

• What is our larger message?

DEVELOP A PLAN

• What is the plan for the action?

Announcement

Setup, making the case

Confrontation, presenting demands

Climax, getting a response

Conclusion, how will we end?

• Can this action draw the media?

Will this action draw sympathy and support for our demands and place the blame for the problem on the target?

Chanting, street theater, visuals, sit-in, speeches, testimonials, enter office, picket home, confront target, present demands, etc.

• Contingency planning.

What could go wrong?
What is our contingency plan?

Target is not there; target won't meet because of no appointment; security or police are called, etc.

ASSIGN ROLES AND OTHER PREPARATION

• Who is scouting the location of the action?

• Who are going to be the leaders out front (e.g., giving testimonials)?

• Who is dealing with the target?

• Who is the chant leader?

• Who is the media spokesperson?

• Who is managing the visuals?

• Other roles?

WRAP UP: Immediately debrief the results of the action and begin follow-up.

• Did we carry out our plan and what actually happened?

• Who didn't make it? Who needs to be called? Who will make those calls?

Source: Adapted with permission from the Center for Third World Organizing.

A large-scale, highly confrontational action is rarely going to be your group's first tactic. Over time, an organization learns to vary the tone, message, and creativity of its direct actions. Our targets do eventually learn improved ways of putting us off, even under pressure, and our people get bored doing the same actions for years.

Illustration: SMART Uses Multiple Tactics

Community members supporting Hotel Employees, Restaurant Employees (HERE) fights around the country regularly conduct water-ins at fancy hotels; they get seated in the hotel restaurant, order water, chant their pro-union message to the wealthy patrons and management, leave a large tip, and march out the door. SMART also forms delegations of allies and clergy who enter hotel management offices and ask managers not to interfere in a union-recognition fight or to end harassment campaigns against individual workers who are leaders in the unionization campaign. Next the tactics center on building visibility and support. SMART sets up a truth commission made up of prominent people who are invited to hear testimony from workers confronted by union busters. Clergy members supervise a mock union election, and union activists conduct a hotel-in-the-streets. Then there is another direct action, this time on a trustee or CEO. Vivian Rothstein of LAANE notes the importance of "a fun-loving and exciting set of tactics," which are more possible when the union skirts the election process and asks the employer directly for recognition. There are two ways to get a union recognized: to have it voted in by the workers according to NLRB rules or simply to have it accepted by management without an election. The election process designed by the NLRB holds many pitfalls for union activists; it can be delayed and manipulated easily by employers. Unions have found such elections with private employers almost impossible to win. Even if an election is in process, Rothstein believes creative tactics can be used.

Illustration: The HDCJ Campaign Keeps Direct Action Focused on Its Main Goal

While fighting for health insurance for day-care providers, the HDCJ Campaign had to expand its tactics without giving up its militancy. A study by the Legislative Advisory Commission on Child Care recommended explicitly that Department of Human Services day-care providers be allowed to join the state employees' health plan. But even these results and the 1994 death of member Yolanda Gonzalez from a treatable, but uninsured, heart condition, were not enough to move the state. From the beginning, the HDCJ Campaign's clarity about its cause shined through the red tape and excuses of its targets.

One bill to finance health insurance had already failed to pass the state legislature in 1994. Earlier, Bob Fallon, the director of the Department of Human Services, had refused to include provider health insurance in his budget request. Because he kept stalling, the providers escalated their tactics. In addition to testifying at official hearings, the committee set up a day-care center in Fallon's office and at the state house, visited Fallon at home on Easter Sunday, and held repeated accountability sessions at the DARE community center with two governors. Accountability sessions are essentially community meetings, designed to put a target on the hot seat in front of a hundred or more people.

Rather than blunting their militancy to engage in these new arenas, the Campaign adapted the tone of its tactics and actions, going hard after the most recalcitrant targets while courting potential allies with no less passion but a more cooperative tone. The Campaign had to develop the sophistication to take on many tasks, both familiar and not, and to figure out the relationship between one tactic and another. It had to conduct or direct original research that measured conditions, tracked funding streams, and clarified the power structure. The group learned how to operate an inside-outside strategy, in which some of the leaders carried the message from their members in government-sponsored bodies. They wrote legislation, testified at legislative hearings, and lobbied state representatives and their staffs. Finally, they communicated their perspective to the media and used the electoral cycle to pressure officials.

Regardless of which tactics were in use at any given moment, the Campaign never abandoned its true goal—to win health insurance for providers in a way that would set the stage for bargaining on additional issues later on. Simply by keeping its central demand consistently visible, the Campaign repeated the point that providers needed and deserved health insurance, while always being internally clear about the incremental concessions it would accept until that demand was met. Shannah Kurland, the first organizer of the HDCJ Campaign, reflects that "if we hadn't had clear fallback positions—for example, on what the study should consider and that we had to review it—or if we hadn't been specific about the kind of health care we wanted, we would have been easily led astray by the things the administration offered to do for us." This focus allowed the Campaign to produce demands that were competitive alternatives to the state's proposals during the negotiations that ended each phase of the campaign.

The combination of many tactics, including a lot of direct action, along with the Campaign's ability to outlast two Department of Human Services directors and two governors, led to the passage of a clause in Rhode Island's welfare package that financed providers' participation in the state health plan.

Exhibit 4.1 is the design chart for a sample campaign. It gives an idea of how direct actions fit with other tactics and how they contribute to the overall campaign. Exercise 4.3 is a blank chart that you can fill out to design your own campaign.

Exhibit 4.1. Sample Campaign Design Chart.

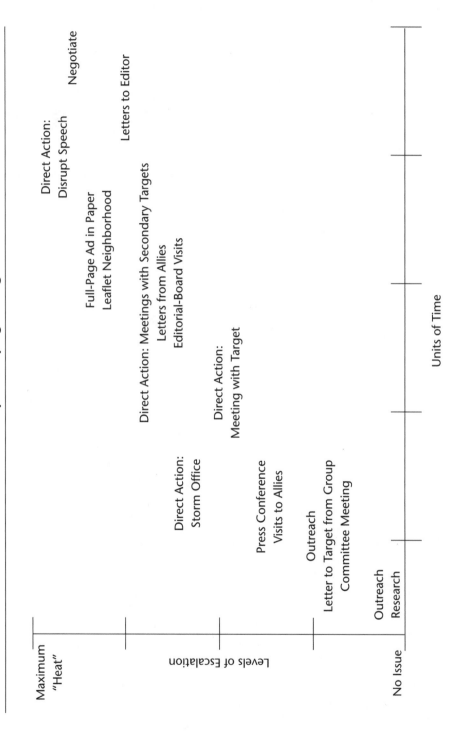

Exercise 4.3. Campaign Design Chart.

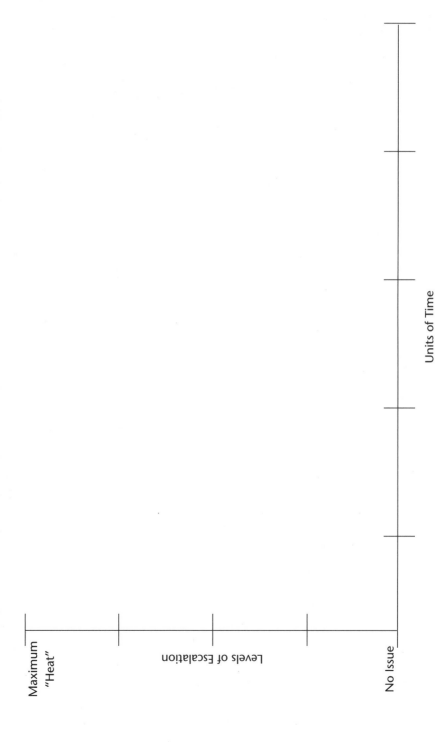

Maximum
"Heat"

Levels of Escalation

No Issue

Units of Time

Conclusion

Mili Bonilla, one of the best organizers I know, told me once that direct action is like an umbrella. "You put it away in the closet when you don't need it, but always in the same place, so you can get to it easily when you do." While all kinds of tactics play a role in a carefully plotted campaign strategy, direct actions are your escalated tool for the intractable target on a clear issue. When direct actions have clear goals, are well prepared and cleanly executed, victories will come while the group builds its cohesion. Places in which direct action is uncommon present rich possibilities for shifting power in this way. Macri and Seed agree that direct action is even more effective in a conservative place like Salt Lake City than in more liberal cities because "direct action [is] very foreign to everyone here."

No matter how experienced an organization is, it can expand or improve its use of direct action. If face-to-face confrontation with a target is new, a group might want to ease its way toward that confrontation by using other tactics that require some of the same skills, such as public speaking, making a case, and presenting demands in a press conference. A less experienced group might want to start with administrative targets on administrative issues that are important but in which the stakes are low, as in the example of winning timely paychecks. More experienced organizations have to guard against boredom and complacency. Such a group might want to test the freshness of its actions, consider rotating its leadership, track the ways in which targets are responding, and evaluate its use of allies during actions. As an organization grows and takes on more sophisticated campaigns, its expertise in other arenas might blunt its willingness to go direct and rely on people pressure.

In the era of the Patriot Act, much of the United States is taking on the character of more conservative places in which direct action is not so well accepted. The excuse of homeland security is being used to limit our most basic rights, the right to assemble and the right to free speech. We can defend these rights, as well as increase the possibility of winning, by taking our issues directly to the source of the conflict.

CHAPTER FIVE

LEADING THE WAY

Although most people agree that good leaders occupy the center of all successful organizations and institutions, from the family to the county hospital to the community-based health clinic, society tends to define leaders narrowly. In this mainstream framework, leaders are easily identified individuals with a public face who work in a fairly self-sufficient manner. They tend to be charismatic, good networkers, able to attract resources. This dominant notion of leadership is essentially elitist: vocal individuals speaking for a voiceless mass. In this characterization leaders are recognized for their individual contributions, not because they are accountable to or represent a larger group. But, Ellen Bravo of 9to5 says, for leaders "to think of power as being lodged within their person rather than lodged in the collective is a problem for the group."

The innumerable programs supporting individual leaders constitute a mini-industry. Most of these programs are geared toward developing the skills of professionals—leaders who are paid to work in their chosen fields. For the most part, they ignore the potential of lesser known leaders, leaders without formal education, leaders who are poor, leaders who are immigrants or of color, and leaders whose mission requires them to be accountable to a larger community or to build organizations in which leadership is renewed.

An organization's leadership reveals a lot about the group. If we see the same three faces at every event, perhaps enough new recruitment is not happening. If an organization has had one executive director for twenty-five years while a string of short-term staff people pass through, perhaps founder's syndrome is preventing the organization from meeting new challenges. An organization in which leaders are always looking and sounding burnt out might be neglecting long-term planning, operating instead in crisis mode and moving from one emergency to another. By contrast, smooth leadership transitions are usually a sign of good planning and respectful turnover.

I consider the leadership of an organization to include both staff and volunteers, and this chapter includes tools and suggestions applicable to both. Innovations in leadership development have blurred, if not erased, the traditional distinctions between staff and volunteer leaders. Organizations and unions are increasingly attempting to hire staff organizers from among their constituencies and members. Increasingly, organizations are realizing that organizers and volunteer leaders have to be able to do the same job, if at different paces and at different times. In the end, the sheer need for capable people, the impossibility of hiring enough people, and the complexities involved in being a good leader drive most organizations to be systematic and creative about leadership development.

In this chapter, I explore the four most important elements of strong leadership development programs: these programs emphasize development rather than identification; establish formal programs; pay attention to race, class, gender, and culture; and actively plan for leadership renewal and rejuvenation. In illustrations from Working Partnerships, Direct Action for Rights and Equality (DARE), the Center for Third World Organizing (CTWO), the Women's Institute for Leadership Development (WILD), and the Southeast Regional Economic Justice Network (REJN), we can see, respectively, how a formal leadership development program that is willing to experiment helps to build a diversified cadre of leaders for community-labor alliances; how a graduated development program prepares leaders to take on increased responsibilities and how members of constituencies can be hired as leaders; how structural changes attract new potential leaders and how creative policies can help a staff remain sane; how to develop leaders rather than simply identify them and how to become a truly multicultural organization; how to diversify leadership and how to rejuvenate leaders.

Principles

There are four key principles of leadership development. First, successful organizations distinguish between leadership identification and deeper development. Second, they formalize their leadership development programs, using popular education methods and grounding development in the daily work of the organization. Third, they pay attention to the race, class, gender, and cultural issues embedded in leadership development. Finally, they actively plan for the renewal and regeneration of leadership, from supporting an individual in avoiding burnout to managing leadership transitions well.

Emphasizing Development Rather Than Identification

As a young organizer, I was taught to conduct my outreach with an eye out for people whose demeanor and speech indicated a fire in the belly. After that, I was taught to identify the established formal and informal leaders in the community, those to whom others looked for direction. Leaders identified in this way are often invaluable, especially to new organizations. But this approach does not take seriously enough the fact that existing leadership is often based on existing power structures. Certain characteristics are more readily given the stamp of leadership—maleness, assertiveness, being employed, having English language skills. This approach often ensures that all the leaders in the organization have the same personality, even if they are diverse in other ways. Additionally, the fire in many bellies has been systematically smothered. These cannot be our only criteria for investing in someone's leadership.

There are implications to the distinction between identification and development. Identification requires matching a person's skills to tasks, but not much more. Development is more time-consuming and riskier. It requires reflection and planning, as well as systematic teaching. According to Amy Dean, the executive director of Working Partnerships, it requires helping potential leaders think through who they want to be, as well as who they are in this moment; having some knowledge of a leader's learning style and history; and designing a cycle of learning that makes room for diverse styles.

I have found it useful to think of leadership development as consisting of stages. The first stage is *assessment* of a leader's strengths and goals and how those match the current needs of the organization. In this stage, the emphasis is on reflection. The second stage involves making an *assignment* that both advances the needs of the organization and stretches the individual to take on new responsibilities. In the third stage, the leader can expect *assistance* from an organizer or another leader, who might share the task with her the first time or two, until she is comfortable performing it herself. In the fourth stage, we *acknowledge* the work the leader has done. Then, the whole cycle starts again, with an assessment based on the results of the latest experience. Exhibit 5.1 details the kinds of tasks leaders with different levels of experience might perform and what they might be expected to know.

Exhibit 5.1. Leadership Development Chart.

Levels of Experience	Recruitment	Research	Action Campaigns	Fundraising	Politics	Planning
New: Getting started	Understands drives and membership recruitment	Reads the newspaper Generates research questions	Attends Enjoys Recruits others	Pays dues Attends fundraisers and brings others to those events	Knows what is going on with self and neighbors Sees unfairness and inequality Is mad!	Participates in a meeting, finds out the organization's plan
Emerging: More responsibility and a base	Recruits new members in one-on-one personal visits Recruits new members wherever they are Recruits new house-meeting hosts Makes turnout calls	Participates in interviews Uses various sources Reports research results Uses research in actions	Is spokesperson at activities Helps debrief Takes role in campaign meetings Understands the role of the media	Volunteers for a committee Asks people to pay their dues Asks foundations for money	Knows how the local and state governments work Understands one issue very well Has bigger picture of world than neighborhood Understands institutional power	Seeks responsibility Attends annual leadership retreat

	Takes out teams to do outreach; Coordinates membership campaign and trains house-meeting hosts; Does personal visits; Chairs membership meetings; Runs a phone bank; Recruits allies; Represents organization in coalitions	Does interviews alone; Packages research usefully; Attends strategy gatherings	Chairs campaign committee; Preps other leaders for actions; Participates in negotiations; Runs evaluations	Helps develop the budget; Develops proposals	Reaches for new ideas; Sees contradictions; Sees the many ways in which issues are connected	Is on board of directors; Participates in staff hiring and evaluation; Leads annual retreat
Experienced: Teaching others						
Super-experienced	Chairs coalitions	Supervises research team	Plans whole campaigns; Chairs large-scale actions	Chairs long-range fundraising and endowment committees	Projects politics outside the organization	Is board chair or on executive committee; Supervises executive director

Source: Adapted from the Northwest Federation of Community Organizations and the Center for Third World Organizing.

Illustration: WILD Encourages Women to See Themselves as Leaders

If leader identification involves finding the people who have already claimed the right to exercise leadership, then the job of a developer "involves taking risks with someone who has the spark of potential but who wouldn't see herself as a leader," says Alison Bowen, the executive director of WILD in Boston. Bowen notes that the usual response to the question "Whom do we think of as leaders?" takes participants outside of themselves. She says, "Women give the names of senators and presidents and sports leaders instead of thinking of ourselves as leaders in the work we do. Development is key to getting women to identify what we do as women for basic survival as leadership and then to be able to use that as an asset." WILD works to develop new leaders by making its programs widely accessible and preparing women to take formal leadership positions in their unions and central labor councils. The organization did not always emphasize formal positions. Former director Susan Winning says that "at first we talked about women just doing whatever they could in whatever capacity, but then we realized that real power lies in those elected positions. If you have the rank and file behind you, you can advance the top-level decisions and make sure that women's issues get dealt with."

Providing Formal but Not Academic Training

To many people, the notion of formality raises the specter of pantyhose and high heels, something disconnected from daily life. In leadership development, however, it means only that there is a systematic program to which resources are devoted and that there are clear time frames and expectations.

There are four substantial reasons to formalize leadership development rather than leaving it to get done in the normal course of organizing. First, significant leadership development tends to fall off the table during the height of campaign work and to stay off the table during lag times when the need for new leaders feels less urgent. When leadership development is casual, people can learn new skills only through trial and error. That's not necessarily bad, but it tends to work best for those who come to the organization with strong self-confidence. Those who need support or encouragement tend to drop out. Second, formality is an equalizer. To the extent that formal leadership development programs are attached to formal responsibilities and clear lines of succession and accountability, the entire process of becoming a leader can be greatly demystified. Third, by formalizing their programs, practitioners are more likely to capture the lessons learned about what works and what doesn't; we are also more likely to document training designs so we don't have to re-create them for every new leader. Fourth, formality forces us to create a diverse toolkit that includes training sessions, one-on-one dialogues, and fieldwork of various sorts. The variety of tools is especially necessary for groups with uneven literacy or multiple languages. Formality is important, therefore, if we're developing nontraditional leaders who live most of their lives on the margins of mainstream society.

Illustration: Working Partnerships Provides Formal Training for Local Leaders

Working Partnerships provides formal training to community leaders as a key element in its community-labor alliance-building strategy. The eight-week Community Leadership Training Institute focuses largely on issue development and organizing. Although participants always get their field experience through campaigns such as living wage and children's health insurance, program designers thought it was important to have a formal program to ensure quality and diversity. Phaedra Ellis, director of workforce development, who ran the program for several years, says, "If it's not formal, it doesn't get done as it should. It's too hard to make time for it in the rush of campaign work. Formality forces you to think about the pedagogy and the content so that it's not haphazard or causing some other contradiction in the organization."

Illustration: DARE Provides a Graduated Program

DARE prepares its leaders in three ways to take on increased responsibilities, whether as future staff of DARE or of other organizations or in continued roles as volunteer leaders. First, DARE, in conjunction with CTWO, hosts three-day Community Action trainings on the basics of organizing. These sessions cover the history of organizing in communities of color, framing and developing issues, direct actions, and door knocking or street outreach. Second, DARE leaders who have been active for at least six months are eligible to enter DARE's own ten-week program, Apprenticeship for Member Organizers, in which they work twenty hours each week for a stipend. The curriculum includes formal sessions on the history of organizing in poor communities and communities of color, the basics of recruitment, facilitating group work, and planning direct actions and campaigns. "The most important part of the curriculum is the time people spend actually going out into the field and doing the work the organization needs done," according to Sara Mersha, DARE's director. Third, the DARE Leadership Institute, which runs for six months, provides opportunities for experienced members to be mentors for new members and for all to explore key political questions. In this program, long-time and newer members get together twice each month, once for skill building and once for a political discussion; they set the agenda for these sessions by identifying their needs. Then experienced leaders are paired with new ones, and these pairs develop six-month projects that allow them to apply what they are learning.

Illustration: DARE Hires Leaders from Its Constituency

DARE has successfully hired many of its staff from its constituent base. In making concerted efforts to do so, it is driven by the need for stable staffing and for increased connections to its members. Organizers who come out of the community bring their existing social networks and direct, compelling experience with the issues; this background supports their recruitment and campaign work. Mary Kay Harris, DARE police-accountability organizer and former member, asserts that the fact that "the DARE staff [is] membership-based shows that our mission is being fulfilled, that people in the community are the ones that drive these campaigns." That quality makes DARE fairly unique among social-change organizations, which, in Harris's perception, hire only people with at least a bachelor's degree for positions like hers. But Harris's experience uniquely qualified her for this position. She joined the DARE police committee in 1996 after her then-teenage son's violent confrontation with officers, and she remained active throughout the struggle to get the Providence police department to open up its complaint records for community review. By the time she joined the staff in 1999, she had already led actions, recruited new members, and facilitated strategy meetings. Although Harris initially accepted an administrative job at DARE, she soon negotiated her way into the empty staff slot left by a departing police-accountability organizer: "Being married to that campaign as I had been," she says, "it became impossible to stay away."

Harris, her colleagues who came up through the ranks, and the organization continue to face challenges. Long-time grant provider United Way "made an accusation that our folks were not qualified to do what they were doing and threatened to cut off our funding," recalls Sara Mersha. Harris notes that gaining the respect of external players remains a challenge; she says, "I've been insulted over and over again, by people writing me off in [policy] meetings. Once while I was meeting with city council members, one said I was ignorant and obnoxious and not even pronouncing some word right." Mersha adds that "now that the majority of staff come from the membership, we have to work to find balance on staff, have enough folks available to do specific nonorganizing things like write proposals or heavy-duty research." Mersha and Harris agree that the change in staff composition has also required a shift in the role of the organizer. According to Mersha, "Now it's not so much that the organizer has to sit back and not talk; we value their experience as well." But Harris notes that even though some redefinition is taking place, "as a member, I had freedom to do a lot more than I do now. The hardest part was realizing that now I can no longer play a lead role, that I have to be on the sideline and push other people to be leaders. I'm learning how to stand back when I was used to being up front."

Popular education pedagogy keeps formal programs from becoming divorced from the organization's daily reality. Popular education is a community-based, participatory adult learning process whose principles have been used for many years all over the world. The work of Brazilian theorist and teacher Paolo Freire, who codified many of the principles in his book *Pedagogy of the Oppressed* ([1970] 2000), popular education pedagogy has the same roots as the secret transfer of reading and writing skills to African slaves in the Americas. Freire was a literacy teacher working with very poor adults in Brazil; he rebelled against the traditional methods of teaching people to read and write by memorization. His essential premises are that people learn better if what they are learning has clear implications for their survival, that people already have the seeds of knowledge within themselves, and, finally, that teaching methods have to break down the authoritarian hierarchy of teachers and students that characterizes childhood schooling experiences. In community organizing, popular education activities are grounded in peoples' day-to-day life experiences and in doing the work of the organization—recruitment, direct actions, research, fundraising. The advantages of popular education include greater engagement of participants in the material, more opportunities to build community among members, and more opportunities to raise participants' confidence by stressing internal knowledge—all in addition to teaching hard skills.

Designing programs based on these principles is both easier and harder than providing lectures and reading materials. Lectures tend to involve fewer people and less preparation. They are usually written and delivered by a single person. Lectures can be a good way to dump information that only one person has. By contrast, the small-group-activity method, one of the most popular techniques used in grassroots organizations, begins with a brief introductory presentation followed by small-group exercises to grapple with a problem or decision based on real experiences; the small groups then report back to the larger group. The principles related to the topic emerge in the combination of all the reports and discussion of their implications. The teacher/trainer's job at that point is to draw the links between the ideas presented in the reports and to add any other information that may not have come out. Ninety percent of the time, the trainer has only to add one or two ideas. Such small-group activities are harder to design than lectures, but they are sometimes easier to execute.

Popular education methodology allows the trainer to get a sense of the information people are retaining from the initial presentation as well of the skills and experiences people are bringing to the session. If in a session about house meetings the small groups keep designing the perfect door-knocking rap, the trainer can see that her initial presentation and the instructions she gave to the small groups were ineffective. Likewise, during a lecture, a trainer is unlikely to find out that someone in the audience has worked in virtually every aspect of campaign development and might be a good source of case studies or a strong small-group leader.

In addition, because small-group-activity methods involve at least a three-way exchange—trainer to participant, participant to participant, and participant to trainer—they have the potential to democratize the learning process and produce new knowledge for all involved. Unlike didactic lectures, popular education allows many people to take teaching roles because the session itself can be broken down into discrete sections.

Popular education is the central pedagogy at WILD. Member Diane Dujon, who got her college education at the nontraditional University of Massachusetts at Boston, has always been attracted to popular education models. She says, "I would always rather have something participatory than have someone talking at me. I like to be able to air my opinion, and it also validates that everybody in the room comes with something, not that one person knows everything and the rest know nothing. You can't get bored, especially when its hot-button issues, and you get to know the people in more than one dimension." Susan Winning notes that designing education in this way allows WILD to break through the intimidation that many strong leaders feel at the prospect of teaching what they know. "Most of our members would be horrified if we asked them to do a one-hour lecture about how to run a negotiation, but they can easily lead people through a small-group exercise about how to decide on the key issues and how to set up the negotiation. Debriefing the small groups especially gives them the chance to reveal what they know because it gets stimulated by what the group knows."

One of the advantages of the popular education methods is that they involve leaders in working together, a first step to creating and deepening relationships between people who will have to work together to move the organization forward. Phaedra Ellis identifies this as a strong guiding principle in the Working Partnerships program that constitutes the first interaction between leaders of diverse Silicon Valley organizations. She says, "We wanted people to learn from one another rather than learn from us. Our role is to provide the tools, say this is how equity might work, and this is how we've gotten it so far."

Filling out the worksheet in Exercise 5.1 will help you organize your leadership development courses in a formal way regardless of what kind of pedagogy you use.

Most formal leadership development programs, whether their goal is to prepare staff or volunteer leaders, include some form of fieldwork that helps the group to bond and provides practical experience to advance participants' knowledge. In part, emphasizing the actual work as a path to leadership helps to build a sense of accountability: leaders are acknowledged because of their work rather than because of their social positions. The great advantage of developing leaders within a community organization is that their work places them close enough to the ground for them to address learning needs and to take up opportunities daily.

Exercise 5.1. Curriculum-Planning Worksheet.

Course Objectives:

1.

2.

3.

4.

Class 1: Topic:

Content

-

-

-

Methods

Outcomes

Materials

Trainers

Class 2: Topic:

Content

-

-

-

Methods

Outcomes

Materials

Trainers

Source: Adapted from Working Partnerships.

Illustration: Working Partnerships Learns Through Doing

Working Partnerships uses class projects to provide a field experience and has experimented with projects that are broad and specific. At the beginning of each class cycle,
the group breaks down into media, policy, research, base-building, and organizing
teams; each team is responsible for one aspect of the project infrastructure and is led
by a resource expert. The groups meet during and between classes, and each individual takes an assignment. San Jose's living wage ordinance was crafted by a diverse
set of community leaders engaged in the Working Partnerships program; they grap-
pled with the hard questions of designing and fighting for the ordinance through the
program's community-project component. Phaedra Ellis is committed to the fieldwork
model because "running sessions without providing opportunities to practice can have
[the] extremely negative effect of anointing people with a certificate before they've
actually experienced the work."

After building the fieldwork assignment around the living wage campaign for two
years, Ellis tried a different approach in 1999. Program leaders charged the teams with
developing a five-year regional plan using four different philosophies. Then the teams
were required to determine whether their economic plans could address specific equity
concerns. Ellis reflects that building the class project around macroissues didn't work
as well as using living wage because it minimized the kind of practical learning that
occurs in campaign-based projects. When living wage is used, "people actually participate in a real campaign and they understand what happens. Their work has real
outcomes and implications."

Ellis also provides follow-up opportunities to strengthen the regional leadership
cadre: "It's not enough to just train people and let them go. There has to be a network of these folks so people can support one another. People can get the framework,
but they need to keep coming back and see how they're applying the framework."
One graduate out of each cycle is always invited back to help deliver the training
and support participants.

Paying Attention to Culture, Class, Race, and Gender

Careful attention to demographics and to equalizing the participation of different gender, class, and racial groups plays an important role in building an effective leadership. Consequently, sophisticated organizations pay attention to the role
of race, class, gender, and culture in their leadership development. They are generally driven to do so by two factors. First, the definition and style of effective leadership vary from community to community, and progressive leaders are often at
the forefront of causing cultural change within a community. For example, some
cultures in all racial groups tightly proscribe the role of women or the poor; those
people are punished for exercising leadership. In other cultures, young people face
taboos against criticizing their elders. Grassroots leadership development is cul-

turally based; it has to resonate with people's lived experience but at the same time influence their understanding of their tradition. This process is best accomplished by grounding leadership development in the day-to-day realities that cause tiny shifts in cultural practice.

Second, leaders of today's organizations have to be able to build bridges across constituencies; consequently, they need support in developing the skills required to resist cultural biases that are likely to kick in if they aren't paying attention. Institutions and allies express their biases in both subtle and obvious ways, and we may have to defend our leaders and their legitimacy. Research and advocacy groups have commented, for example, that it isn't useful to have overly emotional welfare recipients speak at public hearings. Their comments reflect the value attached to rationality and credentials rather than to emotion and experience, the additional strengths from which grassroots leaders operate.

The imperative to remove sexism, classism, and racism from the ranks of movement leaders is not simply a moral one. According to Ellen Bravo, groups find it difficult to win their fights if the people most affected by negative policies and trends are not at the forefront, making strategic, as well as technical, decisions. She says, "You either have this token window dressing or you have an organization built from the ground up, where the campaign itself is led by the people with the greatest stake, [who] won't give up. The demands, the form of organization, everything is shaped by that." While many organizations have struggled with the need to advance women's leadership in a male-dominated world or the leadership of people of color in a racist world, Bravo insists that this goal is strategic, not moral. She continues, "If the power you get comes from making deals or having influence, it's a different kind of power that doesn't change things at their base. If you want change at that level you have to involve the people whose lives would be left out otherwise."

Amy Dean of Working Partnerships, who is known for mentoring highly skilled and dedicated young women, makes the point that looking out for diversity does not mean elevating someone who isn't ready. "That sets people up to fail," she says; "then you've ruined a potentially good experience." Dean emphasizes building organizational structures in which people can advance as their experience and skills grow.

Illustration: WILD Prioritizes Involving Women of Color

WILD makes it a practice to involve women of color at all levels of the organization and of supporting their particular struggles. WILD maintains three committees: anti-oppression, Latinas, and women of African heritage, developed in that order. Winning notes that decisions about which group to start with were based on "where there seemed to be the match between greatest need and opportunity." These committees provide dedicated training programs for specific constituencies through community-based organizations, and they feed directly into union caucuses. WILD also created an accessibility checklist to measure the progress of labor organizations in achieving diversity; women leaders can use this tool to start raising questions about inclusion. Civil rights and women's committees use these checklists to challenge leaders to move on and to justify creating new structures for participation and leadership.

Winning notes that this commitment to multiculturalism in unions called into question the roles of white women on the WILD staff. One of the most important expressions of WILD's internal commitment was the long-drawn-out search for an executive director who could replace Winning. Until WILD was able to identify or develop a woman of color to take the directorship, Winning simply remained in the position. Winning also kept other positions open until they could be filled by women of color. She says that most organizations don't have the patience to become truly multicultural: "We can't be driven only by the need to get the work done. We have to be equally driven by the need to have a diverse, multilingual staff; so some positions stay open until we really find the right person." This approach to organizational development sometimes means that project plans do not move forward at the fastest pace, but "that's a sacrifice we're willing to make to push ourselves on the racial diversity." The delay allowed Bowen, who was already on the staff, to gain the experience necessary to take over as executive director.

WILD member Dujon reflects that having leaders of color makes a substantial difference in who joins. She says proudly, "[A recent WILD event] was so colorful you could tell it really makes a difference." Dujon notes that WILD avoided many of the pitfalls of turning multicultural with help from an active board that wasn't afraid to "work on the issues that a lot of other people run away from." Organizations are often "started by middle-class, white women, who say they don't mind women of color and women of other classes belonging but really think, 'I know how this should run, and you don't really know.' That may work all right for a year or two, and then women of color say, 'How come we can't do that?' That feels like somebody trying to give you something on the one hand but snatching it away on the other."

Illustration: Working Partnerships Watches the Demographics

People cannot just sign up randomly for the Working Partnerships Labor/Community Leadership Institute; they have to be invited to join a particular cycle of the class. Ellis says, "We're thoughtful about the people [who] participate because that determines the success of the class. The diversity is what makes it rich." All the people invited, whatever their gender, economic background, and race, have to meet a specific set of criteria. Ellis asks these questions about potential participants: "Do they have the ability to build or are they already attached to a base? Can they replicate what they learn in the class?" Ellis approaches the diversity question on the basis of organizing strategies rather than with a static quota system. She says, "The ideal mix changes as we get deeper into communities, hear about groups we didn't know about before."

Illustration: REJN Trains Leaders Diversified by Class and Age

From the outset, REJN embraced intentional diversity by considering each potential leader's geographical home, class background, race/ethnicity, religion, age, language, culture, and sexual orientation. For example, in its early days REJN reformulated its leadership body to reflect the range of groups that might be interested in the network. REJN also provided the first grassroots space to incorporate simultaneous translation in English and Spanish. REJN has made specific commitments to diversifying the class backgrounds and age of regional leaders by requiring member organizations to include the rank-and-file, not just paid staff, in REJN gatherings and activities. Although each member organization is normally allowed four spots at a gathering, REJN makes special allowances if an organization brings workers and youth. At some gatherings, groups bring large delegations of poultry workers, farm workers, or injured industrial workers, who help others gain an understanding of that industry from the workers' perspective.

REJN uses its own leadership body to develop new leaders among its youth constituency by making twelve- to nineteen-year-olds board members. Executive Director Leah Wise notes how important REJN is in providing young people with alternative frameworks. She points out that U.S. cultural institutions—the educational system, the media, Hollywood—engage people only in an ahistorical and individualized view of how the world works. When REJN began its youth-leadership program, organizers found that "the popular culture's hold on young people here is very tight. The educational culture here is really horrible; there's a lack of analytical training and lack of exposure. School is for control, so when we have these kinds of settings where you ask kids to think for themselves, they have a really difficult time. Especially in the South, working-class black, Latino, and white kids don't have access to a lot of alternative voices."

Some resistance came from older leaders in the network, who would "get frustrated that the youth had to be doing something with their hands during meetings. The older folk had internalized a culture in which you don't fidget in serious meetings," says Wise. Some of the resistance was worn down when it became clear that the orientation and trainings provided for the youth members of the board "have helped everybody, especially the rank and filers who have literacy problems, less formal education, and are shyer, quieter." Wise notes that REJN aimed to model for its member groups the benefits of integrating young people into the highest ranks of organizational leadership: "Young people have made some very good board members, so we proved that it could be done." While it was exciting to see many of the groups take up that challenge locally, Wise says that "one weakness was not having the resources to help the groups keep developing that work to make it more systematic."

Illustration: CTWO Makes Structural Changes to Diversify Leadership

Over the years, program directors of CTWO's Movement Activist Apprenticeship Program (MAAP) have worked to expand the program's reach to organizational members who want to make the transition to staff. Former MAAP Director Sonia Peña recalls that "because of the way the program was organized we initially attracted a lot of middle-class people of color, some of whom became organizers, but many . . . went on to graduate school and other institutions. We realized that the people who would have the greatest commitment to this work were the people who came from the communities themselves."

To accommodate the needs of members, MAAP staff made significant changes over time. The program started out as a summer program geared toward students, but it now offers a fall cycle also. It initially had a strong ethic around sending people away from their home communities, but it now has some placements in which people work at home. The early MAAP curriculum was delivered lecture style, but today's curriculum includes small-group exercises, popular theater, written reflections, and fieldwork. MAAP's early recruitment process—consisting of postings in college job-placement offices and word of mouth, an application and an interview—also underwent major refinement. Today, CTWO offers a three-day basics-of-organizing training in cities across the country, hosted by local community organizations. These trainings expose potential interns to the range of activities the program will require of them, including recruitment and political analysis. The participants include not just applicants but emerging leaders from the community organization involved. The stipend offered for the program is $250 per week. All these changes, notes current MAAP Director Irene Juaniza, have "made the program a lot more attractive to single mothers and people who are just not mobile enough to leave their homes for two months."

Planning for Renewal and Regeneration

The purpose of all this developmental work is to produce leaders who can be active in our organizations for the long haul. Unless leaders are provided with significant resources and support, communities and organizations find themselves in untenable situations because of leader burnout, isolation, founder's syndrome, lack of leadership renewal, and lack of accountability from recognized leaders. Established leaders often suffer severe stress-related health problems as a result of their isolation and lack of ongoing skill development, and emerging leaders often turn away from leadership for fear of "ending up like my executive director."

If those leaders have to step away from the work forever because they are mentally or physically burnt out, our hard work to develop the right programs will have been for naught. Many people feel they cannot let go of organizational roles even for an instant. This feeling comes from a sense of responsibility, but also some fear of being replaced. Organizations have to address issues of rest and burnout to create a standard of rotation and renewal, rather than leaving those decisions solely to the individual.

Part of burnout prevention is establishing organizational habits that encourage people to have a life outside the organization and allow them to integrate their life in some way into that of the organization. For example, young women organizers, knowing that they will have primary responsibility for raising children, constantly ask me whether it will be possible for them to pursue a family life and have an organizing career. One colleague, a brilliant organizer and leader, told me once that she would love to have children but finds our political culture so unfriendly to mothers that she doesn't want to put herself and her children through that. Perhaps out of commitment to the work or perhaps out of a sense that she cannot change the parameters of the work, this woman has decided to forego motherhood. It is hard not to wonder how resentful she might feel later, how that resentment might affect her leadership, and how many other women have already been forced out of organizing because there was no acknowledgment that they work a triple shift. This is obviously a question not just for women but also for men who are committed to performing their fair share of household tasks and child rearing.

Organizations have found many creative ways to reward long-term leaders by integrating a concern for physical and spiritual health into their organizational cultures and policies. Some groups provide sabbaticals for their long-term staff people; other organizations build altars by having participants place meaningful objects on a table as they introduce themselves to a new group, or the organizations conduct rituals by adding some formality to the beginnings and endings of their gatherings; and others try simply to provide working conditions that approximate the standards for which we fight in the larger economy.

Illustration: CTWO Has Innovative Vacation and Sabbatical Policies

CTWO has two innovative time policies. First, although employees have a standard amount of vacation time ranging from one to four weeks, the entire organization closes down for the last two weeks of the year, a beloved tradition since the organization's early days. During those two weeks, a few people are assigned to check for urgent messages, which they pass on to the appropriate person. Executive Director Mark Toney says, "Not very much happens in those two weeks in any organization, and people who are working are distracted by holiday pressure. In this setup, people get to enjoy the holidays." Second, CTWO was one of the first organizations to institute a sabbatical policy for its staff members, who can take three months of paid leave after serving five years and making an additional one-year commitment; after that year they can take another two months.

Illustration: REJN Establishes a Wellness Team

REJN was forced to consider questions of rest and renewal because "we had a lot of injured workers and had to pay attention to how we meet—ample breaks and comfortable chairs. Tackling the ravages of oppression and internalized racism had us searching for intentional healing practices," says Wise. REJN eventually began to pull resource people in to help. Wise hired a massage therapist to come to major strategy sessions and provide brief shoulder massages. She invited a First Nations Canadian healer, who conducted native women's healing circles, to lead the group through a ritual engaging the physical elements of earth, fire, water, and air "in a way that was very intentional and grounded in her spirituality and culture," according to Wise. These experiences led Wise to organize a wellness team composed of people from various traditions; they lead Native American rituals, African drumming and dance, meditation, and Christian and nondenominational prayers. Wise says these activities manifest "the nexus of spirituality and justice," although she acknowledges that all the resource people she has brought in have not understood the connection. When they do, however, all members benefit from someone "articulating in plain language what it mean[s] to be able to take some time to allow yourself to relax and reflect; what the connection is between mind, body, and spirit; and how that affects practical things in the organization." Wise recalls that "it all came together perfectly when the wellness team developed a process of beginning the day with drumming, smudging [burning sage to anoint spaces and people with the smoke], deep breathing, [and] ending with self-massage and sometimes storytelling. That became our opening ritual. We did closing rituals as well. People said, 'Man, I feel healed.'" "Organizing for justice," she asserts, "is spiritual practice. It is about creating right relations and unleashing creative potential that renders life more whole for all."

Conclusion

Leadership development is not just a sideline to the real work of organizing, but rather a critical element in generating the human energy that builds strong progressive organizations. A commitment to leadership development involves replacing status quo definitions of leadership as individual talent with the notion of group accountability. In order to regenerate leadership, established leaders must see the encouragement and training of new leaders as one of their central responsibilities, and they must add teaching and mentoring to their own sets of organizing skills.

Organizations will face different challenges in implementing strong leadership development programs. Ironically, although foundations are often attracted to our leaders, they aren't equally attracted to funding the programs that support those leaders. As funding for community organizing goes through cycles, foundation expectations will sometimes push groups to deliver campaigns and victories rather than new leaders. In addition, the U.S. culture of individual leadership often runs counter to the qualities we need in organizational leaders, and negotiating those expectations in a multicultural, mixed-gender, cross-class context can put a lot of pressure on organizations.

If your organizations want to do more in leadership development, a good place to start is by thinking through the skills and experiences the organization needs from its leaders at various stages. If your leadership is too small or is stuck in other ways, you might need to consider structural issues—for example, how to combine fieldwork and leadership development or how to formalize activities. If you already have formal programs, consider evaluating them from the perspectives of participants as well as other parties, such as allies and new members.

Many community and labor organizations use intermediary training organizations to expose their staff and members to new skills and to stretch their boundaries politically and intellectually. Using an intermediary is often the most practical option for a group with limited resources, but it doesn't replace local capacity. There is a cost to overreliance on intermediaries, who are one step removed from the daily realities of an organization. Wise acknowledges that, as an intermediary, "in creating a specialized setting, we sometimes create a false space in following principles together that people do not pursue at home. There is a cost when people can't repeat these settings when they got home."

Challenges aside, leadership development is one of the most rewarding aspects of organizing. Everyone of us has something important to teach, and there's nothing like watching a great leader model effective action and inspire others to take it.

CHAPTER SIX

TAKE BACK THE FACTS

While political organizations have always done research, technological developments and the growth of conservative intellectual capacity have raised the bar significantly. Community organizations should increase their research capacity for three major reasons. First, we have to have information in order to develop solid issues and validate our constituency's instincts and experiences. For effective organizations, research is critical to their issue choices. Second, we need research to counteract the opposition's misinformation campaigns. We have to be able to respond, intellectually and pragmatically, especially when the "facts" that our opponents put out about our constituencies fly in the face of reality. Because social-justice research is often attacked as biased while conservative research is not, it is important that our research be systematic enough to allow us to describe and defend our methodology and data. Third, we can use research to generate press.

Although I know that some researchers will take me to task about this, I assert that, in politics, all research is led by ideology. I participated in a telephone poll in spring 2002. Pressing buttons to respond to conversational recorded questions, I rated the performance of President George W. Bush, confessed to unfavorable feelings about Bush, Tom Daschle, and Trent Lott, and commented on the likelihood of victory in the war on terrorism. My suspicion that I was participating in a conservative poll was confirmed during the spate of questions on immigration. Should people from Canada be able to immigrate to the United States permanently if they want to? Okay. How about people from Mexico? Fine. How about people from Israel? Fine. Should people from "Ay-rab" countries be able to immigrate permanently if they want to? Of course, I said that even "Ay-rabs" should be able to immigrate. But I had no hope of influencing the poll results. This experience reinforced my most cynical ideas about the "objectivity" of research. Clearly the questions asked, and how they were posed, would influence the answers of most respondents and skew the results.

No matter who conducts the research, it can be manipulated for ideological ends. This reality was driven home to me when I read a research report on welfare by the American Enterprise Institute. In it, the authors review all kinds of progressive and liberal research showing that welfare reform pushes people further into poverty, that the number of people on the rolls who have deep-seated problems—people such as substance abusers and victims of domestic violence—has not been reduced, and that who gets benefits is racially determined. On the basis of this research, conducted by our side, the authors conclude that, indeed, welfare reform has not worked as predicted; their solution is to dismantle the programs completely.

Understanding how research is used to advance political ideologies does not mean that we can't be vigorous and accurate or that we can't provide alternative explanations when the "facts" contradict what we believe or what would be helpful for our campaigns. It just means that we need to approach all research with a healthy skepticism, knowing that the ideology of the researcher and of the messenger can influence the results and how they are spun. If we want to control the information that influences public opinion, we have to be able to produce our own research and supervise how it is used.

Organizers and activists are often intimidated by the prospect of having to conduct or digest research. We believe that we have to have Ph.D.'s to claim the validity of the data we generate, and we have fallen asleep trying to pinpoint the relevance of archaically written research reports. While undoubtedly credentials help in many arenas and our own analysis has to withstand scrutiny, we have far more resources available to us than we might think, starting with our own members and expanding to include universities and research organizations. Research can be an exciting part of the organizing process.

In this chapter I discuss how to develop research capacity by integrating research into an organizing plan, emphasizing human sources, and deciding whether to conduct the research in-house or through a partnership. The illustration from Direct Action for Rights and Equity (DARE) shows how members can be involved in research projects and how useful human sources are in researching policy proposals. The illustrations from the Center for the Child Care Workforce and the Center for Third World Organizing (CTWO) explain how research can help in outreach efforts and in issue development. The illustration from Wider

Opportunities for Women (WOW) emphasizes the importance of an organization's producing its own credible research, and that from 9to5 indicates how it used research to reframe policy debates. The illustration from Working Partnerships delineates the benefits an organization can gain from doing its own research. The illustration from the Women's Association for Women's Alternatives (W.A.W.A.) shows how an organization can develop tools for applying research data.

Principles

There are three basic principles for conducting research for organizing purposes. First, consider the ways in which you can combine your research with outreach and issues development. Second, use human sources rather than paper as much as possible. Third, figure out whether you are better off doing your research internally or creating a partnership with another organization.

Integrate Research with Outreach and Issue Development

Integration of functions allows us to involve members in designing and implementing research plans. When we go out to survey teenagers about their recreation and job needs, or welfare applicants about their experiences, we can get names and phone numbers and go back to those people to recruit them for our campaign. They, in turn, can conduct surveys with other people. When we combine research and outreach, the conversation has to further the goals of each. The research part surfaces information, and the recruitment part moves commitment.

There are always dozens of contributions members can make to research projects, regardless of their level of experience. They can generate research questions and prioritize them, track newspaper coverage, read books, do Internet searches, interview experts, and make presentations to campaign committees. Members can also help negotiate research contracts with other organizations and individuals, and experienced members can supervise new researchers. Often, members are the best source of inside information—for example, in uncovering unwritten policies in a workplace or locating the owner of a sweatshop. Develop a timeline, and hold people accountable for their research tasks. Over time, you may want to have trainings for your folks in order to develop your internal capacity, at least so they can understand research reports if not produce them. One organization held trainings on how to read census data and how to do investigative journalism. Everyone in the organization won't be doing those things, but they all now have a sense of the questions to ask and the resources to consider.

Illustration: DARE Involves Members in Research

DARE developed its living wage proposal through a collective process that helped build members' ownership of the campaign. In order to calculate a fair hourly wage, members spent several months keeping track of their own expenses and conducting surveys with relatives, neighbors, and friends to identify "what it really costs to live" in Providence, according to Jobs with Dignity leader Jeannie Russell. "We asked people to include their monthly expenses for food, personal items, child care, clothing, transportation, health care, all the basics. We asked people for the low number, which is what they actually spend, and a high number, which is what it really costs. We know that people find a lot of different ways to subsidize what things really cost." When the survey results were tabulated, DARE members came up with a living wage figure of $16.58 per hour. In search of a figure close to that number that was defensible by some officially recognized standard, further research surfaced a rate of $19.30 per hour, 200 percent above the official poverty line. When confronted with resistance to such a high figure from allies, campaign leaders settled on a compromise figure of $12.30 per hour.

Illustration: Research from the Center for the Child Care Workforce Moves a New Constituency

Critical research reports from the Center for the Child Care Workforce broadened the child care debate from a narrow focus on private consumer access to a broader focus that included child care workers. The Center forged a link between the quality of child care services and the quality of child care jobs; it showed that the wages and working conditions of staff were directly related to children's experiences in care. In the process, the Center encouraged more child care workers to become involved in advocacy. The lack of public funding that could ensure good wages along with access has created miserable and isolating conditions for the workforce. Low wages, the lack of benefits, and the lack of respect drive much of the workforce to abandon the field if they have other options. Although child care teachers and providers are likely to be better educated than the average for the rest of the labor force, those with a bachelor's degree and several years of experience earned on average only $8.94 per hour in 2000; "fewer than 1% of the professional occupations, among which kindergarten teachers are classified, earn an average wage of less than $8.50 per hour, and 59% of professional workers earn a mean wage above $19.25 per hour. Child care workers are classified as service workers, the lowest-paid division, in which nearly 44 percent of workers earn less than $8.50 per hour" (Center for the Child Care Workforce, 2000, p. 17).

The notion that providers should be selfless nurturers permeates the thinking not just of outsiders but of workers themselves. The social self-effacement that is supposed to accompany child rearing, along with the fact that most teachers and providers have close contact with their bosses and clients, prevents many providers from running the gauntlet. Training Director Rosemarie Vardell explains: "Our field is about caregiving and nurturing and sacrifice. Imagining that we would do something that would make parents feel uncomfortable when we're there to serve parents, something that could be construed as not good for kids, makes it difficult for people to think about strategies and tactics that they can use" to improve their wages and working conditions.

The Center's research has raised the visibility of the workforce, educated providers about their conditions, and bolstered organizing efforts among workers. The Center's research on turnover proved particularly important in persuading workers themselves about the need to fight for higher wages. Marci Whitebook notes that "the only way we were going to activate some workers was by showing the effects on the kids." In 1990, the Center's National Child Care Staffing Study documented an annual turnover rate of more than 30 percent. Almost one-third of the field's workers are leaving it each year, to be replaced by a new crop of poor and working women (who often have less training) at the same, or even lower, wage rates. In some parts of the country, turnover rates exceed 50 percent. Turnover is a tremendous drain on the industry, which has to spend time and money finding, training, and integrating a huge new pool of people each year, without the support of experienced teachers. Turnover also has a negative effect on children, who require stability and routine to thrive.

The Center's list of model work standards (Center for the Child Care Workforce, 1999) supports self-organization and consciousness raising among workers. A group of workers can assess their work situation against the list of characteristics under each category and identify priority changes to fight for or to establish. Stars are placed next to characteristics considered essential for an effective child care workplace. The standards themselves provide an organizing tool, as all standards can't be met through individual action alone: sometimes workers have to apply pressure that loosens up resources from state and local governments as well as businesses.

Child care workers supplied the empirical evidence for much of the Center's groundbreaking research. The model work standards were developed by small groups of child care workers and center directors, recruited through the Worthy Wage structure and in other ways, who answered two questions: "What is a high-quality work environment? What needs to be changed to improve your job and your capacity to be a good teacher?"

Keep in mind that integrating new data into your organizing or advocacy work may require developing tools that help people apply the data or analysis.

Illustration: W.A.W.A. Develops Tools for Using Research Results

The Self-Sufficiency Standard was developed by an economics scholar and is extremely rigorous in its research methodology. Yet W.A.W.A. has developed simple, user-friendly tools for service providers who employ the standard when working with clients and institutions in Pennsylvania. In Pittsburgh, the standard has been used to determine water and sewage rates. Eastern College has used the standard to lobby for raising the wages of campus housekeepers. Susquehanna County has used it to determine whether a low-income family can pay back school loans or they should be forgiven. The Pennsylvania Department of Public Welfare increased economic support policies based on information from the standard. Through the state's Community Action agencies and others, W.A.W.A. has trained hundreds of people on the standard, a process that proved invaluable in expanding the project into rural Pennsylvania. Carol Goertzel, executive director of W.A.W.A., says that Community Action agencies are often "the only antipoverty network in [a] rural area. We were so urban until we took on this project, we would not have known what we were doing."

Patty McClone, Gwen Robinson, and other staff provide family advocacy through several elementary schools in West Philadelphia. They use the Self-Sufficiency Standard to counsel clients trying to get off welfare. McClone and Robinson have found the standard a valuable tool in helping clients think through their job training and work options. W.A.W.A. has developed a budget worksheet that the family advocates use to help clients evaluate their options, including those being pushed by caseworkers. McClone says, "It makes me so mad to see people in training for dead-end jobs that they couldn't possibly survive on." While she recognizes that developing new jobs in a comprehensive economic-development plan is beyond the scope of her work, having clients use the standard as a measuring stick gives them a bit more self-confidence to challenge their caseworkers about their placements.

The use of the standard has led to an innovative model of public-benefits advocacy and "packaging" to assist families on their paths to self-sufficiency. W.A.W.A. has also developed a benefits tool, the "Human Resources Packet," which case managers and counselors can use to help low-income families access public benefits and services.

To use research to work on issues, we have to know where we are in the issue-development process before starting the research. Are we choosing an issue, reframing it, or developing a campaign plan? Choosing an issue requires a research process that determines what the constituency cares about, whether a solution is available, and whether we can craft an issue that meets our criteria. Reframing an issue requires detailed data, sometimes stories but often hard numbers, that dispute or discredit information put out by the other side. Developing a campaign plan requires tactical research—gathering specific information about targets and potential pitfalls embedded in our demands. (To get an idea of how you can use research to identify and develop a profile of targets/decision makers, complete Exercise 6.1.)

Research for issue development raises lots of questions about ethics and accuracy. What if you uncover information that is unflattering to your constituency?

Exercise 6.1. Target-Research Worksheet.

What power does the decision maker have to meet your goals/demands? By what authority?

What is the decision maker's background and history?

What is the decision maker's position on your issue/goal? How did this position develop?

What is the decision maker's self-interest?

What is the decision maker's history on the issue?

Who is the decision maker's boss?

What/who is the decision maker's base of support?

Who are the decision maker's individual allies?

Who are the decision maker's opponents/enemies?

What other social forces influence the decision maker?

Reprinted with permission from the Environmental and Economic Justice Project.

For example, progressive researchers once discovered that most welfare recipients supplement their welfare checks with undeclared income, a practice that counts as welfare fraud. In another example, analysis of the 2000 National Election Study results by the National Gay and Lesbian Task Force revealed that Americans support gay rights in unprecedented numbers, except for the right to marry. Organizations often decide not to release such information, but that option brings the potential for being outed by our opposition. I advocate putting out the research and interpreting it ourselves for opinion leaders, decision makers, and our own constituencies. Far better we explain it before the other side does. In the case of the welfare-fraud study, researchers explained that benefit levels were so low that women had to supplement their welfare checks in order to meet basic food, housing, and health needs, not to buy Cadillacs. In the case of gay marriage, it turned out that the majority of Americans supported the rights associated with marriage, such as expanded workplace benefits, the right to visit a partner during emergencies, and a tax break, so their resistance was largely to the religious symbolism of marriage.

Illustration: CTWO Combines Research with Direct Actions to Develop Police-Accountability Issues

Prior to launching the Campaign for Community Safety and Police Accountability, five organizations throughout the country committed to conducting a series of participatory research projects and a standard set of discussions to develop a definition of responsive policing. Craving action through this long phase of research, organizers came up with the idea of conducting direct actions using the Freedom of Information Act (FOIA). Most states require documents such as legislative debate records, public contracts, legal decisions, and more to be turned over to the public on written request. Typically, institutions have ten days to respond to such requests, either with the information or a clear timeline for providing it or with clear reasons for not providing it. Small groups of members at each organization wrote letters requesting their police department records, such as the number of misconduct complaints that had been filed and the policies governing the use of force. Rather than being delivered by anonymous postal workers, the requests were hand delivered by the group, who demanded a signature from the chief of police as proof of delivery and conducted follow-up actions. Gwen Hardy, a long-time leader of People United for a Better Oakland, recalls that "these FOIA actions were great for us. People did it all over the country, so we had the same experience, and it showed us how much the police departments hide from us all the time. It made us mad and more confident!" The results of these and other research tactics were discussed in local and then national settings and eventually fed into a platform of demands on which local groups could take action.

Illustration: 9to5 Reframes the Relationship Between Temp Agencies and Welfare

When 9to5 decided to take on welfare reform and contingent work as priority projects, the Milwaukee chapter conducted a groundbreaking study testing the link between welfare reform and the growth of temp agencies. Temp work is one of the fastest growing forms of contingency work; it constitutes 25 percent of all new jobs created since 1984 (Cook, 2000). Temps make up 3 percent of the overall labor force, more if we account for the turnover in temping. Employment in the temp industry rose from a quarter of a million workers employed daily in 1973 to three million by 1997 (Campaign on Contingent Work, 2000, pp. 8–9). 9to5 has a particular interest in temp work because over half of all temps are women. Clerical workers comprise 45 percent of temps, the single largest portion, and the top three temp jobs for women are secretaries, data-entry workers, and assemblers (Economic Policy Institute, 1997). Temporary workers are contracted by agencies. In 1999, forty-four thousand temps out of seven hundred thousand workers in Milwaukee, 9to5's national home, were employed by more than eighty agencies (9to5, 2000).

Temp agencies have also played a major role in implementing welfare reform. Of the Temporary Assistance for Needy Families (TANF) population 42 percent used temp agencies during the first year of the implementation of Wisconsin Works. In the first quarter of 1997, 30 percent of TANF single parents hired were employed by temp agencies. Of the new hires employed by temp agencies, 45–55 percent failed to post even $500 in total wages that quarter (Campaign on Contingent Work, 1999). The welfare-to-work tax credit provides a one-time incentive to encourage employers to hire recipients. To get the credit, temp agencies have to contract someone who has been on assistance for at least eighteen months prior to being hired or who has been cut off benefits because of time limits; assign that person to at least 180 days part-time or 400 hours full-time to get the first $2,400 of a possible $3,500; and get certification that the worker qualifies from the Department of Workforce Development Work Opportunity Tax Credit Office.

Designing a testing project to connect abuses in the temp industry to evaluations of welfare reform allowed 9to5 to find new opportunities to educate workers and recipients, apply existing legal standards, and initiate a public debate about the role of temp agencies in employing former recipients. Linda Garcia-Barnard, a former teen mom and current law student who utilized welfare and 9to5 to escape an abusive relationship, oversaw the testing project. Requiring more than a year and a half of preparation and research, the test surfaced illegal and unfair practices at two-thirds of the twenty-five agencies tested. Garcia-Barnard recruited and trained testers, developed a methodology, and worked with agencies like the Equal Employment Opportunity Commission (EEOC) to design solutions.

Garcia-Barnard built the testing project through focus groups with welfare-to-work participants and other temp workers. For the initial testing round, Garcia-Barnard sent two pairs, each consisting of one African American woman and one white woman, to apply for unskilled, entry-level industrial work. Although each tester had or was about to get a college degree and had no children, one member of each team presented herself as a welfare recipient and said she had her high school diploma. The other stated she had her General Education Diploma and did not claim to be a welfare recipient. All included children as part of their constructed résumés and referred to child care issues as the reason for gaps in employment. The pairs applied and were interviewed the same or the following day, usually within minutes of each other. The control group (those not claiming to be welfare recipients) always applied first, and all the testers audiotaped their visits (Wisconsin is a one-party consent state) and wrote detailed reports.

The results were dramatic. 9to5 found race, sex, pregnancy, marriage, age, and disability discrimination in clear violation of federal law. Many demanded that applicants take any job, no matter the wage or the location. Most had partnerships with check-cashing establishments where their workers had to pay fees to cash their checks, and others required workers to consent to investigations of their personal lives. Testing surfaced illegal questions about marital status, which violated Wisconsin's fair-employment law, and questions about health status before a job offer, which violated the Americans with Disabilities Act.

To give some examples:

- Company A offered employment to all the white applicants at the time of the application and then again during follow-up. The black testers, who applied the same day, were told that nothing was available and that they would be called when a job came in. A pair called the agency within minutes of each other five days after the initial application process. The white woman was offered an assignment at $7.60 per hour; the black woman, who called first, was told nothing was available.
- Company D told one tester that the "higher paying jobs are for men only." The interviewer then asked another staff person, "Do you have anything available, but for women?"
- Company H told the white tester "she didn't look like factory material" and " looked like she belonged in an office setting." They offered her a position as a dietary aide at $8.50 per hour and a second position doing clerical work for the same pay. When she indicated that she could not type, the interviewer responded, "That's OK, you can learn as you go." The black applicant was told nothing was available.

To make the findings stick the EEOC encouraged 9to5 to conduct another round of testing, using actual applicants, because testers may have no legal standing. Garcia-Barnard recruited new teams at entry-level job fairs funded by welfare-to-work agencies. When Garcia-Barnard had her teams together, she focused on the ten agencies with the most flagrant race violations in the first round and found that six of them repeated those violations.

The testing project helped 9to5 to reframe the relationship between welfare leavers and temp agencies, a frame they used to good advantage. First, 9to5 integrated the testing project with ongoing efforts to file complaints with the EEOC, got temp agencies to adhere to a code of conduct, trained agencies in antidiscrimination regulations, and launched a campaign to increase public scrutiny of temp agencies with welfare contracts.

9to5 also used the report to challenge the substantial welfare contracts of two temp agencies, Maximus and Employment Solutions. Maximus had been exposed for misspending $400,000 of public funds on parties and perks for agency staff. Although an internal legislative audit concluded that this figure was a bookkeeping error, Maximus has also been hit with three EEOC complaints on discriminatory pay rates for women. 9to5 further argued that Maximus and other temp agencies had not fulfilled their contract to work with community groups in placing former welfare recipients.

Third, the group worked with State Senator Gwen Moore to try to get the state attorney general to investigate the agencies and their welfare-to-work contracts. Although they were not successful, the effort bolstered 9to5's relationship with Moore and gave the group a legislative toe-hold. The attempt to have the attorney general investigate the discrimination was diverted because the attorney general lacked civil rights enforcement authority. When the Department of Workforce Development, which administers welfare contracts, was charged to investigate, it declined.

Fourth, despite these setbacks, 9to5's protests made welfare contracts somewhat less attractive as a cash cow for agencies and resulted in the establishment of a citizens' advisory council. When the nonprofit Employment Solutions decided not to renew its contract for two regions of the state after it was also fined for financial improprieties, the state was deterred by public outcry from awarding those two regional contracts to Maximus. 9to5 continues to work with Moore to argue that the unequal pay Maximus gave to women affects all welfare-to-work participants as a group.

Using People as Primary Sources

The best way to use research to generate analyses of policy and of the power structure is to talk to people. It is important to talk to people on all sides, especially when we are researching a new issue. Remember that there may be more than two sides and try to understand where they all fit in the bigger picture. Reporters are great sources; they amass a lot of information about particular topics—city politics, for example. It's often especially easy to talk to those who work for the ethnic or alternative press or those in smaller cities and towns. Although the Internet is a good way to gather background data on targets, and it is conceivably available in the middle of the night, going to human sources offers greater advantages. We can ask a human being to translate her own jargon into language that makes sense to us. In addition, we begin to build relationships with potential allies and supporters or to identify those who are likely to compete with or oppose our group.

Illustration: DARE Talks to an Attorney to Design a Policy Demand

To develop policy language for the Providence living wage proposal that would prevent discrimination against ex-prisoners, DARE tracked down an attorney in Pennsylvania who reported that a new Pennsylvania law prohibited consideration of a record unless there was a justified business necessity, such as the seriousness of the offense, or a relationship between the offense and the kind of job being filled. Long-time DARE leader Dale Jackson, someone who knows firsthand the difficulties of finding work after serving time, notes that this "was really hard to create because [until we spoke with the attorney,] we couldn't find any other ordinance that had anything like it."

Sometimes getting people to agree to talk to you can be tricky. It's important not to assume that people do not want to talk to you—for example, if you are an immigrant-rights organization going to visit the conservative Federation for American Immigration Reform. You can use subterfuge—for example, claim that you are a student working on a paper—but persistence will generally get you further than a new identity. If you do pretend to be an unaligned student, don't leave the organization's phone number for a call-back. If you are a frequent spokesperson or a staff person for the organization, you are likely to show up in an Internet search yourself, so don't lie about your identity.

Deciding Whether to Do Research Internally or Through a Partnership

Most organizations need a combination of internal capacity and external partnerships to get all their research needs met. Start with as much clarity about your research requirements as possible. Do you need on-the-spot research that can be done quickly to feed into campaigns? Do you need an occasional analysis of the power structure? Do you have a regular need to have government data analyzed for their implications? In what form do you then need the research produced—a simple report to your organization or a fancy report with pictures for the press? Consider what you might get out of a research process besides the data themselves. Is there a potential outreach, media, or alliance benefit? Think about how difficult or time-consuming the data gathering and analysis are likely to be. Do you have the ability to analyze lots of numbers, such as those in the state budget? Is finding the data a matter of reading lots of academic reports? Would the imprimatur of a Ph.D. make a huge difference in how the data are perceived by key audiences? If benefits can be gained from matching research closely to your organization's image of itself, then it might make sense to invest in doing the research internally. For example, if your grassroots organization wants to prove that its solutions are well-informed, you may want to collaborate with a scholar or even hire a Ph.D. to be the internal research director. But if the costs outweigh the benefits, you might want to recruit a partner.

Illustration: WOW Supports the Research for the Self-Sufficiency Standard

As a result of new research, WOW was able to initiate one of the most successful interventions in the debate on jobs and welfare. WOW had to establish a relationship with a credible researcher who understood the political implications of the project. It challenged Diana Pearce, Ph.D., at the time director of the Women and Poverty Project at WOW and author of a 1978 article that coined the term *feminization of poverty,* to develop a new wage standard to measure the effectiveness of Job Training and Placement Agency (JTPA) programs. Eventually, Pearce decided to return to academia specifically to be able to have university credentials to back up the standard; she is currently a faculty member at the University of Washington. In her earlier research, Pearce had found that the federal government allowed JTPA to set lower wage standards for women and for men of color on the premise that these groups earn lower median wages. The lower wage standard provided incentives for JTPA programs to serve these marginalized constituencies but created a low-wage sex and race ghetto within JTPA. Cindy Marano, former WOW director and senior organizer on self-sufficiency, affirms that "we were just going crazy about the fact that all of this training money was being used to train people for nonexistent jobs or jobs that paid people at the very bottom of the wage scale."

Pearce formulated the Self-Sufficiency Standard—the income necessary to meet basic needs—which became the cornerstone of WOW's family self-sufficiency program and state-level organizing strategy. Although WOW started out addressing local JTPA programs, it soon became clear that the organization faced a significant obstacle in the widespread use of the federal poverty line as a national standard. Many public-assistance programs, such as the Child Health Insurance Program and food stamps, as well cash assistance programs, use the federal poverty line as their base. The federal poverty line was devised by using family spending on food as the basis for other expenses, which were determined according to an assumed fixed ratio to food costs. Pearce says, "The poverty line is not accurate and has nothing to do with cost of living."

The Self-Sufficiency Standard differs from the poverty line significantly. First, rather than assuming replicable costs nationwide and that the average family composition includes a working father, a stay-at-home mother, and two children, the new standard is geographically based and adjusted for different family types. Second, it does not attempt to set a national figure, although WOW does embrace the goal of getting the standard into national use. Third, Jennifer Brooks, director of self-sufficiency projects and programs at WOW, says the standard provides a "unique methodology, with more precise measures than others." Pearce attributes the great reception that the standard has received to its grounding in reality: "We always started from the ground up; we didn't just take a traditional approach and tweak it."

The standard is developed at the county level to measure the cost of living, including transportation, housing, and child care; it uses actual costs as opposed to what people are accustomed to spending. Brooks notes that, "by including what child care actually costs, versus what people spend, we're saying something that's really radical. What people spend is controlled by their decision to spend or not to spend. In going by what quality child care costs, we are pointing to what people really deserve." The standard recognizes, for example, that children raise family expenses according to their age: a young child needs child care for more hours than does an older child who is in school. And, in contrast to the general assumption that rural areas are less expensive places to live than urban areas, measuring county by county often revealed that "rural resort towns are actually very expensive places to live," says Brooks.

WOW is now pushing to produce it for as many states as possible before "states decide to do it themselves," according to Pearce. Although she sees no problem with a state managing the updating process, she does believe that government motivations can undermine a standard's accuracy at the beginning. She says, "The state . . . has a strong interest in the standard being much lower than it should be. The lower the bar, the easier to get to success, whether it's wages they pay their own workers or what welfare leavers make." Pearce notes, "In a couple of states, people brought me in after they had done their own versions. They can get pretty close, but then it gets trashed [because of credibility problems]." Pearce's reports are academic, with twenty pages of text, two pages of footnotes, and "virtually no advocacy." In part, the greater the credibility of each report, the less likely that the idea will be taken up inadequately by a state government.

It isn't realistic to think that every community organization or small workers' center will be able to generate all the research it needs with only internal resources. These organizations have to find research partners that can generate and package information. There are several ways to go about this search. You can review reports produced by state, national, and regional think tanks, such as the Joint Center on Policy, the Urban Institute, and the Center for Policy Alternatives. Many of these, as well as academic research institutions, produce research for government agencies, and you can locate them by going to the agency websites and searching for research or evaluation. In some states, fiscal-analysis groups break down state budget proposals and the effects of budget decisions. While such organizations produce some useful reports, be prepared not to be able to influence their research agendas.

There are also research organizations willing to customize research for movement needs. The Data Center in Oakland, California, provides background research on corporations and public officials for a small fee. CTWO and the Northwest Federation of Community Organizations use the Applied Research Center for their race-based research needs. Santa Monicans Allied for Responsible Tourism hired the polling firm Lake, Snell and Perry to poll Santa Monica residents about living wage issues; the results greatly influenced their campaign. Universities often provide helpful resources for your research needs, as college professors seek fieldwork for their sociology, public health, and social work students. If there isn't a research outfit near you, consider getting together with some other organizations to start one.

When planning a research program, it is a good idea to decide first which questions you need answered, then what kind of research format will best answer those questions, and finally who will do the research. Exhibit 6.1 is a research worksheet; it poses these questions and others to guide an organization in planning. It is filled out by a community organization that wants to determine whether and why the welfare department is diverting applicants. After reviewing the exhibit, use Exercise 6.2 to start outlining your organization's approach to research.

Illustration: Working Partnerships Reframes with Internal Capacity

Working Partnerships has built a six-person research team that surfaces groundbreaking information on economic development for the community-labor coalition in San Jose and the Silicon Valley. Amy Dean, executive director, believes that Working Partnerships needed to build substantial research capacity to meet the challenges of a new economy. Research Director Bob Brownstein affirms that research has helped the alliance to understand the structure of the new economy and to develop policy initiatives. Dean credits research capacity with allowing Working Partnerships to "break the ideological hold of business in the Silicon Valley and debunk the Silicon Valley daily millionaire myth."

A prime example is the research that preceded the 1998 living wage campaign. Before initiating the campaign, Working Partnerships produced two key reports debunking the myth and introducing the concept of a living wage. *Growing Together or Drifting Apart?* (Working Partnerships, 1998a) highlighted the gap in wealth and income and tracked that gap by race, age, and sex. The living wage report (Working Partnerships, 1998b) addressed comprehensively all the questions related to living wage. Brownstein says those reports helped the ensuing campaign "put the issue of the working poor on the regional economic agenda, where it had never been . . . before that." Living wage has opened the discussion of a whole subset of issues that "make life feasible for the working poor, and now that's on the agenda too. It's not going back in the closet." Opponents of progressive wage and tax policy now have to argue over methods and means for dealing with the problems of low-wage work, as the existence of the gap itself is no longer debatable.

Accurate data also proved strategic during the campaign itself, which started without the necessary votes on the city council. The city council was split three ways—one group supported the ordinance on principle, another wanted proof, and a third was philosophically opposed to it. The vote was 8–3, so "we won over the group in the

Exhibit 6.1. Sample Research Worksheet.

Question	Source	Research Format	Who Will Do It	Training Required	Additional Benefits	Goals/ Timeline
Is the welfare department diverting potential applicants?	Applicants	Survey	Welfare Rights Committee designs and conducts survey	Elements of a good survey? How to conduct a survey	Names and numbers for outreach	200 surveys by June 15
On what grounds are applicants denied?	Caseworker	Interview caseworkers	Interns	How to conduct an interview	Potential allies	15 caseworkers by June 30
What are the legal grounds for denial?	Administrators	Interviews Legal materials	Welfare Rights Committee conducts FOIA action on director of social services, does follow up	How to conduct an interview What is FOIA?	Demystify officials	Interviews by June 30 FOIA action by July 15
What are the legal grounds for denial?	Welfare advo- cacy groups	Materials search Interviews	Two committee members conduct Internet search Committee chair plus emerging leader interview welfare advocate	How to search the web How to conduct an interview	Potential allies	Web search by June 30 5 advocates by June 30

Source: Adapted with permission from the Environmental and Economic Justice Project.

Exercise 6.2. Research Worksheet.

Question	Source	Research Format	Who Will Do It	Training Required	Additional Benefits	Goals/ Timeline

Source: Adapted with permission from the Environmental and Economic Justice Project.

middle, partly through the thoroughness of our research. That wouldn't have helped with the third group, 'cause they're not influenced by proof," says Brownstein. Dean says that, for San Jose activists, "living wage was the perfect issue for marrying the folks doing the heavy lifting and those doing the heavy thinking. It taught us how to be strategic about language and communication. It's about incorporating research and technical information into our work, so we're not just morally right."

Working Partnerships is now proposing expansions of the living wage based on new research. Brownstein plans to review all the theoretical arguments used by the opposition in 1998 and test them against the results. He is clearly confident that the facts belie the myths. He says, "They said, 'business will flee San Jose,' but enormous numbers of new businesses were created. There was a historic high in commercial construction." Working Partnerships will propose closing loopholes and adding new categories of coverage, such as city partnerships with private firms and city redevelopment programs. And it will also try to connect new research to the need for policies that supplement living wage: child care, health care, affordable housing.

Working Partnerships also relies on research to identify windows of opportunity. Brownstein spends a lot of his time meeting with activist groups to talk about their needs; he calls this a process of "heuristic thinking about what we should do research on." Mostly, he says, organizers want to know how research can surface solutions to the most intransigent problems. He offers the example of the poor person's search for affordable, quality health care. In that case, Working Partnerships research revealed a funding handle that would allow the county to provide health insurance for every child: tobacco-settlement money. That campaign led to a new policy that made seventy thousand children eligible, with thirty thousand signed up in the first fifteen months. Brownstein says proudly, "Santa Clara is now the first county in the nation to insure all its children"; but, he warns, "you can't just do wishful thinking, you have to do analytic work."

The decision of Working Partnerships to internalize research—what Brownstein calls the capacity to join research, policy analysis geared toward feasible implementation, and organizing and advocacy—has some clear benefits. He says that, without that tight linkage, "there's the possibility of researchers not looking at the things that people on the organizing cutting edge need looked at. . . . Our research model has a connection to [a] real constituency and understands the relationship of the research to the power dynamic."

Conclusion

The case studies in this chapter showed how conducting our own research significantly strengthens our ability to shift the terms of debate and advance our campaigns. Research plays a critical role both internally and externally. Internally, research can help us understand our constituency and develop our issues. Externally, it can help convince policymakers and potential allies that we are correct, and it can force opponents to respond to our frames. Although not everyone will be influenced by accurate research, without it we are at the mercy of conservative think tanks. We have the potential to get a lot of research done by using resources we already have, starting with our own members. Whether we do it all ourselves or develop partnerships, research will help our groups be more than morally correct.

CHAPTER SEVEN

UNITED WE STAND

Alliances and their looser form, networks, constitute an important part of movement infrastructure. When groups work together, they share the costs of doing business and can take roles that play to their strengths to achieve a productive division of labor. A collaboration can spread one group's expertise, contacts, and reputation to benefit more people. Although these resource considerations are always present, they aren't the most important reason for us to work together. If each organization is like a finger on a hand, only working like a fist will allow us to avoid being smashed by the opposition. No matter how successful any given organization is, we have far more potential to make change together than apart. Working separately, we are more vulnerable to being pitted against each other, especially in the heat of policy negotiations, or to diffusing our power in uncoordinated campaigns and actions.

As exciting as the concept of collaboration is, alliances and networks are difficult to build and maintain. Each problem we might encounter in building an organization can be multiplied when we have to deal with the interests and dysfunction of many groups. Alliances can be slow to act, have bland politics, take the edge off the best organizing, and exploit talent without providing credit. Alliance work can eat up the time of your best staff members and leaders. The bottom line is that collaborative work is worth doing only if it produces more in political action than it takes up in trouble and resources. Applying the key principles of alliance building will help us to decide whether and what form of collaboration we need and then to build it.

In this chapter I discuss the importance of clarifying the purpose of any new collaborative effort, of having each partner in an alliance enter it with a healthy and direct self-interest and compatible politics, of having each partner bring a substantial resource, and of giving the collaborative its own staff and other resources. In illustrations from the Campaign on Contingent Work (CCW), the Southeast Regional Economic Justice Network (REJN), the Workplace Project, the Los Angeles Alliance for a New Economy (LAANE), the Center for Third World Organizing (CTWO), and the North American Alliance for Fair Employment (known by the acronym NAFFE for its previous name, the National Alliance For Fairness in Employment), we can see these principles at work and learn why building an organization specifically to be a network sometimes makes sense, how an exchange network operates, how to work with just a few tactical allies rather than a large coalition, how to build successful community-labor alliances, how to negotiate on race in a network, and how groups that coordinate alliances can contribute resources.

Principles

There are four key principles to remember here. First, a group has to distinguish between different forms of collaboration and choose the one that matches its goals and capacities. Second, each partner in a collaboration has to have substantial self-interest and similar politics, although the need for political negotiation is ongoing. Third, organizations need to bring resources into an alliance or network, and those contributions have to be structured to equalize power and credit among the partners. Fourth, these formations work best when one party is responsible for staffing them; long-term alliances and networks require their own staffing and infrastructure.

Choosing the Appropriate Form of Collaboration

Any collaboration has to meet our needs. To determine whether the collaboration we have in mind does, we should determine the form it will take, identify the purpose of the collaboration, and decide whether we need an alliance at all.

What do we mean by *coalitions, alliances,* and *networks*? People define all these words differently, and often use them interchangeably, but different forms offer different advantages. Two important distinctions stand out: the degree of formality in the relationship and the level of political alignment. Before entering into joint work with another organization, it's important to know whether we are moving to a tactical or strategic relationship. Tactical allies come together for a specific campaign or for a specific amount of time, as in an election campaign. Most of the unusual alliances we see—for example, between workers and a group representing business interests—are tactical in this way. Strategic allies are those groups with whom we share so many similar analyses of situations and so many visions and goals that it makes sense to craft long-term projects. Such allies tend to do their organizational planning together and take on ambitious issues. Often, tactical alliances allow groups to test out potential strategic partners. Whether a collaboration is tactical or strategic then determines the level of ideological unity required.

Coalitions and alliances are the most formal and permanent of these organizational forms—they are organizations of organizations. While individuals might represent organizations in coalitions or alliances, these forms do not typically allow individual membership. Groups might contribute different resources to coalitions, but usually one group has one vote, and whatever majority the group has agreed to carries a decision. When an organization joins an alliance or coalition, that organization's own members or leaders generally have some process for providing input and ultimately voting to support the larger formation's positions and actions. The larger a coalition is, the more organizational self-interest it has to accommodate and the more unwieldy it is likely to be.

Networks are generally looser formations that require fewer sign-offs from their members, which might include organizations and individuals. Networks are often built on a general statement of principles that are basic enough for lots of people to buy into. They also generally don't require members to have the same level of involvement. Some people participate in every campaign, and others pick and choose those that appeal to their politics and fit into their time constraints. Because every decision does not have to be approved by every member, networks often require less of a common analysis of situations than alliances do.

Illustration: CCW Organizes as a Network

When Tim Costello first decided to build an organization for contingent workers, he recalls that "originally a lot of us thought we'd do a membership organization; the funders were really promoting this." But Costello found himself resisting the urge to build a traditional membership organization. His read of the landscape led him to a different conclusion. "In this issue," he says, "we saw that people were in motion all over the place. It was not so important that we create a new thing, it was more important that there are resources for struggle." So Costello built a network of individual activists rather than a formal coalition of organizations or a membership-based organization of contingent workers. Because CCW's constituency, labor and community activists concerned about contingent work, is diverse—by occupation as well as race, gender, and class—the looser network form was required. In some ways, CCW serves the same functions as a membership organization: it provides a gathering place for activism, political education, and mobilization, and it can work in larger coalitions. Quarterly meetings regularly draw seventy people for committee reports and educational sessions. But the network form also allows CCW to act as an intermediary, available to "get called in on anything" and to work with multiple constituencies. Reflecting another difference between organizations and networks, Costello notes that CCW can move quickly, despite the range of views held by its members, because it doesn't require majority votes or consensus in order to lend assistance on a fight as long as the issue meets the basic criteria. If network members like the fight, they participate. If not, they sit out.

Illustration: California Organizations Build a Strategic Alliance

Four California organizations (LAANE, Working Partnerships, the Center for Policy Initiatives, and the Environmental Health Coalition) have developed a strategic alliance to take the excellent work they all do in different parts of the state to a new, more ambitious level. Jessica Goodheart, LAANE research director, notes that the four groups have a lot in common but are different enough so that they can carve out their own niches in the larger alliance. All four have emerged out of the labor movement, have experience building community-labor alliances in their own cities, and have won model policies influencing economic-development decisions and laws locally. These victories consist largely of passing living wage ordinances, unionizing workers, and making it easier to organize. In short, these four organizations are equally powerful in their local contexts, and they share ideology and methods. The four had already been collaborating informally; their first joint activities were organizing and designing policies around local development projects. They are now exploring the possibilities for winning state legislation that would increase their power regionally by providing additional leverage to use in local fights. The first step, says Goodheart, will be to develop a tool that can measure the community benefits of any contract, tax subsidy, or economic-development decision. A potential legislative campaign may grow around getting such a tool adopted by the California state assembly. In spite of their close alignment, Goodheart says the groups face challenges. All are extremely stretched by the demands of their own projects, and they require the funding that will allow them to gather more frequently and develop projects together.

Groups get together in collaborations for three common reasons. The first is to take action; the second is to provide public education; and the third is for exchange, to share best practices. If action is the goal, is your group defining a new agenda or trying to defeat an oppositional agenda? Creating a new agenda

often requires strategic allies, while defeating an opponents' agenda can sometimes (not always) be accomplished with tactical allies. In conducting public education, groups might complement each others' language skills or ability to reach
different audiences. Exchanges between organizations working on similar issues
in different parts of the world are increasingly common. Mostly, groups visit each
other or meet in a central place to compare notes, look at each others' work firsthand, and, as in the next illustration, strengthen their relationships.

Illustration: REJN Sets Up an Exchange Network

Groups participate in the REJN network mainly through annual meetings that last several days. Sessions at REJN's annual meetings follow popular education guidelines, and
they also provide additional time for people to build relationships through informal
exchanges. Executive Director Leah Wise says, "We began to figure out how to make
relationship building a simple part of the meetings." REJN gatherings generally start
with "a good bit of time on introductions so people can find someone to connect with,
then we give them three hours in the middle of each day for one-on-one time, usually after lunch." Building that time into the course of the day, notes Wise, prioritizes
relationships, so that participants don't have to stay up late or get up early to engage
each other. Each gathering is planned by the REJN board, in a process that requires
board members to think as a movement, rather than for their own organization.

An alliance or coalition is no substitute for organizing a constituency and
building a powerful organization. Too often, groups that are frustrated with the
lack of attention paid to an issue in their own community step outside that community and look for support elsewhere. Although alliances, coalitions, and networks are hard to build and sustain, often we find it easier to recruit support from
the staff and leaders of another organization who don't need to be convinced of the
issue's importance than to struggle with individuals in our own communities over
what our priorities should be. My mentor Tim Sampson used to object strenu-
ously to the coalitions built by service providers that moved on an issue but did little to build an active constituency out of those they served. These groups might
have provided great services, but their lack of organizing made them weak, he
said. Adding them to other weak groups, he argued, built no power among the
powerless and led to frequent political failures. He believed that the energy put
into sustaining coalitions of service providers would have been better spent in political engagement and leadership development among poor people themselves.

There are other reasons for avoiding alliances. Quite often, people ask me
why half a dozen organizations all appear to be working on the same causes. Reasons range from the diverse needs of various constituencies to the distinct

approaches of different organizations—all of which mitigate against the formation of successful alliances. Perhaps it isn't easy to convince potential allies to hook up, and differences in culture, gender, and class sometimes can't be overcome even by strong self-interest. Or our own constituency may be overshadowed or replaced by allies who are more palatable to decision makers. If we feel intimidated by experts, alliances with stronger groups can lead us to compromises that water down what we want and that we aren't prepared to make. Perhaps our constituency needs only a few tactical allies that we recruit to an agenda that we control. In addition, an organization that is relatively small or under significant attack might want to avoid an alliance while continuing to build itself.

Illustration: The Workplace Project Works with Tactical Allies

In 1997, the Workplace Project won the strongest wage-enforcement law in the country, the Unpaid Wages Prohibition Act. By organizing immigrant workers directly, the campaign projected their voices into the labor debate, counteracting stereotypes with real-life images of immigrants working to improve their situations. The campaign also isolated right-wing critics by organizing other allies around their specific self-interests, such as that of government agencies in having more revenue and that of business associations in creating a level playing field. The Long Island Association, the most respected local business group, was motivated by the need to remove unfair competition. The New York State Restaurant Association was more reluctant because restaurants are notorious nonpayers of wages, but the Long Island chapter joined to promote good business.

The Project retained control of the campaign's frames and tactics by not expanding to a coalition around the issue. The worker leadership was thus not under pressure from allies to reduce their demands, hide their immigration status, or muddy their messages. Gordon (1999, p. 23) writes about that decision: "In a coalition, the bill might have been diluted by the variety of interests represented, instead of coming directly from immigrant workers. Our members might not have had the chance to deliberate and make their own decisions about bill revision and strategy. Furthermore, if we had launched the bill from within a labor/community/religious coalition, we might have been unable to gain business support; if business had been included at the outset, the bill might never have been written. Finally, it is quite possible that a coalition would have initially rejected this campaign as too unlikely to win or ended it prematurely."

Determining That Each Partner Has Healthy Self-Interests and Compatible Politics

Collaborative formations work best when the participating groups bring substantial self-interests and similar politics to the work. Nevertheless, groups in an alliance must be prepared for almost constant negotiations over political differences. Many people forming an alliance spend a lot of time crafting fancy political statements, hoping to weed out those who are not with the program. While these statements are sometimes helpful, requiring each group to clearly state its self-interest in the formation, as well as any costs it might incur, would probably take us further toward successfully negotiating around our political differences. If it is clear that a group's self-interest is compatible with those of the other groups, then people have an incentive to work out their political differences. That self-interest doesn't have to be narrow, but it does have to be direct and clear. Alliances built on altruism tend toward negative, unequal dynamics. For example, a middle-class, white organization might have an interest in fighting segregation, but it would have to be clear about why fighting segregation was good for its own constituency.

Illustration: GROWL Negotiates on Race in Welfare Network

GROWL's focus on race has attracted many groups involved in the welfare debate, according to Sandra Robertson, director of the Georgia Coalition Against Hunger, and Lee Ann Hall, executive director of the Northwest Federation of Community Organizations. Robertson, who is black, says that race has become even more central to welfare debates than it was before 1996. "It used to be that when people would attack welfare as a crutch for the colored, we could point to the fact that most recipients were white to kill racist arguments," she says. "But now those numbers are reversed, like a self-fulfilling prophecy, forcing black people to rely on welfare more than whites." Robertson raises a core dilemma facing antipoverty activists—stubborn institutional refusal to acknowledge the effects of discrimination on economic prospects and the use of a welfare underclass to suspend hard-won civil rights laws. Hall, who is white, agrees that race is central, but says, "I think most white organizers don't know how to deal with race with their constituencies."

But the race frame, while easily accepted in principle, is not without controversy in the GROWL network. Dana Ginn Paredes, former coordinator of GROWL, says that "most of the groups really put a class or gender frame on the issue, and they're not so used to looking at it from a race angle." At times both women of color and white women resist the race frame because of their perception that it isolates both of them. "Black women do not want to [be] stigmatized as welfare hogs, and white women don't want to be pushed out of the leadership on the debate," says Hall.

In addition, addressing both the racist and the patriarchal aspects of welfare policy has created the need to watch for and struggle over potential conflicts between policies that appeal to different constituencies. For example, says Hall, "many of the white-led organizations have been big on child-support enforcement. Studies show that white women who are left by white men move deeper into poverty but that women of color and men of color are both likely to be poor already before their split. You can't get blood out of a stone, even by putting it in jail, so many women of color resist solutions geared toward child support."

CTWO, the initiator and coordinator of GROWL, does not use the race question to limit a group's participation in the network, as long as it signs onto all the GROWL principles. Although a racial justice frame is high on the CTWO agenda, "we haven't pushed it as a bottom line for our participation in the network. It's not where the majority of the groups and their leaders are at," says Mark Toney, CTWO's executive director. Instead of pushing for a high level of agreement, CTWO has opted for a basic agreement and to "work more closely with the specific groups that want to strengthen that dimension of their work."

Groups involved in community-union coalitions often need to evaluate their self-interests in new ways. Madeleine Janis-Aparicio, the director of LAANE, maintains that unions engaged in alliances need to broaden their definition of important issues, just as community organizations need to acknowledge the critical role of good union jobs. "Community-labor coalitions will work only if people are brought to see the parts as one and the same, that the community program is the labor program, and vice versa. Unions have to see that access to these jobs is really crucial to creating a whole program of economic justice and that affordable housing is the other side of that. And, community people have to fundamentally believe that unionization is a solution to low-wage poverty. There's a lot of education that has to take place on both sides to generate mutual respect."

Illustration: NAFFE Brings Union and Community Groups Together

To help build public demand for reform in contingent work, CCW and 9to5 were both active in pulling together an informal network of local organizations that eventually became the formal NAFFE. Ellen Bravo, executive director of 9to5, supported the idea of starting a national network that could educate and mobilize union members, organize temp workers into unions, organize contractors using temp firms, and level the playing field through legislation and other public policy initiatives.

NAFFE represents an important step in the consolidation of two different approaches to the problem of contingent work. On the one hand, unions have sought to "hold onto things they've won legally, after many years of actually ignoring contingency or even encouraging its use to prevent lay-offs," says Costello of CCW. On the other hand, community organizations, many of which have roots in civil rights and racial justice movements, stepped in to "fill the gaps that labor left open, trying to organize the workers who are in those jobs." These strategies began to resemble each other as organized labor took up some organizing challenges in highly contingent industries, as with the Justice for Janitors and United Parcel Service campaigns. Costello notes that "historically there was a lot [of] tension between those two types of approaches," but says that by the late 1990s some commonalties had begun to emerge, including the "belief that you [have] to produce standards for the contingent economy so those workers are not super exploited as a way to protect the standard workers." As union and community-based approaches began to overlap, Costello thinks that it "opened some social space for developing new strategies. NAFFE's goal is to serve as the nexus where that discussion can take place and where various streams can figure this out."

NAFFE has taken up two major tasks in encouraging national action: research that exposes the depth of industry violations and the diversity of contingent workers, and collective action to set new standards and explore legislative options. In March 2000, NAFFE rolled out its groundbreaking study on the conditions resulting from widespread discrimination against temp workers. NAFFE has also consolidated into one national code many of the regional and local codes of conduct that have been developed to control temp agencies. NAFFE is negotiating with a large national temp agency to jointly develop a code of conduct. Bravo recalls getting the call from the agency saying that it was not going to sign onto the NAFFE code. "Since I was expecting an attitude of 'we're not going to let 9to5 push us into anything,' it was surprising to hear the CEO say, 'Why don't we develop a code together?'" Bravo agreed to a negotiation process with the conditions that the joint work would take place with NAFFE rather than just 9to5 and that whatever was developed would not be subject to approval by the temp industry's American Staffing Association.

Requiring the Contribution of Resources and Managing Them Equitably

Each partner in an alliance must bring resources. Then the project has to be structured in ways that maximize each group's contribution and equalize power and credit among them. Collaborations should set a minimum standard for contributions of money, people, and staff time. The resources don't have to be the same—that would eliminate one of the major benefits of achieving a more efficient division of labor. One group might contribute people while another contributes money; one might produce research while another carries it to legislators. But everyone has to contribute specific resources and get credit for it.

However, alliances and networks, especially if they have a political purpose, usually involve groups whose existing power and resources are unequal. When this inequality is combined with a vast difference in political values, a lot of time and money can be wasted building an alliance that turns out not to be particularly radical. When conflict arises in such an alliance, often the group with the most power and resources wins, regardless of the decision-making structure. The easy answer is simply to avoid collaborative work with groups that wield more power than ours or have more mainstream politics, but broad avoidance doesn't amount to much of a strategy.

In community-labor coalitions part of the challenge is that unions have many more resources and much more power than community organizations do, so they can virtually set the agenda unchallenged. That difference in power can lead to token positions for community people and can determine how conflicts will be resolved. Community members are often recruited to lend their prominence to a fight, but they are not involved in the strategic planning of its course. The power differential, along with the potential racial, economic, and gender conflicts built into any effort involving multiple constituencies, makes the job of building such alliances complicated.

Several measures can equalize the power relations among groups in community-labor and other coalitions. First, the decision-making structure has to be clear and transparent to all. Second, throughout the project it is critical to conduct honest and principled evaluations of how the alliance is working. Conducting evaluations on an ongoing basis ensures that they become part of the collaborative culture. Third, the benefits of collaborative work have to be distributed evenly. Issues of credit and acknowledgment can make or break a collaboration. Finally, while all the parties have to be on their best behavior, groups with more resources have to be especially vigilant. With power comes the responsibility not to use it casually or destructively. These measures can mitigate against the power imbalances that haunt so many collaborations.

Assessing the contributions of potential allies needs to be combined with knowledge of their self-interests and the costs to your organization of collaborating with them in order to determine whether you want to invite them to be part of some kind of joint effort. Exercise 7.1 gives you a chance to make such an analysis for groups that might become allies. The example is one organization's assessment of having the Chamber of Commerce as an ally.

Setting Up Staffing and Infrastructure

While lots of collaborations are sustained by the voluntary contributions of member groups, they need dedicated resources in order to maximize their potential. Having dedicated resources also ensures that the nitty-gritty work gets done. When only one partner is coordinating the alliance, dedicating resources within that organization can ensure that the larger alliance has its own identity. Building an independent structure has the added advantage of helping to define a culture and structure not bound by any single group.

Illustration: CTWO Provides the Infrastructure for the GROWL Network

With sixty organizational members, GROWL is the largest effort to align welfare rights organizations since the National Welfare Rights Organization (NWRO) was launched in the 1960s. As the initiator and coordinator of GROWL, CTWO provides an infrastructure,

Exercise 7.1. Potential-Allies Assessment Sheet.

Constituency	Organization	Self-Interest	Contribution	Cost	Invite? Y/N
Business	Chamber of Commerce	Support for probusiness policies	Deliver Politician X Credibility with media	We sell out Lose left allies	Y

opportunities to develop a joint analysis and strategy, and organizing resources. CTWO began to strategize with GROWL about welfare reauthorization at the end of 1999—nearly three years before reauthorization was scheduled to take place. The early gatherings of GROWL groups laid out political principles, built a common analysis, and began to provide training sessions in campaign planning, media, and direct action. CTWO pays for the travel costs related to each gathering, as well as for many regional and national events. In addition to organizing these ongoing strategic gatherings, CTWO conducts research, produces materials, and coordinates campaign activity among the GROWL groups.

CTWO also provides services to GROWL groups through the Movement Activist Apprenticeship Program. MAAP serves two purposes: to provide human resources and organizing consultation to groups in the GROWL network and to encourage welfare recipients to become paid welfare rights organizers. (The combination of political goals and the goal of advancing infrastructure by training new organizers mimics one of the greatest contributions of NWRO, which also ran a program for new organizers of color in addition to recruiting and training dozens of white organizers, many of whom went on to become prominent movement leaders.) Devoting five MAAP class cycles to the issue of welfare "has created a great sense of solidarity among the graduates of those classes and gave us a great way to develop their political sense," according to Paredes. MAAP interns have helped groups recruit new members, gather intelligence about their welfare departments, and confront local decision makers in New York, Chicago, Oakland, Seattle, and San Francisco.

Illustration: CCW Devotes Resources to a Partner Organizing Contingent Workers

In 2001, CCW worked with the Chinese Progressive Association (CPA), itself a formidable local organization with a strong track record and media connections, in an emblematic struggle over globalization and the conversion of good jobs into bad jobs. CPA called on CCW after it was approached by a group of workers from Power One, a heavy-electronics factory. Before initiating contact with CCW, CPA had organized two hundred of the three hundred workers in the plant, all about to be laid off and "already in trouble with management," according to Jason Pramas, CCW organizer. Karen Chen of CPA says, "There were other workers at the plant who were more or less in management or were white; native-born workers were being laid off some months later and getting a much better severance package."

CCW did target research, helped kick off picketing, helped recruit lawyers to begin negotiations on behalf of the nonunionized workers, brought in other groups, and connected CPA with the Massachusetts AFL-CIO. As the company stalled, workers called a second picket, larger than the first. Pramas also worked the media, getting a local community radio to do a live broadcast of the very untraditional picket line in the working-class and student-dominated section of Boston, which happens to be visible from a major highway. Says Pramas, "You never see 150 Chinese immigrants and 50 assorted labor and public officials marching right next to the Mass[achusetts] Turnpike, chanting in Mandarin, English, Spanish." Just before the third picket, management shut down the factory, so the picket was transformed into a rally at the statehouse to get the Commonwealth of Massachusetts to do the right thing.

The alliance led CPA to make visionary demands in this unclear labor situation. Pramas's early research had revealed that the factory was moving to China and Mexico; this relocation plan made the workers eligible for NAFTA benefits. Ultimately, the company laid off the workers but agreed to pay two years of unemployment under NAFTA, to pay for English as a Second Language classes and teachers, and to leverage the money necessary from the state and federal governments to pay for job-training and placement specialists. The state provided $100,000 and the Federal government $1 million toward retraining.

Conclusion

More than anything else, our ability to work with other groups indicates both our readiness to work as a movement rather than as separate organizations and our ability to upgrade our organizing. But alliances are tricky, and not all are worth pursuing. There are a lot of external pressures to build alliances, networks, and collaborations. Foundations would like to fund one coordinated effort on an issue rather than thirty. Conservatives try to split us, and so we often get together because we're all under attack. Other groups ask us to lend support to their causes. But if the building of an alliance is externally driven, it cannot survive the inevitable conflicts over time, money, and politics. While we need alliances to succeed, we have to build them on our terms.

Tactical alliances and networks allow for the greatest flexibility and generally do not require much ideological unity. But strategic alliances give us increased leverage over time, as we consolidate our base of knowledge and work together more efficiently. Our collaborations can be successful if we are clear about their purpose, every partner brings its own self-interest, resources are equitably shared, and the collective formation itself has resources devoted to it.

CHAPTER EIGHT

Speaking Truth to Power

Tracy Jones fought her temp agency and won. A former shop steward, Jones filed sex-discrimination charges with the Equal Employment Opportunity Commission (EEOC) when she discovered that MaxStaff, a subsidiary of Maximus, the nation's largest temp agency, paid male co-workers $1.12 more per hour than it paid her. Armed with one of the men's pay stubs for proof, Jones raised the issue with her supervisor, only to find herself suddenly unemployed. In August 2000, the *New York Times* covered the EEOC finding in Jones's favor (Walsh, 2000). Jones's story mirrors that of thousands of temp workers. Her story got into the *New York Times* because of her organization's media capacity.

Most progressive organizations are uncomfortable with mainstream media, and for good reason. In an environment of dwindling media diversity and democracy, it is extremely difficult for grassroots community organizers who want to affect deep social change to get their stories heard. Often, the mainstream media have been downright hostile to these groups and their constituencies. Mainstream media are generally acknowledged to be politically conservative, not in party affiliation but in their unwillingness to put forth major challenges to the current political and economic system. Backed by huge multinational corporations in search of profit, they have no interest in changing the status quo. The ongoing creation of a media oligarchy further limits opportunities for alternative voices to be heard. Six corporations now own the majority of this country's major media outlets: AOL Time Warner, Walt Disney, Bertelsmann, Viacom, Vivendi Universal, and News Corporation (owned by the flamboyantly conservative Rupert Murdoch). The same six to eight corporations that dominate the U.S. market are coming to dominate the global market as well (Granville, 2001).

The Telecommunications Act of 1996 kicked off an intense period of corporate mergers and joint ventures; as a result the number of television-station owners dropped by half in subsequent years (Granville, 2001). The FCC, whose original role was to regulate the communications industry, has moved to further weaken broadcasting rules that safeguard media diversity. In April 2001, the FCC eliminated the "dual-network rule" preventing one television network from buying another. Consequently, Viacom now owns CBS and a part of the UPN network, and with current trends as they are, the way is open for further network consolidation (Fairness and Accuracy in Reporting, 2001).

Yet progressives cannot afford to avoid the mainstream media. Positive media coverage can lend great momentum to an organizing campaign and credibility to the organizations behind it. The elite news media are where the agendas for public policy are set and the "official story" is cast. Not to be overlooked is the power of the media to let people know that progressive, grassroots organizations are here and that they're proposing solutions. Given the current atmosphere, however, grassroots organizations have to back up their media work with accurate documentation and preparation because they won't get many chances and the stakes are high. According to media consultant Kim Deterline, "Bad coverage can mean the death of an organization. It can mean loss of funding, loss of a campaign—it can affect people's lives directly."

We have a responsibility to try to influence the coverage of our issues. Many organizers have proven that this is a challenging but not impossible task. As Makani Themba, with the Bay Area Praxis Project, explains, "We can tap into the knowledge people have of the problems with the system. People know about racism, they know about injustice, but we have to challenge the notion that there's nothing that can be done about it and there's nobody trustworthy to do it."

Given the compelling reasons for progressive groups to improve their media capacity, I use this chapter to cover the basics of media planning: adjusting messages and materials according to the audience; developing messages; designing our own media; understanding the media; and, finally, developing our organizations as sources. In our illustrations, we learn from the Women's Association for Women's Alternatives (W.A.W.A.), the Workplace Project, the Campaign on Contingent Work (CCW), and 9to5 as we observe the importance of creating a systematic media plan and of integrating it with programmatic goals; the gains that can be made from using the media for our own purposes; the benefits of creating our own media, such as websites and videos, to educate both our own constituencies and the broader public about key issues; the value of not compromising the terms of the debate when crafting media messages; the advantages derived from maintaining our own information about the media; and the benefits of taking the time to prepare our members to be spokespeople.

Principles

There are five key considerations in expanding organizational media capacity: crafting a strategy that adjusts messages and materials according to the audience; developing sharp, polarizing messages based on shared values; recognizing the importance of designing our own print, radio, and electronic media; understanding the media and building relationships with reporters, including challenging outlets when necessary; and, finally, using people within our own organization as sources.

Designing a Strategy

Like everything else in a policy-change effort, our work to get media coverage will be more productive if it emerges from a strategy rather than a last-minute mad scramble. As an organization crafts a media strategy, it should consider the kind of coverage it wants and for what purposes. Whether we are trying to mobilize our own constituency, apply pressure on a target, or gain public sympathy determines the media we work with. Most groups have the option of approaching three kinds of media outlets—ethnic, alternative/political, and mainstream—or developing our own. There are also different forms—electronic (radio and television), print, and computer.

Illustration: CCW Uses the Media to Put Pressure on an Opponent

Jason Pramas, CCW organizer, has made media work a central function of the network. He says, "We've become the go-to people for everything from writing press releases to pitching stories. This is part of our way of doing things based on the old labor principles of mutual aid and solidarity. We try to help out directly and teach some skills." For Pramas, flexibility and responsiveness are the watchwords that guide both his media work and his organizing work.

CCW's press strategy is to look for opportunities where it can make a point not just about injustice but also about resolution and action. Because welfare is one of CCW's primary issues, Pramas recalls forcing himself to read the weekly political summaries of the Massachusetts legislature after hearing that the lieutenant governor, Jane Swift, had received a great deal of negative media attention for having her staff members take care of her children. Although he almost overlooked it, he came across a news blurb stating that Swift was slated to speak to a group of government employees. With further research on the Internet, he uncovered more details and secured passes to the event for six people. "Here was an opportunity to expose an opponent, a woman who was pushing policies to kick women off of welfare while she used state resources for her own personal needs, for child care, no less," says Pramas. The group shifted into high gear to prepare for the meeting. One press release, with the slogan "Child care for all, not just for Lieutenant Governor Jane Swift," alerted media contacts to CCW's message. An hour before the meeting, CCW sent out a short press release that read: "Working Massachusetts has called a surprise demonstration outside the FEDERAL BUILDING TODAY AT NOON, where Lieutenant Governor Jane Swift will make a speech entitled, 'A More Family Friendly Government Equals Better Government.' We don't think we need to explain this situation any further. Come down and join the fun." This press release would have been inappropriate if Swift's reputation in the media was not already severely challenged or if CCW had no relationships with reporters. As a result of CCW's action, Swift's entire media strategy got derailed that day, with welfare recipients in the room where she was speaking, fifteen to twenty people from CCW outside, and, in a sheer stroke of luck, a chance for Pramas to ask the first question, which was followed by a series of hard-hitting questions from the *Boston Globe* and other local media. As Pramas describes it, "We all read a lot and keep a look-out for opportunities, and often people feed us tips." In this case, reading a lot allowed CCW to expose the opposition, create a dramatic event that garnered great media attention, and build momentum to propel its campaign forward.

If our resources are limited, we might want to focus on one element of the media for a time. Although we tend to consider mainstream media the key to power, ethnic and alternative outlets frequently pursue stories for months and force the mainstream media to pick them up. For example, when Gerrold Hall, a black sixteen-year-old, was shot to death by transit police in the San Francisco Bay area in 1995, the mainstream media repeated wholesale the police officer's story of chasing a thief with a gun in the train station. But Tim Redmond, of the *San Francisco Bay Guardian*, an alternative weekly, followed the story for months and eventually reported that no gun belonging to Hall had ever been found and that Hall was shot in the back of the head; neither fact was reported by the mainstream press. The regional dailies then had to print the real story.

In addition to making decisions about audiences and outlets, we need to think about how to garner the resources we require for our media work and what the timeline for carrying out that work will be. A group should determine the human resources it will invest, whether in staff time or in a functioning media committee, and budget for hard costs, such as a database, materials with high production value, and consultants. CCW tries to bolster its members' commitment to media work. CCW leaders engage regularly in discussions about the appropriate use of the media, what groups can expect to get out of it, and how to deal with its limitations. Pramas notes that, as important as media work is, "the resources in many groups [are] not allocated as effectively as possible to make it happen."

Illustration: The Workplace Project Systematically Builds Media Capacity

The Project began implementing its five-year strategy for building media capacity by tracking and generating contacts in all three parts of the print media—the ethnic, alternative, and mainstream press—all of which had provided decent and frequent coverage of the Project's campaigns and actions. Although the Project does not have a dedicated media person, executive director Nadia Marin-Molina says, "We try to think it through as a part of every campaign strategy: how are we going to get the press out?" Because it systematically seeks out opportunities to get coverage, the Project has also trained dozens of immigrant leaders to craft messages and to stay on message. Articles on the Workplace Project have helped build public sympathy by describing the horrific conditions in which immigrants work; as a result, the Project has been able to polarize day-labor and domestic-work issues and deflect immigrant bashing. The Spanish-language press, in particular, is a staple outreach tool. The Project steadily built capacity and relationships by regularly mining its ongoing work for good media stories, even outside of campaigns. For example, the legal-clinic staff constantly reviewed cases brought by immigrant workers for a possible media story; they asked, Would this case bring out the intended message, paint a sympathetic picture, and stand up to scrutiny? Occasionally, the Workplace Project works first in an exclusive way with one reporter to unveil a story, knowing that other outlets will follow up.

Illustration: 9to5 Integrates Media and Program Planning

Few organizations have the good fortune to have had a Hollywood movie written and produced about their work, much less one with three major stars that has continued to run for more than thirty years on cable television. My introduction to clerical organizing came from Jane Fonda, Dolly Parton, and Lily Tomlin. Although 9to5, National Association of Working Women, got major name recognition from the movie and was able to prevent through informal channels the plot's culminating in the boss's murder, the movie did not replace the need for a strong and systematic media program based in 9to5's real agenda.

Despite the repeated dilemmas encountered in negotiating between the activities that are guaranteed to get press and those that actually get the message out, integrated planning can make all the difference. At the beginning of new projects, Meg Lewis-Sidime's job as the public-affairs coordinator is to ask questions: Is this newsworthy? How can we frame it to be more newsworthy? How can we make it visual?

What's the timing in relationship to newsroom schedules? Lewis-Sidime communicates closely with the organizing and program staff so that she can contribute media-related ideas to the work plan and help formulate messages. She then creates training plans that support members in putting out those messages so that they coincide with organizing activities and press outreach.

It also helps to have regular activities that generate good media stories. 9to5 alternates annually between the Rate Your Job contest and an electoral education campaign. The Rate Your Job contest, which has been going on for more than twenty years, provides workers with a scorecard for rating their jobs based on a variety of different policies. People send in their stories, receive a set of negotiation tips in return, and celebrity judges like Senator Christopher Dodd rate them. 9to5 promotes the contest in women's magazines and other outlets, then publicizes the best companies and the worst practices. In alternate years, the election campaign operates in a similar way; 9to5 distributes cards on which people can send a newly elected official a message and state how they voted. Regional media trainings use those two campaigns as a springboard for teaching media skills.

Developing Our Own Media

In addition to thinking about how to get our work into the external media so we can influence the larger public, we also need to improve our own communication mechanisms. Ironically, the same technology that has built media conglomerates enables us to produce our own media. Media that are increasingly available to us include print, such as zines and tabloids, video, radio, and the Internet. Print media are still important vehicles for communities that don't have access to the Internet. People do read our newsletters, so they need to be attentively put together. Websites are increasingly key for reaching both our own constituencies and the press. To be most effective, they need to be visually appealing, easy to use, and frequently updated. Despite the consolidation in radio, a number of community-based radio stations, such as the nationwide network of Spanish-language stations, will still carry our stories. In rural communities, radio is often the favored medium. If a group tapes a two- or three-minute news piece about its work, many radio stations will run it as is.

Illustration: 9to5 Produces Its Own Media to Appeal to Internal and External Audiences

Lewis-Sidime takes a broad approach to 9to5 media work that differentiates between "our own and earned media." She notes that the audience differs for these two types of media, and she can't always use the same language—for example, "our mission statement says *economic justice,* which means nothing to reporters." A look at the 9to5 website reveals that it is designed to appeal to both internal and external audiences. The website is updated regularly. The first page has some appealing features. The boxes for sections of the site include only the most important four—how to join, a sign-in, a link to local chapters (which gives a sense of scale), and the Raise the Score Award, which sounds like fun. The next lines provide contact information for the national office, the hotline, and media calls. Then there are two action alerts. At the beginning of 2002, the first was entitled "Confronting Terrorism"; it was a brief piece decrying the rise in hate crimes after September 11th and relating the need for vigilance around hate crimes to 9to5's fight against workplace discrimination. The second was about recent 9to5 victories. The webpage leads to the "Profile of Working Women," which combines up-to-date facts and statistics on issues. The topics include women in the workforce, women in traditionally female jobs, women and politics, pay equity, working families, nonstandard workers, employee benefits, discrimination, poverty, women in unions, violence on the job, and retirement security. The website will eventually include resources for journalists.

Illustration: W.A.W.A. Makes a Video

W.A.W.A. has developed methods for reaching out to the general public as well as administrators. With funding from the Ms. Foundation, W.A.W.A. conducted the New Voices study, which documents the experiences of welfare recipients with "work first"; the study became the basis for a widely disseminated video, "New Voices in Welfare Reform," featuring three women in their struggles to move off the rolls. The video, made by filmmaker Sharon Mullaly, describes the experiences of three women, Kay, Mayra, and Linda, as they struggle to feed their children and meet the work-first requirements of the state of Pennsylvania. The video is accompanied by a discussion guide geared toward other recipients, including questions about their own experiences in moving out of poverty and with the programs that are supposed to help them. The most common use of the video has been by social services programs in orienting caseworkers so they can help recipients most effectively and in motivating the clients themselves. W.A.W.A. has distributed the entire first run of the sixty-minute video and plans to send out another 250 copies. "It's been great to be able to use the video to humanize the issue, to train caseworkers in how to deal with the changes," says Executive Director Carol Goertzel.

Making the video, which cost about $25,000, involved finding the women (who received new computers as compensation for their participation) and designing the storyline. W.A.W.A. paid for the project largely by allocating a small portion of grants for general support and for self-sufficiency work from a wide range of foundations. Jane Eleey, project director, recommends that organizations be clear about how they are going to use videos and other such tools. "Because of staffing issues we were not able to use it as much as we had hoped to help us move the policy agenda. It was a great general education tool, but the filmmaker also wasn't able to get it wide exposure—for example, on PBS or in film festivals." Eleey notes that a group should not underestimate the staff time and skill required to ensure excellent production and distribution, as well as the importance of clear goals at the beginning. Although the process of making the video was "very new for us and fraught with small challenges," Goertzel says she would encourage other groups to explore visual and other methods of getting their messages out.

Developing the Message

Message development is a matter of polarizing the issue, speaking to shared values, and maintaining discipline. One should not underestimate the power of a well-stated, strategic message to redefine the debate. Every media campaign has two targets, one being the institutions of power and their power brokers, who should be challenged and exposed, the other being the people whom progressives want to win over to their side. The message should put pressure on the power brokers but be directed toward the sympathies of the people. From one strategic message, people should be able to figure out exactly what happened and what the proposed solution is. This message should always be grounded in issue development and in campaign goals.

The most common mistake groups make is to water down messages to meet the conservative standards of the press and general public. Deterline feels that many progressive organizers have not put forth hard-hitting media messages for two reasons. One is that they are reluctant to take the moral high ground and speak about shared values, perhaps because they are afraid to confront disagreement, and the other is that they have been afraid to ask for what they really want because they might lose. In the attempt to sustain winnable campaigns and create messages most people can agree with, the issues have been compromised, and the messages have been diluted.

This tendency has been greatly aggravated by the public-relations firms that progressive groups sometimes hire to advise their media campaigns. Often firms that lack connection and accountability to the communities affected have recommended watered-down messages that are ultimately ineffective in either winning on the issue or reframing the debate. For example, one public-relations firm hired to help develop media strategies in opposition to Proposition 187, which made undocumented immigrants ineligible for many public services in California, conducted a poll and found that most Californians had ambivalent or even hostile feelings about immigrants. The firm's problematic response was to concede that the voters' fear of illegal immigrants was valid and that blame should be shifted to the federal government for not patrolling the borders properly. This proposal did nothing to advance the campaign against 187 and did not attempt to reframe the issues to counter the propaganda coming from the right, according to Deter-line. It did not change the way the public viewed undocumented immigrants or shed light on the complicated issues behind illegal immigration.

When we craft media messages, we need to be aware of where the general public stands on an issue and identify shared values we can use to move the conversation, rather than let public opinion compromise the terms of the debate. Rather than speaking to people's fears, we can appeal to their highest shared values and their belief in fairness and human dignity. Many of our beliefs—police should not kill unarmed men, children should not be poisoned by the dirt in their playgrounds, people who work full-time should not live in poverty—are not extreme and are probably shared by most people. Once we appeal to people's basic belief that it's not OK to kill unarmed men, for example, we can craft media messages that move them to see the need for addressing police brutality.

It's all right to polarize the people on different sides of an issue in your media campaign. Do not be afraid to point the finger. Themba, a longtime organizer and media activist, likens a news story to a comic strip. "You have the people who are on our side, we hope they'll look like the good guys, and the people on their side, you hope they'll look like the bad guys. You have to think, as an activist, what do you want your comic strip to say? Who are the best people in the pictures and what will be the best bubble, because that's all the time you're going to get." Themba points out that in a campaign to get rid of tobacco billboards targeting communities of color, the message was carried by a pediatrician who talked about how awful smoking is for children and by regular folks on the frontlines who testified to the human costs of this billboard policy. Then, she says, her group found "the sleaziest, weirdest, most callous opponent" and tried to get reporters to interview that person. The tobacco industry provided perfect villains who used one set of practices in white communities and another in communities of color.

Perhaps the most important rule has to do with message discipline. The only way to come close to ensuring that the media will carry your message is to repeat it endlessly. Conservatives have effectively repeated their overarching message of individual responsibility and racial scapegoating through a variety of outlets. Let's look at the media's coverage of welfare as an example. The backlash against welfare mothers was clearly agitated by the media's willingness to embrace one image—that of the black welfare queen. Ronald Reagan's 1980 election ads featured a black woman, supposedly from the South Side of Chicago, who had been arrested for an elaborate welfare fraud that encompassed the creation of eighty names, thirty addresses, twelve Social Security cards, and veterans' benefits for four deceased "husbands." This image was repeated each time a press outlet covered the campaign and even after the electoral contest was over. In a short time the image of the black welfare queen took hold among white Americans. Repeated efforts to undo the faulty image have had minimal effect. Deterline says, "The right is good at coordinating their message and effort so that many of the same messages come out of many different places, whereas on the left, you could hear thirty different things from thirty different people." The lesson is that progressives need to take a more systematic, disciplined approach to media.

It's generally easier to achieve consistency in our message if we use only a few spokespeople; they should be trained to figure out what the message is before the press calls, and they should practice. They should also remember that they are not required to answer every question from the press and that they should not equivocate. In an interview on April 12, 2002, with the Lebanese ambassador to the United States on *Hannity and Colmes,* the interviewer asked repeated questions about the ambassador's feelings about Israel, but all the ambassador would talk about was Palestine. The interviewer would ask if he supported Israel's right to exist and the ambassador would respond that he believed in the right of Palestine to exist (foxnews.com/story/0.2933.50344.00.html). Our spokespeople should be unafraid to be just as blatant. They also should not use the phrase "yes, but." Instead, they should simply repeat the message. A "yes, but" statement can be quoted out of context, and if the reporter's frame is not ours, the quote can be used to reinforce the reporter's frame.

Illustration: The Workplace Project Undermines Immigrant Scapegoating

Strong media work made a huge difference in the campaign to pass the 1997 Unpaid Wages Prohibition Act in New York. The Workplace Project had to get the bill sponsored by a Republican state senator from Long Island and passed through the Republican state senate. In the beginning, there was no overwhelming tide of support publicly or politically that could fuel the legislative campaign. Rather than accepting the prevailing political climate and giving up on its goals, the Project launched a media campaign that would bring the reality of immigrant workers' struggles into public consciousness. Before it could promote its ultimate message—that unscrupulous employers should be held accountable for nonpayment of wages—it had to credibly expose the situation. Jennifer Gordon of the Workplace Project describes this initial campaign as building "a climate of outrage about the treatment to which immigrant workers were subjected" (Gordon, 1999, p. 20).

By allowing the most vulnerable workers in our society to tell their stories, the Project attempted to win the public's sympathies without creating a divide between workers—documented and undocumented, American and immigrant, skilled and unskilled. The Project persisted with this strategy until it had an overwhelming amount of sympathetic media coverage and got the necessary sponsorship for the bill. In the end, the Project got its message out so effectively that there was not much vocal opposition to the bill. Opponents would have had to clearly come out in favor of employers who continuously failed to pay their workers. Given the fact that this bill could have easily gotten caught in the anti-immigrant quagmire, its passage was a remarkable achievement.

Understanding the Media

Because we can't influence any institution that we don't understand, we need to build a systematic base of knowledge about media outlets. First, we must know what reporters and editors are looking for in a story. Largely, outlets want stories of individual successes and failures, incidents and conflicts. They are not oriented to collective action and systemic analysis, in part because of the conservative bias in many outlets and in part because the media is in the business of news, not analysis. The best way to understand the characteristics of a good story is to read, listen to, and watch the news regularly and to take the time to analyze the incidents, sources, and data presented. Knowing what makes an attractive story will help tremendously when we are pitching our own to reporters.

Second, it is useful to know the basic power structure in a newsroom or outlet. Generally reporters don't have total control of their assignments or of how their final stories read. These decisions are made by city-desk editors. If we want to influence an outlet's coverage in a major way, we need to be talking to the editors as well as to the reporters.

Systematic research on all relevant media outlets can be conducted in many ways. I recommend keeping a file of editorials and articles organized by reporter or outlet so we can check for patterns in the coverage and signs of sympathy, resistance, or interests. Having an updated database with contact and basic information about reporters and editors will save huge amounts of time when we send out materials or make calls. It's also a good idea to keep track of reporters as they move from one outlet to another, just in case our favorite alternative reporter gets a job at the local daily. Finally, we can reach out to reporters with resources even when we don't have a story to pitch. The Expose Racism and Advance School Excellence (ERASE) program of the Applied Research Center published a handbook for journalists about race and education and developed many great contacts that way. In another example, when a nationwide network of tobacco-control activists in communities of color conducted a media campaign to support their organizing, they built relationships with their local reporters over time by looking for those who would be most sympathetic to their message and inviting them to compelling and creative actions or offering to give them tours of the tobacco billboards in certain neighborhoods.

Illustration: 9to5 Builds Relationships with Reporters

Lewis-Sidime sends out monthly reports to journalists to maintain an ongoing relationship. She explains, "People look at this job and think that you have to be a good salesperson. You do have to be able to pitch and sell your stories, but systems make it possible to do this. You need to know who you're calling and be able to provide resources to reporters because you're the one who knows what those resources are."

The media often contact 9to5 on women's work issues because they know that 9to5 has systems in place that make for smooth communication between its spokespeople and the media; these systems include a file of up-to-date facts and statistics; accessible, prepared spokespeople; and the Voices Project database (described on page 163).

Lewis-Sidime spends a lot of her time cultivating media contacts. "You have to read what reporters write and watch what they do. And when you read something that is close to what you're doing, send them a packet and follow it up with a phone call saying, 'That was a really good story on reproductive rights. I just wanted to introduce myself and let you know we're out here. Here's what we're thinking about and how it intersects with what you're talking about.'" Lewis-Sidime describes it as doing prospect research on reporters, the way fundraisers do prospect research on funders. "I look for people who cover labor or women's or poverty issues, and if they seem to have a political awareness, that's great. But my general approach is to look for what their self-interest is and try to provide them with what they need."

If we are persistent and methodical about following the media, we will find it easier to challenge inaccurate or biased reporting. Our members might learn a lot from tracking the coverage in one outlet for a period of time. The media consulting group We Interrupt This Message conducted a study of welfare coverage in three major California outlets for the first five months of 1999 (Avalos, Bervera, and Cutting, 2002). It found only thirty-seven articles on welfare, compared with forty stories about pets, and only one article devoted to children, although the number of children living in poverty continues to climb. Furthermore, it found that when outlets report racial differences, they gloss over discrimination. Interrupt used the study to point out inaccuracies to those outlets and to generate new press on welfare issues (quoted in Avalos, Bervera, and Cutting, 2002, p. 109).

Understanding the media is key to CCW's strategy. Pramas notes that reporters work under difficult circumstances: "The media increasingly use contingent workers, reporters are under a lot of pressure, and they have short attention spans. We try to keep a positive relationship with the media. We don't hassle them." He further notes that the mainstream media generally like conflict, but only the simple two-sided kind, and they aren't good at covering collective action, so "our job is to trick them into covering it." But the media's willingness to cover collective action differs from issue to issue. Pramas notes the difference between trying to get media to cover contingent-work issues versus welfare issues. He says, "Most media people don't have a lot of experience with welfare; with contingent work they have their own experience, which is a great advantage. We have to use a different strategy in each case."

Once you have researched the media outlets you will be dealing with, use the suggestions in Exhibit 8.1 to decide how you will pitch your stories to them.

Developing Our Own People as Good Sources

One of the limitations of commercial media is that they want stories about individuals, usually told in the simplest manner possible. Organizers have to decide who will be the heroes of their stories and what they will say and to find a way to compare them with the target. If groups understand this framework, their media training should help them to develop the right cast of characters, to keep the dialogue crisp, and to take on the opposition's arguments. Anyone facing the media needs to understand the importance of stories, but grassroots organizing groups have an additional, unique objective in story framing—to bring out the marginalized voices of their members and leaders and to shed light on their issues.

However, no group wants to set up its members for failure and have them enter, unprepared, an environment in which they could be subject to slander, ridicule, or intimidation. This is just as much about preparing good storytellers as it is about presenting a good story. Preparing members to deal with the press takes the same discipline and planning as any other aspect of media work. As groups work to frame their stories effectively, it's important not only that the spokespeople be trained to take on the opposition but that they be focused in their commitment to the framing of the story. Themba says that sometimes people lose their focus by expanding their dialogue with the media to include too many irrelevant details. "If you talk to a reporter for an hour, even you can't remember everything you said. Then people get mad that they are quoted out of context, as if the media is responsible for editing them." Remember that nothing is off the record, and anything you say can appear in the press.

DARE has tried several methods to increase members' comfort levels. It has invited sympathetic reporters to an informal conversation with key leaders of a campaign and has conducted training in public speaking, which is crucial in developing the confidence of new leaders. DARE often takes time to prepare for media events even in urgent situations, buying a few minutes by promising to call a reporter back, huddling with leaders about the message, preparing one designated member to talk to the press. It also trains members to stay calm and to keep the feelings of the wider audience in mind when dealing with oppositional interviews.

Exhibit 8.1. How to Pitch Stories to the Press.

Strategize Beforehand

Think Like a Reporter

Reporters and editors are interested in stories rather than issues. Think about how you can turn your issue into a story. What are some story elements: good guys and bad guys, plot, controversy, tension and resolution? How do larger social forces shape people's personal experiences? What are symbols, metaphors and/or visuals that give your story meaning and make powerful images for cameras?

Find the News Hook

Besides all its story elements, what makes your story newsworthy? . . . The more elements of newsworthiness the better chances it will be covered. Assess the timeliness of your story. How is it relevant today? Does it relate to other news?

Frame for Institutional Responsibility

As an advocate always frame your story around institutional accountability. How are institutions exacerbating the issue? What can they do to improve conditions? Offer solutions.

Identify Reporters

Pitch stories to reporters you know would cover your story. Refer to your press list. When calling outlets, ask specifically for these reporters.

Look for Audience Angle

Does the paper have a certain constituency to whom this issue is most relevant? Race and education will be hot topics with the ethnic press.

Write Out Your Pitch Beforehand

This will help you prepare your thoughts. You should expect a pitch to last no more than 30 seconds. That's the amount of time you have to get a reporter's attention.

Practice Your Pitch with Another Person

Use a friendly, positive and persuasive tone. Ask for feedback from your partner.

(continued next page)

Exhibit 8.1. How to Pitch Stories to the Press, *continued.*

When Pitching

Be Patient and Persistent

Not every reporter will be interested in your story. Pitching to several people in a larger media outlet is quite common.

Offer Pauses to Allow Reporter to Respond

By pausing briefly, you get a chance to gauge reporters' reactions. You also create a dramatic effect in delivering the news hook.

Know the Issue

Be prepared to answer reporters' questions and provide additional information or contacts.

Be Courteous and Professional

Remember you are establishing relationships with reporters. The more contact you have with them the better your chances of their covering your issues.

Source: © Copyright 1996, 1999, We Interrupt This Message. Reprinted with permission.

If a group is setting its members up as a major source for the press, it has to prepare for the logistical realities of that charge. Reporters write under demanding deadlines, especially if they work for daily outlets like radio, television, or print news. An organization can develop a reputation for being reliable if it makes sure that reporters are able to get consistently good quotes on time to meet deadlines. Phone and e-mail systems should provide quick options for media callers. One person who is always available by phone should know how other spokespeople can be reached and be able to broker a conversation between spokespeople and reporters. An organization should figure out how to meet logistical challenges, especially during a media push. For example, many people lack the time and technology to be in constant touch. Organizations should consider availability when assigning speaking roles and should train multiple spokespeople so that someone can always be reached. If no member is available, staff people should be authorized to provide interviews. In addition, the person who answers phones for the organization should be trained how to deal with media calls.

Illustration: 9to5 Prepares Members to Be Spokespersons and Communicates Their Availability to the Press

9to5 develops its members as sources by providing substantial training in media work. First, Lewis-Sidime designs regional trainings and action-alert packets to help members understand and develop a whole media system rather than just one portion of it. For example, if she is helping chapters think through how to pitch the organization's Raise the Score contest to the local press, she sends not just the press release but information about how to develop a press list, track contacts, and prep spokespeople. Second, Lewis-Sidime says it's important to categorize people by their stage of activism. At leadership conferences, she might conduct one training session for Voices members and another for chapter leaders on how to put together a complete media plan.

Lewis-Sidime says 9to5 also works hard to resolve the logistical problems that might limit its ability to put members in front of the press. "We pay attention to representing a diverse range of voices, and that's hard when you're dealing with poverty issues, hard to reach women [with a] three-hour deadline who live in homeless shelters. People don't have phones, or they've been cut off. We deal with that by doing everything possible to reach them." For example, 9to5 has on file a number at a relative's house or meets the member somewhere and provides a cell phone for speaking with the press. Lewis-Sidime says that members themselves are often willing to make adjustments to do the media work if they understand the benefits: "What is most critical [is] for members to get comfortable and media savvy. Having them understand what kind of impact it can have on other people's lives, how it can create social change. People with great stories to tell are often afraid . . . because they fear consequences. If they think it'll help others in their situation, they're more eager to do it."

9to5 also has the Voices Project, a database of women's stories and of contacts who are willing to tell their stories to reporters. This database can be searched by topic and geography, and a template sent out to activists continually generates more stories and contacts.

Conclusion

While there are many lessons to be learned from the media-savvy work of groups, we still face challenges. Funding for effective, on-going, politically sophisticated media work is scant, and monies for media training are the first to be cut when budgets are tight. To get issues of race, class, and gender raised in a hostile media environment requires an enormous amount of time, labor, practice, and money. For a group that is just starting to develop a media program, the best investment is training and a good, regularly updated database. Several groups might consider sharing the maintenance of such a contact list. With these tools, we can establish and maintain regular contact with the press. With a little experience, we can start calling on those contacts to reframe debates and increase coverage for our issues.

Traditionally organizers concentrated on what got said in the neighborhoods, over the fence, and this strategy is still important. Organizers should continue to get messages out to the people on the streets and to make those messages even more political, more inspiring. On the other end of the spectrum, there are the news media, controlled by the most powerful corporations. Groups like CCW, the Workplace Project, and 9to5 have shown that it is difficult but possible to slowly but surely enter that arena.

CHAPTER NINE

EDUCATION FOR ENGAGEMENT

Ideological development strengthens progressive organizations. In truth, a non-ideological organization does not exist. Far from being an abstract crutch comforting the organizer with a weak self-image, ideology constitutes a necessary aspect of the internal struggle to set the political direction of an organization. Some organizations are designed to expose racist, capitalist patriarchies and to push in the opposite direction, and others are designed, perhaps unintentionally, to collude with those systems in order to accumulate benefits for their own members. Organizations composed of people who think that capitalism basically works and that U.S. democracy needs only loud voices to crack its bureaucracy reveal that analysis in their campaigns and positions. Those that think capitalism can and has to be dismantled reveal that belief, probably in a long-term strategy.

The accusation that political discussion imposes a viewpoint on members that they would not have come to themselves is specious. My own experience says that if people don't think a cause is relevant to them, they won't join it. Most poor families include welfare recipients; most poor immigrant families include both legal and undocumented immigrants; and most poor people of color have family members in prison, and many of them have lost family members to police brutality. So-called peoples' organizations have avoided many of these issues and more, while people suffer.

Furthermore, it is virtually impossible for an organization to achieve long-term change without a coherent picture of the world and a theory of how change is effected. Given the resurgence of the New Right, and the contest of ideas it has started, the organization that pretends to have no ideology is not going to cut it.

Ideological development, what I refer to in this chapter as political education, strengthens organizations that espouse progressive values in three ways. First, we need political education because it helps us hold onto our members. Without a way to build political understanding and commitment among members, organizations often find themselves rebuilding the membership at the end of each campaign. Campaigns have a necessarily narrow focus; they advance specific interests of specific groups of people in a specific time frame. While there is nothing wrong with attracting members on the basis of self-interest, as soon as the campaign is over, folks go back to regular life, and we have to start all over again. While an organization cannot hope to hold on to every campaign activist for the long haul, it is in our interest to help them see the relationship of the campaign to other issues. In addition, political education helps to connect activists to history, to a sense of how long it takes to make fundamental change. That connection to history inspires us and keeps us going through the inevitable losses and attacks.

Second, political education supports our long-term strategic planning. Leaders of organizations are responsible for a lot more than getting people together and making a list. In an increasingly complicated world, leaders have to help organizations understand the implications of their actions, integrate changing demographics into their image of their neighborhood, recruit allies from different constituencies, and identify threats to their constituency, even if those threats are not pressing at the moment. To fulfill these responsibilities, leaders have to know how the whole system works, where it has holes, and why it makes sense to take an organizing approach to effecting change instead of some other approach.

Political education is a must for organizations engaged in movement building because it helps us connect one issue to another and allows us to be good allies of other constituencies. The conservative backlash has focused on particular "wedge" issues around which Americans have conflicted feelings. This often divides constituencies who actually have common interests. For example, by making racial profiling acceptable again, the stripping of suspected terrorists' civil rights threatens the rights of all people of color. When confronted with these kinds of attacks, only organizations representing the specific constituency can be mobilized for the hard fight. Multiconstituency organizations that do not invest in political education for their members often sit out these fights or, worse, take positions that work against the best interests of their constituencies.

Third, political education helps prepare us to get our ideas out into the world. It should also be clear by now that resolution of the problems affecting people requires more than a facile critique of bureaucrats and politicians. The New Right is extremely well connected and has thousands of outlets for its ideas, from textbooks to television. Some of its more persuasive spokespeople look just like disenfranchised moms, immigrants, and people of color, and they provide cover for harmful concepts. Conservatives also have the power to test their policies in privately financed projects. Because media consolidation means that people have less access to information from nonmainstream sources than they ever did before, it becomes the responsibility of community organizations to provide the space for people to question and to come to an understanding of how the world is organized and of who benefits from or pays the costs of that system.

Political education in community-based organizations and labor unions has a rich history. Marion Steeg, of Working Partnerships, an organizer for nearly thirty years, told me, "I was raised to believe that every single thing that happens is the organizer's responsibility. The organizer has to lead in leadership development, not just let people choose. If they make bad choices because they're not educated about how the system works and what is likely to happen next, then they don't grow." Steeg's point is not that organizers should impose their ideals but that in the current political context they must create space for the ideological and political discussion to take place.

In this chapter, I explore the most exciting work currently being done in political education. To make the best use of this work, we need to be clear about the purpose of political education as well as avoid dogmatic rhetoric, balance the time we spend on education with action and organizing, and explore solutions. In illustrations from Direct Action for Rights and Equality (DARE), 9to5, the Workplace Project, the Center for Third World Organizing (CTWO), and the Southeast Regional Economic Justice Network (REJN), we can observe the use of political education to respond to current events and to prevent demoralization by stressing solutions to political problems; the use of strategic planning and other organizing activities for political education; an effort to balance education with organizing; attempts to vary the methods of education and to use political education in developing issues; and the use of education to create and expand alliances.

Principles

If we are going to engage in political education, we need to keep four principles in mind. First, clarity about the purpose of our political education will help define the approach we take and the questions we ask. Second, we need to avoid dogmatic rhetoric by grounding our political-education work in fact and inquiry. Third, we need to balance education with our primary goal, political organizing. Fourth, varying the medium of education will keep people engaged. Fifth, exploring solutions will help prevent our members from becoming depressed after political-education sessions.

Defining the Purpose, Content, and Approach

Most often, the need for political education emerges in one of three situations—when developing issues, when exploring a new constituency or alliance, or during what I call momentous events, which requires an approach that differs somewhat from the approaches we use in the first two situations. When we are developing issues and relating to a new group of people, the organizing context will lead us to what we need to know. In these situations, our questions are geared toward helping us make decisions or take action. If we're looking for policies that address racism in education, then we probably want to know the history of affirmative action and desegregation, and maybe we also want to find out about other ideas that were floating around but didn't get implemented. We also want to understand the power structure in our public schools right up to the top, including the informal power brokers, such as corporations doing business with our schools. In this case, political education is distinct from run-of-the-mill issue research because it is long-term. We might be fighting on issues of immediate concern while working out a strategy to do more. With a new constituency, we'd want to know how it was organized, what the key institutions were, who provided leadership, how that community came to be rubbing up against us, and so on.

Illustration: CTWO Uses Political Education to Explore a Dangerous Issue

The uprising in Los Angeles in 1992, after the acquittal of four police officers accused of violating the civil rights of Rodney King with a brutal beating, woke many people to the realities of police control in communities of color. Throughout the 1980s neighborhood associations and community groups had demanded responsive policing while ignoring the ongoing problem of police violence and the new problem of the booming prison-industrial complex. While CTWO and its member organizations had taken on some big institutions, none of them had guns, so members were understandably intimidated by the notion of confronting police departments. It was clear that the issue-development process would require a lot of education if people were going to get behind a police-accountability campaign.

To get a handle on how to approach this issue, CTWO, the Applied Research Center, and five organizations on the local level entered into a political-education and issue-development process that took more than a year, the longest a CTWO campaign had been in development. Leaders from each partner organization framed the questions for the process at an initial national gathering. Local research teams composed of members investigated the role of the police in society, police practices and training, the limitations of community policing, and the financing of police-brutality lawsuits. Each team sent its findings to designers at CTWO and the Applied Research Center, who then crafted ninety-minute discussions for issue study groups. These discussions ultimately produced the policy platform for the campaign.

For CTWO, convening issue study groups has become standard practice when organizations are investigating a new issue or a new aspect of an old issue. Each study group is designed with clear objectives, a process for reflecting on the experience of the people in the room, and one for adding new information to that experience. Sessions are designed to be easily replicated and to be led by people who are not necessarily deeply embedded in the topic. A series generally includes information about the history of the issue, competing theories about the role of the institution being targeted, its standard practices, and precedents for reform.

By the end of the 1990s, political education had become central to every CTWO program. The three-day Community Action training starts with a session on the history of organizing in communities of color. Each strategy session of CTWO's newest national effort, GROWL, includes a review of the policy landscape and recent research. CTWO staff members are not exempted; they attend regularly scheduled education sessions on theories of racism and antiracist struggle, the racialized history of immigration, and welfare policy. CTWO has added a training for trainers, as the role of an organizer now includes political thinking and education.

Illustration: REJN Designs Educational Programs for Alliance Building

REJN's intentional discussions addressed the politics of sexuality and the resistance to women's and youth leadership among member groups. Work on sexuality was divisive, as there were no gay/lesbian groups in the network at the beginning. Leah Wise, the executive director, recalls that when homophobia started disrupting gatherings and local discussions, the lack of visibility among sexual minorities presented a real barrier. She notes that the role of religion in the South creates a fearful atmosphere for sexual minorities and that communities have a wide range of negative attitudes. Because REJN is centered on the principle of relationships, the first thought was "if we can get some folks into the room, then we can create spaces for people to recognize each others' humanity." REJN leaders tried to recruit gay/lesbian groups but could not find any at the time that were working on economic justice. Then, says Wise, "we talked about what would make it safe . . . for gay and lesbian people within the current groups to be more vocal." As gay people in member organizations began to come out at network gatherings, REJN made space for those discussions, which in turn set the stage for new groups to form and join the network, as in the case of Southerners on New Ground, a gay/lesbian/bi/trans group of activists who work on various issues. Wise notes that the role of REJN's leaders has been critical in the organization's taking on these issues.

REJN has also equipped itself to deal with international-migration and free-trade issues largely by building international exchanges; it has invited organizations of low-wage workers and activists from outside the United States to participate in strategic and analytical dialogues since 1992. REJN has also sent delegations of members to Mexico, Cuba, China, Chile, and South Africa to visit organizations and attend international conferences. These exchanges have emerged as one of the network's most popular programs and have led to new southern leadership on U.S. foreign and trade policy, a topic few domestic organizations address. Wise notes that, despite some initial resistance to investing the time and attention required to conduct these exchanges, "that was the only place where people got to interact with their peers, and that kind of exposure was very good."

"Immediately after the first gathering, people were armed and took off on the NAFTA fight," says Wise, who notes that NAFTA was considered largely a Latino issue. In Durham, REJN members hosted three televised community forums on the impact of free trade on local workers and communities. Rank-and-file delegations of REJN organizations testified at congressional hearings. REJN provided much of the presence of African American voters and grassroots people at those hearings, and these folks were able to engage with real confidence. Wise supplies the reason: "We had actually read NAFTA and had learned about the realities on the ground from people outside the country, so we could go toe to toe with the head of Nations Bank, who was arguing for NAFTA. People felt steeled that they knew what they were talking about." Although REJN did not single-handedly battle the globalization of capitalism through NAFTA, it did help to challenge the perception that only Latinos on the other side of the border were concerned about its effects. Wise acknowledges that much still needs to be done but proudly calls it "a good fight and a good piece of work."

Fighting racism plays a central and historically important role in the REJN network. Wise asserts that the history of the South, as well as its current conditions, demands that groups address racism and conflict. She notes that otherwise effective movements have been brought down by racial conflict and white supremacy. She offers the examples of the populist movement, in which the racism of populist leaders drove away the black base, and the southern tenant farmers union, which has been identified only recently as a primarily black organization rather than as "a movement of white socialists leading black workers." Wise notes that many REJN leaders have their own experiences in the civil rights movement to consider, including the ways in which the organizing of black folks "wasn't getting at recalcitrance in the white community." The focus on race carved out a critical role for REJN as the demographics of the South changed to include more Latino and a small number of Asian immigrants.

The work on race and the international work helped REJN members prepare to address changing demographics in their local areas. Wise says that "when the immigration here started, our folks were not the ones to say 'those are our enemies.'" REJN conducted a number of educational projects that helped in particular to bring Latino immigrants and black workers together. It hosted an exhibit of photos of black Mexicans by Ron Wilkins, organized a demonstration at INS offices in Durham to protest racist immigration policies ("Southern black folks doing that was a big leap," says Wise), sponsored a dialogue between black family farmers and immigrant farmworkers, and started the Resisting Rivalry: Black/Latino Organizing Project in North Carolina, which emerged out of conflicts and cooperation in contingent-work organizing. With the help of REJN, among other factors, groups doing service and advocacy around poverty have become more sensitive to immigrant issues, says Wise, and Latinos have been able to advance their organizing beyond the farmworker groups. But Wise says that REJN is committed to staying on top of this particular cross-racial relationship. She notes that "you can't sit on your laurels, you have to keep at it; . . . the forces tearing people apart are very powerful. When immigrants started coming into factories, construction, and service industries, black workers took a big hit, and that's real. Even though people didn't hate Mexicans, they still had a gut reaction of feeling threatened." She adds that dealing with international-economy and domestic-immigration issues has forced REJN to "think about vision and what kind of policy would be helpful for the people. Our space is a place to model what we want to be and have; [we] can't just continue to be against stuff."

Approaches to political education become a little less clear when we are confronted with momentous events, those incidents that shake the world, even if for only a minute. If our organization is the place where people get their political stimuli, then that is where they're likely to go when President Bush declares war on Iraq, the men who brutalized Rodney King are acquitted, the Berlin Wall falls, AFDC turns into TANF, or the World Trade Center is attacked and Bush declares war on Afghanistan. Often, people have conflicting feelings about, reactions to, and analyses of world-changing events, and they head straight for their community organization in order to express their thoughts and feelings. Organizations tend toward two opposite reactions. One set ignores the momentous event, fearing a discussion that will reveal cracks in the organization's mask of unity. Perhaps there are some informal discussions, but nothing is organized. Another set rushes to design a comprehensive two-hour discussion that is to end with an organizational statement of outrage or solidarity. After these formal sessions, the organizer often reports, "We had our discussion. It didn't go well." That's usually code for saying that people who worked together perfectly well on yesterday's issues were calling each other names. Some organizations even squeeze out a statement from this process, at the cost of lost members and bad will.

To address the implications of current events, sometimes we need a break from the requirement to take action. The need for action raises the stakes of any discussion. And if the momentous event is not widely understood by members, the rush to unity and action might cut off a fine opportunity for inquiry, education, and greater long-term unity. Taking the time to conduct a discussion without the expectation of immediate action will reveal how ready an organization is to make a statement. If opinions are closely aligned, the desire to do something will become clear. If they are not, people have the time to gather more information and organize each other. Some will accuse me of giving us an out on issues that require widespread support and timely action. However, a public statement that amounts to nothing more than ink on paper, that doesn't have a unified, educated base behind it, is relatively meaningless. Organizations are much more likely to take solid positions on issues if the members are accustomed to having deep political discussions that sometimes involve a lot of conflict. Most of those issues will still be there in six months, when the organization will have the knowledge base to say something intelligent. In the meantime, a thoughtfully constructed program designed to engage members in current events will go a long way toward broadening members' world-views.

Illustration: DARE Takes Multiple Steps After September 11th

DARE's history of ongoing political education helped the organization conduct an effective education and decision-making process after September 11, 2001. The early reactions and discussions were characterized by great emotion on the part of both the staff and the membership. For example, while some people focused on the great harm that the U.S. military had done with impunity to thousands of their own people in other parts of the world (such as the Dominican Republic, home of many DARE staff and members), others were frightened for family members who might be affected by terrorism because they were flying that very day. Director Sara Mersha says that among the staff "emotions were raw, and people felt hurt at seeing opposite reactions from others. We took a break and then talked about why different people might be reacting the way they did, but it was still difficult."

DARE held its first membership discussion about the events on September 12th, during a regularly scheduled meeting. Mersha reflects that the same dynamics emerged again to generate heat. That discussion, which aimed only at surfacing peoples' feelings about the event, revealed the fact that while most of the members saw the previous day's shocking events in the context of a history of U.S. economic, political, and military interventions around the world, some members had another perspective.

The next night, a small group of DARE staff and members attended a meeting of activists who worked with a variety of organizations but who were representing only themselves. The people attending decided to take concrete steps toward disrupting the use of grief and anger to further U.S. military violence, but only as individuals. They hosted a press conference on the theme of being "united for peace." This activity allowed DARE members who wanted to to take some action without pushing the organization to arrive at a position prematurely.

DARE staff and members spent the next four months having conversations internally and with allies across the country, and they worked as well to understand ongoing events. By January, the war in Afghanistan had ended, and other policies had emerged. In DARE's January meeting, members identified the elements of the war on terrorism and initiated discussion about the racial implications, then generated next steps for DARE. At a February workshop, leaders explained in more detail the major components of the war on terrorism—the Office of Homeland Security, the Patriot Act, the war in Afghanistan, and international law enforcement—before participants broke into small groups to consider the potential effects on DARE's campaigns. After assessing the themes of those reports, members did an exercise in which they wrote one thing they were for and one thing they were against. The workshop revealed the costs and benefits to DARE's constituency of these policies.

The ideas emerging from these activities then formed the basis for a consensual decision that DARE should develop a statement. A team of people drafted it, and it was discussed and adopted at the next membership meeting. The statement itself reflects the complications of the issue and is closely tied to DARE's base of unity and strength—the organization's issues and campaigns. The statement expresses sadness over both September 11th and the War on Terrorism; it has five clauses that state the conditions that will and those that will not create real justice and peace. The clauses address race and religious profiling, military spending and aggression, corporate behavior and the role of the media. DARE used the statement frequently within the organization, as well as during the May 1, 2002, March for Immigrant Rights and at a September 2002 local action at a prison protesting civil rights violations involved in the push to detain suspected terrorists.

Mersha names two factors that led to consensus on the statement. One was members' base of knowledge about U.S. military and economic history, which had been built through several years of political-education programs. The other was the inclusiveness of the organization's process for studying the issue, deciding to write it, and then producing it. She says that having enough time was critical: "We could not go straight to a position in September, or even October." She further notes that involving lots of people in making and implementing the decision prevented a backslide:

> At first, some of us were reluctant to think about making an organizational statement because of the potential backlash. But involving members in developing the conversations and workshops and meetings led to a lot of different people playing roles; they got invested in the process and the outcome. Once we started, the people who had been reluctant changed their minds, seeing how this was helping the organization make sense of things and remembering as a group that sometimes we do need to take a stand, even if there are risks involved. And the process was an outcome in itself in accountability to our membership in terms of what we said at public events and with other groups.

Many groups hire outside organizations to supply education about economic and social systems. These organizations offer a great service, especially for young groups with little capacity that haven't developed a good way to deal with internal conflict yet. Political education that comes from other sources can raise the level of engagement without generating ideological fights that an organization isn't ready for.

While your organization is defining the purpose of its political-education program, it is useful for you to think about your own educational goals. Completing the survey in Exercise 9.1 will allow you to specify what you would like to gain from and contribute to a political-education program.

In addition to determining the purpose of our political education and the approach we want to take to it, we need to think about the content of that education. Exhibit 9.1 outlines the basic goals of a curriculum for political education.

Starting with Inquiry and Sticking to Facts

In conducting political education, start with inquiry, stick to the facts, and avoid vague rhetoric. Rhetorical discussions are those that have no practical application or answers. We can spot rhetoric from these signs: the lack of facts or evidence, an unclear relationship of the discussion to the organization or constituency, the lack of a solution, and vast overstatements. To be effective and vigorous, our political-education program has to be based on facts and evidence. It has to present multiple sides to an issue so that people can compare their validity. This doesn't mean that we have to give equal time to the local antichoice group, but it does mean that we cannot misrepresent or overstate what the antichoice group says. Research and accuracy have to reach the highest standards when organizations take on political education.

Political education works best when it starts with inquiry rather than with answers. Focusing on what we want to learn and advancing the idea that everyone has something to learn in every situation do not in any way counteract the agenda to which we relate our political education. In fact, inquiry helps us identify why we are engaging with a topic in the first place. When we start with the answers, there is no need for education and reflection; leaders might as well just give the answers and be done with it. Starting from inquiry means we have to be prepared for ideas to emerge that we did not expect or with which we are uncomfortable, but even that is an important capacity to build among our organizations.

Balancing Education with Organizing and Action

The most effective political education works in concert with an organizing plan and is balanced with collective action. It is important to remember that the relationship of education and action is not simply a matter of one leading to the other:

Exercise 9.1. Survey for Political Education.

Date:

Name:

1. Campaigns I'm involved in:

2. Five topics I am interested in learning about and why:

Topic	Reason	Resources

3. Topics I can share knowledge about:

Exhibit 9.1. The Seven C's of Curriculum Design.

1. Culture	An organizational culture of learning and action must be created.
2. Climate	A conducive learning climate must be established for each learning experience.
3. Critical Consciousness	Teaching people to think critically is essential. Constructive conflict and analytical challenges can move people from their comfort zones to stimulate critical thinking and new ideas. Awareness of ourselves and our surroundings (our political, economic, social and environmental reality) is necessary before we can truly transform it.
4. Connections	Identifying connections *between* ideas, issues, constituencies, and communities; and *across* histories, cultures, identities, and geographic areas, can help people form new frameworks of understanding.
5. Collective Consolidation	By engaging in a collective learning process, people can consolidate their experiences, knowledge and ideas into shared understandings of problems and agreements about strategies and solutions.
6. *Capacitación*	Learning has many by-products that expand the action capacities of organizations and the individuals of which they are composed.
7. Concrete Change	Substantive and lasting societal change is the goal of action education.

Source: Copyright 1996 by Applied Research Center.

they influence and enable each other, and their timing shifts according to what is happening in the organization at any particular moment. Sometimes we get so caught up in the intricacies and enjoyment of designing education we lose sight of the educational aspects of taking action. If our primary goal is to build political organizations rather than schools, we have to carefully balance our education program with our organizing program.

Illustration: The Workplace Project Balances Education and Organizing

The Workplace Project has provided substantial political education since its beginning. When an immigrant worker came to the Project to take advantage of its legal services, he or she would be asked to sign a contract pledging to attend the Project's workers' course and then to organize other workers. The workers' course, which took place over eight weeks, was designed to be accessible and was centered mainly on the rights of workers, the function of unions, and the reasons for organizing. Each class lasted two hours, with teaching provided by the Project staff. For many immigrant workers, the course provided not only an orientation to the philosophies and analyses of the Workplace Project but also an introduction to the United States and an explanation of the contemporary immigrant experience.

The course supplied information and reflection opportunities for people as they organized in their own communities and workplaces. Jennifer Gordon, the Project's founder, writes that "the class need[s] to be linked to action, so that participants can test out what they are learning and practice being politically active in a real context. Imagination in the classroom only goes so far" (1999). Through the legal clinic and workers' course, Workplace Project constituents and members engaged in key policy debates over the rights of day laborers, the practices of employment agencies, and the nonpayment of wages.

After five or six years, the Project decided that the workers' course was too slow and didactic compared with the dynamism of the growing organization. In addition, involvement in the workers' course did not offset the essential client-service relationship established in the legal clinic. Gordon says, "No matter how great a relationship you developed, once the person's problem was solved, they were gone." As the membership and leadership continued to grow, Project leaders eventually saw a gap between the members and workers going the legal services/workers' course route. Saru Jayaraman, legal intern, says, "The idea was that once you come to the course, you become a member, but that didn't happen. The membership developed out of campaigns. The legal program became entirely separated from the liveliest base of the organization. Plus, when people got legal service, there was dependency on the lawyer, whereas that wasn't true in the day labor and other committees." (For a fuller discussion of the implications of providing services to aid organizing, see Chapter Two.) Organizer Carlos Canales puts it this way, "Start with doing, rather than talking. Don't forget that most people need a long process of education, but, in the meantime, we have to get changes. One worker says to me, Carlos, you take me on a long journey (education) but if you don't give me food (action), how are we going to survive on the trip?"

Taking lessons from their successful organizing on local and state policies, the Project decided to change the order of engagement and adjust the length of the course. The legal clinic, with its individual in-take system, was replaced by ongoing Friday workshops, in which people share their legal problems and solutions. Jayaraman notes, "This was an easy way to handle an influx of people and not take them on as cases." The first interaction people have with the Workplace Project, then, affects consciousness. When people see others with the same problems, they begin to perceive that all these people can't be at fault; something larger must be at work. After the Friday workshop, rather than move into meeting with an attorney, workers get the option of joining an industrial team. At the end of this two-to-three month process, members take a condensed version of the eight-week course.

Jayaraman, who was in charge of implementing the new system, notes that it was difficult to make the shift. She says, "The workers' course was a revered part of our program for years. Workers felt a sense of pride in passing the course. The staff loves every opportunity to stand up in front of a room and be a teacher." But these benefits were far outstripped by those emerging from the change. Whereas the workers' course curriculum required the training of teachers, the Friday workshops "can be done by a volunteer, a member, anyone who can get people a basic orientation and referral to one of the teams." Rather than having an "expert" expounding on the ins and outs of wage and hour enforcement, the new system requires workers to educate each other about their industry, the results of efforts to gain back wages and deal with other problems, and new issues that might be cropping up. The official course materials, then, reinforce and challenge people from the basis of their organizing experience rather than of their problem.

Using Multiple Methods of Engagement

People learn in different ways and reflect on issues at different speeds, so it's important that your political-education program offer lots of different options for learning and reflecting. Having a variety of methods allows you to reach people who have different levels of exposure to and knowledge about a particular topic, and popular-education models allow your more experienced members to be leaders in an education process. Some organizations have study groups, in which people get together, read or watch something, then discuss it. Others have developed curricula using popular-education principles. Still others use conferences, films, lectures, travel, and articles to explore different topics. Many organizations are now experimenting with cultural production as a political-education tool, which results in murals or CDs created by community members in collaboration with artists. Although it can be expensive, organizations get real mileage out of visiting other organizations either in the United States or abroad. Strategic planning also provides many excellent opportunities for people to learn about what is going on in the world around them and to reflect on the implications.

Illustration: 9to5 Builds Education into Strategic Planning

As happens in many groups, founder Karen Nussbaum's leaving the executive directorship in 1993 gave the National Association of Working Women an opportunity to take stock of its membership, issues, and operations. A strategic planning process helped consolidate the organization's emerging identity as a national organization made up of all kinds of working women, a move that broadened its early base of university-based clerical workers. Devising the strategic plan required members to understand what was at stake for working women with a variety of other identities and to determine what kinds of issues would be most important in the next period.

The planning process included a number of educational discussions, including a vigorous antioppression training process that enabled the organization to take up new issues and engage new constituencies. Ellen Bravo reflects on the need for such work: "Regardless of the fact [that] we'd always been multiracial, we were in fact white, [including the] top staff and decision makers, and the board was not so active." Work groups composed of members in each chapter drafted elements of the strategic plan. These were then circulated for feedback, rewritten, and discussed in national meetings, where a final version, including an evaluation plan, was affirmed. This process led 9to5 to describe its constituency as low-wage, low-income women, women in traditional female jobs, and anyone who experienced discrimination on the job and to define its mission as strengthening women's ability to win economic justice. It also led 9to5 to its current set of five issues: welfare, workfare, contingent work, work/family, and antidiscrimination.

The decision to take on welfare, especially before 1996, was unusual among groups of workers. "People said why would we discuss that? That's not what we do," Bravo recalls. "For us it wasn't an issue of is it what we do or not; even if you [aren't] involved with welfare, and [are] only low-wage workers, you still want to understand the economy, the connection between the way work is organized and how welfare fits into it."

Illustration: 9to5 Inserts Political Education into All Its Activities

9to5 builds political education into as many activities as possible. Grounded in popular-education principles that stress the exchange of experiences, the sessions often start with an individual reflection, then move to collective analysis. Bravo considers the 9to5 newsletter and action alerts as political education, along with strategic planning and specific trainings. She says that each activity is designed to advance multiple kinds of knowledge: "Even our nitty-gritty trainings about how to build a campaign [are] designed so that you're not just learning a technique but also something about how the system works—for example, in thinking through allies and targets."

We can see this concept at work in a number of 9to5 projects. The 9to5 "Voter Guide" opens with having the reader reflect on key election issues so she can see her points of unity with and isolate her differences from the larger 9to5 agenda. Then the reader is encouraged to recruit people to use the literature in order to get five other people to become involved in the election. After the election, local leaders meet and generate a theme, draft and finalize a message, and insert it in the 9to5 "Send a Message with Your Vote" envelope to newly elected officials.

In 9to5's three-day training session for leaders, the same principles are applied. The weekend starts with trios sharing how they developed their sense of justice and how they have acted on that, then moves to having participants identify what people need and why they don't have it, and ends with their suggesting solutions. Each person reflects on her own list with a small group, the group chooses the top five reasons for members' developing a sense of justice, then those are all gathered together. The responses to the question of what people don't have and why are also collected, followed by responses to the question about what needs to be done. Then participants make a step-by-step plan for their outreach efforts.

9to5 trains members to replicate these designs on their own. While Bravo acknowledges that being a good trainer requires a special skill, she also recognizes that there's a lot of hidden talent out there. When new trainers are learning, they receive a script of the training, conduct it with experienced trainers watching, and then conduct it on their own. New trainers often watch their practice sessions on tape to evaluate themselves.

Although all political education at 9to5 does not take place in such an organized way, the formal sessions open up space for members' curiosity. Amy Stier, 9to5's organizing director, notes that people are hungry to learn more about economic systems and justice. "After a training session one of the things that always happened is that people would come to me, college kids and workers, and would always ask me for books." Stier recommends a number of works that "help people to develop politics," such as *The Wretched of the Earth* (Fanon, [1961] 1986), *The Grapes of Wrath* (Steinbeck, 1939), *The West Virginia Mine Wars* (Corbin, 1990), *Labor's Untold Story* (Boyer and Morais, [c. 1955] 1977), *Us and Them* (Carnes and Tauss, 1996), and *Memoirs of a Race Traitor* (Segrest, 1994). 9to5's attention to political education, formal and informal, enables it to meet the challenges posed by conservative policies, both economic and social, through projects that are grounded in but not limited to the workplace.

Illustration: CTWO Uses Many Forms of Education

Coming out of its experience with police accountability, CTWO started the Winning Action for Gender Equity (WAGE) program to build feminist analysis and experience among members of community organizations of color. The goal was to strengthen women's leadership and challenge the division of labor and issue choices within mixed-gender community organizations. WAGE was centered around model campaigns designed to attack the intersection of race, class, and gender, while gathering leaders from across the country to explore the theories supporting those intersections. To develop the capacity to look at the intersection of major systems, CTWO greatly expanded its facility with popular education and documentation. WAGE gatherings featured activities involving drawing and theater, while organizers and leaders added group and individual journal writing to their tool kit for reflection. These documents helped groups participating in WAGE evaluate their campaign progress, assess their leadership development, and create an organizational history that could be used in orienting new members and staff and in strategic planning.

Countering the Doom and Gloom

Often, political education is depressing. It is one of the few times in communal life that people look at the big picture and get a real sense of the power of the conservative agenda, and it is easy to become overwhelmed and feel hopeless. If that happens, our political-education program will drive people away rather than inspire them to go to the next level. Obviously, we cannot play down the strengths of the other side to avoid depressing people, but we can reveal the opposition's vulnerabilities and explore the ways in which people have resisted that agenda, the solutions that folks have generated. These features will distinguish a program from the vast majority of other educational efforts.

Illustration: DARE Connects Political Education to Solutions

DARE's ongoing political-education programs, while loosely connected to campaigns and activities, always stress the solutions that people are working toward. For example, DARE includes three political-education sessions in its ten-week leadership-training program in the skills of organizing: a class on the World Bank/International Monetary Fund (IMF) and alternatives to capitalism, one on sexuality, and one on immigration, imperialism, and white supremacy. Each discussion has some grounding in current policies that affect DARE members. The sessions on the IMF/World Bank and alternatives to capitalism help to illuminate the lack of good jobs in Providence; the sexuality discussion allows DARE to explore issues affecting its gay members and allies; the immigration, imperialism, and white supremacy discussion highlights contemporary racism.

One of the discussions DARE conducted on the international financial institutions occurred just before local actions in September 2002 on economic justice issues; the discussion was held as a teach-in in conjunction with Jobs with Justice. The two organizations took action by pressuring a local hotel developer to meet with HERE and not to try to influence workers against a unionization effort (neutrality agreement). A sexuality discussion ended with agreements to challenge homophobic and heterosexist remarks in the organization, to make resources for fighting homophobia available to members, to adopt an antidiscrimination policy, and to seek out opportunities to address those issues in DARE's campaigns. A discussion on immigration, imperialism, and white supremacy affirmed the role of DARE's existing demands and campaigns in fighting white supremacy throughout society.

Conclusion

We are heading toward a time in which people are going to need their community organizations as places where they can have political discussions that question that status quo. The war on terrorism has undeniably chilled intellectual debate in this country. Examples abound of attempts to control and monitor our thinking. Just after September 11th, a group of conservative academics released a report criticizing the curricula of colleagues whose material was deemed "unpatriotic," and the editor of the *Sacramento Bee*, a mainstream daily, was shouted down when she questioned limits on journalistic freedom during a speech. The Office of Homeland Security released plans to have librarians turn over borrowers' reading lists, and colleges have been required to submit to the government the class choices of foreign students. Meanwhile, people are frightened and confused by terror attacks. Clearly, the harder it is to gain a balanced perspective about the world from regular sources the greater the burden on community organizations to make room for the big questions.

Little organizing practice has fully integrated campaigns with programs that develop politics, and there is a danger of moving too far into political education without any grounding in an action plan. Some feminists and racial justice organizers, for example, have reacted to Alinskyist limitations by creating programs that are heavy on leadership training and political education but light on campaigns and action. I can understand the temptation. Providing extensive developmental programs for twenty people we can count on is much easier than constantly recruiting and politically orienting new people so that they too can confront the power structure. Likewise, it is often easier to simply recruit those new people over and over again than to deal with the contradictions residing in the ideas of our members. The beauty of innovation in organizing emerges from the marriage of the two: political education creates the reflection and growth opportunities that motivate action, and action provides the expression of newly clarified values.

CONCLUSION

Community Organizing—Tomorrow

One message overwhelmed me as I researched and wrote this book. Progressive activists can be most successful if we focus on two things: paying attention and taking action. One of these without the other will limit our success. There are many ways to organize our people, to gain attention for our issues, to enforce existing social-justice policies, and to make new policies that count. We can choose from a huge variety of tactics and organizational forms. But those choices have to be guided by a real understanding of what is going on around us and of how our people are affected now and will be affected in the future. There's a lot to pay attention to: changes in the economy, implications of identity, the connection between local communities and global trends, the tactics of the opposition, as well as how our organizations are shaping themselves. Paying attention is about being self-conscious in the best sense—having a heightened awareness of what's going on with us and around us. It does not mean knowing everything about everything, but it does mean expanding our notion of what is relevant to our work.

But being aware without a commitment to action divorces us from real life and keeps us from distinguishing what requires our attention from what doesn't. In this age of rapid information diffusion, that is a dangerous thing. Much of the information coming our way catalogues the horrors of being a regular person, the terrible consequences of the policies that control our lives. Without a commitment to taking action that will improve conditions, we don't demand the kind of information we need to make changes, and we become paralyzed by what we know. To avoid being bothered, government and corporations frequently send us the message that things cannot be different. Capitalism cannot be reformed. Prisons cannot be closed. Child care cannot be subsidized. Racism cannot be eradicated.

As much as we get those messages from the higher-ups, progressives are also guilty of letting our cynicism limit our options. Largely, we think of threats rather than opportunities. We isolate ourselves by not having the fundamental conversations about values with our constituencies as well as opponents. We narrow our language. We decline to take up projects because no foundation will fund them. While I would not say that we are our own worst enemies, the other side often gets us to believe and repeat their hype.

We have to do better. Something can be done to reverse the injustices caused by capitalism, racism, and sexism, and we have to do it. No one else will do it but us. And once we have done it, we will have to do it again. After the next movement comes and goes, we will have to leave behind people who are prepared to keep pushing for more. Our work is about the most basic questions facing world society; we cannot think the other side will give up if we just start winning a little bit. Resting on our laurels will never take us the whole way to justice. The law of inertia means that we will continue to do what we have been accustomed to doing—providing services that should rest in government, making the call ourselves rather than taking five members to make a demand, designing actions that look just like last week's. Especially in today's context of raging patriotism and wartime hostility to dissent, paying attention and taking action require courage and discipline. The groups profiled in this book have taught me the value of taking a calculated risk. The calculation is in paying attention, and the risk is in action.

RESOURCES

This section is designed to give readers additional references to helpful organizations, websites, and written materials. It begins with contact information for each of the Ms. Foundation grantees profiled in the book, then lists training centers and programs in which one can learn about organizing. The last part is a list of recommended readings.

Current and Former Ms. Foundation Grantees Profiled

Campaign on Contingent Work
33 Harrison Ave., 4th floor
Boston, MA 02111
Phone: 617-338-9966
ccw@igc.org

Center for the Child Care Workforce
555 New Jersey Ave. NW
Washington, DC 20001
Phone: 202-662-8005
ccw@aft.org

Center for Third World Organizing
1218 E. 21st St.
Oakland, CA 94606
Phone: 510-533-7583
www.ctwo.org

Chinese Staff and Workers Association
5411 Seventh Ave.
Brooklyn, NY 11220
Phone: 212-619-9752

Direct Action for Rights and Equality
340 Lockwood St.
Providence, RI 02907
Phone: 401-351-6960
www.daretowin.org

Justice, Economic Dignity and Independence for Women
150 South Ambassador Plaza, 600E
Suite 5B
Salt Lake City, UT 84102
Phone: 801-323-9452
www.jedi4women.org

Los Angeles Alliance for a New Economy
548 S. Spring St., Suite 630
Los Angeles, CA 90013
Phone: 213-486-9880
www.laane.org

9to5 National Association of Working Women
Ellen Bravo/Tracy Jones
231 West Wisconsin Ave., Suite 900
Milwaukee, WI 53203
Phone: 414-274-0928
naww9to5@execpc.com

Southeast Regional Economic Justice Network
P.O. Box 240
Durham, NC 27702
Phone: 919-683-4310
serejn@rejn.org

Wider Opportunities for Women
1001 Connecticut Ave. NW
Suite 930
Washington, DC 20036
Phone: 202-464-1596
www.wow.org

Women's Association for Women's Alternatives
225 South Chester Rd., Suite 6
Swarthmore, PA 19081
Phone: 610-543-5022
ww.womensassoc.org

Women's Institute for Leadership Development
33 Harrison St., 4th floor
Boston, MA 02111
Phone: 617-426-0520
www.wildlabor.org

Working Partnerships USA
2101 Almaden Rd., Suite 100
San Jose, CA 95125
Phone: 408-269-7872
www.wpusa.org

The Workplace Project
91 N. Franklin St., Suite 207
Hempstead, NY 11550
Phone: 516-565-5377
workplace@igc.org

Training and Resource Centers

AFL-CIO Organizing Institute
815 16th St. NW
Washington, DC 20006
Phone: 800-848-3021
organize@aflcio.org

Center for Community Change
1000 Wisconsin Ave. NW
Washington, DC 20007
Phone: 202-342-0567
www.communitychange.org

Grassroots Leadership
P.O. Box 36006
Charlotte, NC 28236
Phone: 704-332-3090
www.grassrootsleadership.org

Midwest Academy
28 E. Jackson St. #605
Chicago, IL 60604
Phone 312-427-2304
www.midwestacademy.org

New York Organizing Support Center
180 Varick St., 12th floor
New York, NY 10014
Phone: 212-627-9960

People's (formerly, Pacific) Institute for Community Organizing
171 Santa Rosa Ave.
Oakland, CA 94610
Phone: 510-655-2801
www.piconetwork.org

The Southern Empowerment Project
343 Ellis Ave.
Maryville, TN 37804
Phone: 865-984-6500
www.southernempowerment.org

Western States Center
P.O. Box 40305
Portland, OR 97204
Phone: 503-228-8866
www.westernstatescenter.org

Networks and Coalitions

Asian Pacific Islander Environmental Network
310 8th St., Suite 309
Oakland, CA 94607
Phone: 510-834-8920
www.apen4ej.org

Jobs with Justice
501 3rd St. NW
Washington, DC 20001
Phone: 202-434-1106
www.jwj.org

Living Wage Resource Center
1486 Dorchester Ave.
Boston, MA 02122
Phone: 617-740-9500
www.acorn.org

National Network for Immigrant Rights
310 8th St., Suite 303
Oakland, CA 94607
Phone: 510-465-1984
nnirr@nnirr.org

National Organizers Alliance
715 G St. SE
Washington, DC 20003
Phone: 202-543-6603
www.noacentral.org

North American Alliance for Fair Employment
33 Harrison Ave., 3rd floor
Boston, MA 02111
Phone: 617-482-6300
www.fairjobs.org

Southwest Network for Environmental and Economic Justice
117 Seventh St. NW
Albuquerque, NM 87102
Phone: 505-242-0416

Research and Education

Applied Research Center
3781 Broadway
Oakland, CA 94611
Phone: 510-653-3415
www.arc.org

Center for Law and Social Policy
1015 15th St. NW
Suite 400
Washington, DC 20005
Phone: 202-906-8000
www.clasp.org

The Data Center
1904 Franklin St., Suite 900
Oakland, CA 94612
Phone: 510-835-4692
www.datacenter.org

National Environmental Justice Resource Center
at Clark University
223 James P. Brawley Dr.
Atlanta, GA 30314
Phone: 404-880-6911
www.ejrc.cau.edu/

United for a Fair Economy
37 Temple Place, 2nd floor
Boston, MA 02111
Phone: 617-423-2148
www.ufenet.org

Websites

Alliance for Justice (rules for nonprofit lobbying)
www.afj.org/fai/non-profit.html

The Black Commentator
www.theblackcommentator.org

University of Ohio at Toledo (papers on community organizing)
www.comm-org.utoledo.edu

Recommended Reading

Abrams, K. *Don't Give Up the Fight: The Story of the Fight for Health Insurance for Family Daycare Providers.* Providence, R.I.: Direct Action for Rights and Equality, 1999.

Armstrong, P. "Professions, Unions, or What? Learning from Nurses." In L. Briskin and P. McDermott (eds.), *Women Challenging Unions.* Toronto: University of Toronto Press, 1993.

Bacon, D. "The AFL-CIO Reverses Course on Immigration." Nov. 14, 1999. Available at LaborNet: newsline11/14/99 www.labornet.org/x/copy-of-site/news/11.14.99/01.html

Bonacich, E., and Cheng, L. *Labor Immigration under Capitalism.* Berkeley: University of California Press, 1984.

Brooks, J., and Pearce, D. "Meeting Needs, Measuring Outcomes: The Self-Sufficiency Standard as a Tool for Policy-Making, Evaluation and Client Counseling." *Clearinghouse Review,* May-June 2000, pp. 34–48.

Calpotura, F., and Fellner, K. *Square Pegs Find Their Groove.* Self-published in 1997; available at comm.org.utoledo.edu

Campaign on Contingent Work. *A Workplace Divided: Understanding Contingent Work for Activists.* Boston: Campaign on Contingent Work, 1999.

Davies, M. W. *Woman's Place Is at the Typewriter: Office Work and Office Workers 1870–1930.* Philadelphia: Temple University Press, 1982.

Howes, C., Phillips, D., and Whitebook, M. *Who Cares? Childcare, Teachers, and the Quality of Care.* Berkeley, Calif.: Center for the Early Childhood Workforce, 1990.

Johnson, O. "Activist Credited with Helping to Pass Living-Wage Measure." *Los Angeles Times,* June 4, 2001.

Kwong, P. "American Sweatshops 1980s Style." In C. Cohen and others (eds.), *Women Transforming Politics.* New York: New York University Press, 1997.

Piven, F. F., and Cloward, R. *Poor Peoples' Movements: Why They Succeed, How They Fail.* New York: Vintage Books, 1979.

Pollin, R., and Luce, S. *The Living Wage: Building a Fair Economy.* New York: New Press, 1998.

Quadagno, J. *The Color of Welfare: How Racism Undermined the War on Poverty.* New York: Oxford University Press, 1994.

Ramirez, M. "Dead Ends on Mean Streets: Workers Often Wander into Scams." *Newsday*, Mar. 5, 1988.

Sen, R. "Winning Action for Gender Equity: A Plan for Organizing Communities of Color." In C. Cohen and others (eds.), *Women Transforming Politics*. New York: New York University Press, 1997.

Theodore, N., and Mehta, C. *Contingent Work and the Staffing Industry: A Review of Worker-Centered Policy and Practice*. New York: Ford Foundation, Oct. 1999.

REFERENCES

Alinsky, S. D. *Rules for Radicals: A Pragmatic Primer for Realistic Radicals.* New York: Vintage Books, 1989. (Originally published 1970.)

Alinsky, S. D. *Reveille for Radicals.* New York: Random House, 1991. (Originally published 1946.)

Ambinder, M. J. *Vast, Right-Wing Cabal: Meet the Most Powerful Conservative Group You've Never Heard Of.* May 2, 2002. Available at http://printerfriendly.abcnews.com/printer-friendly/print?fetchfromGLUE=true&GLUEService=abcnewscom

Avalos, J., Bervera, S., and Cutting, H. "Silencing Poverty: A Study on News Coverage of Welfare." In *From Poverty to Punishment: How Welfare Reform Punishes the Poor.* Oakland, Calif.: Applied Research Center, 2002.

Bacon, D. *Latinos Making Their Mark Through Unions—Not Ballot Box.* Dec. 1995. Available at www.pacificnews.org/jinn/stories/1.04/951229-unions.html

Bacon, D. *Why Some Employees Can't Protest Slave Wages.* Nov. 3, 1998. Available at www.pacificnews.org/jinn/stories/4.22/981103-immigration.html

Blake, K., ed. *The Ark NOA Special Gathering Report, #14.* Washington, D.C.: National Organizers Alliance, 1999.

Bobo, K., Kendall, J., and Max, S. *Organizing for Social Change.* Minneapolis: Seven Springs Press, 1990.

Boyer, R. O., and Morais, H. M. *Labor's Untold Story.* New York: United Electrical Radio and Machine Workers of America, 1977. (Originally published c. 1955.)

Brown, D. "AIDS Groups Feel Heat After Demonstration: Federal Funding Probe Follows Barcelona Protest Against U.S. Health Secretary." *Washington Post,* Aug. 19, 2002. Available at www.commondreams.org/headlines02/0819-02.htm

Campaign on Contingent Work. *What's Wrong with Temp Work: A Report on the Temp Industry in Massachusetts.* Boston, 1999. Available at www.fairjobs.org/report/mass/probs.php

Campaign on Contingent Work. *Temp Work, Tempfare, and the Decline of Good Jobs in Massachusetts.* Boston: Campaign on Contingent Work, Mar. 2000.

Carnes, J., and Tauss, H. *Us and Them.* New York: Oxford University Press, 1996.

Center for the Child Care Workforce. *Creating Better Family Child Care Jobs: Model Work Standards for Teaching Staff in Center-Based Child Care.* Washington, D.C.: Center for the Child Care Workforce, 1999.

Center for the Child Care Workforce. *Current Data on Child Care Salaries and Benefits in the United States.* Washington, D.C.: Center for the Child Care Workforce, Mar. 2000.

Chang, G. *Disposable Domestics: Immigrant Women Workers in the Global Economy.* Boston: South End Press, 2000.

"Combahee River Collective Statement." In *Home Girls: A Black Feminist Anthology.* New Brunswick: Rutgers University Press, 2000. (Originally published 1983.)

Common Sense Foundation. *Common Sense Says,* 2000, *3* (11).

Conger, K. H. "Spreading Out and Digging in Christian Conservatives and State Republican Parties: Special Study Feature." *Campaigns and Elections* (published by the *Congressional Quarterly*), Feb. 2002. Available at www.findarticles.com/cf_0/m2519/1_23/82757259/print.jhtml

Cook, C. D. "Temps Demand a New Deal." *The Nation,* Mar. 27, 2000, *270* (12), 13–19.

Corbin, D. A. *The West Virginia Mine Wars, an Anthology.* Charleston, W.Va.: Appalachian Editions, 1990.

Crittenden, Ann. *The Price of Motherhood. Why the Most Important Job in the World Is Still the Least Valued.* New York: Metropolitan Books, 2001.

Davis, A. Y. *Women, Race and Class.* New York: Random House, 1983.

Delgado, G. *Organizing the Movement: The Roots and Growth of ACORN.* Philadelphia: Temple University Press, 1986.

Delgado, G. *Beyond the Politics of Place.* Oakland, Calif.: Chardon Press, 1997. (Originally published 1993.)

Economic Policy Institute. *Non-standard Work, Sub-standard Jobs.* New York: Economic Policy Institute, 1997.

Fanon, F. *The Wretched of the Earth.* New York: Grove Press, 1986. (Originally published 1961.)

Fairness and Accuracy in Reporting. "FCC Moves to Intensify Media Consolidation." *FAIR Action Alert,* Apr. 20, 2001.

Fellner, K. *Is Nothing Sacred?! The Ark, #10.* Washington, D.C.: National Organizers Alliance, 1998.

Freeman, J. "The Tyranny of Structurelessness." In A. Koedt, E. Levine, and A. Rapone (eds.), *Radical Feminism.* New York: Quadrangle, New York Times Book Company, 1973.

Freire, P. *Pedagogy of the Oppressed.* New York: Continuum, 2000. (Originally published 1970.)

Gapasin, F. "Beyond the Wage Fight: Social Movement Unionism and Latino Immigrant Workers." *ColorLines,* Summer 1999, pp. 31–34.

Gitlin, T. *The Twilight of Our Common Dreams: Why America Is Wracked by Culture Wars.* New York: Metropolitan Books, 1995.

Gordon, J. *The Campaign for the Unpaid Wages Prohibition Act: Latino Immigrants Change New York Wage Law.* Working Paper 4. Washington, D.C.: Carnegie Endowment for International Peace, Sept. 1999. Available at www.ceip.org/files/;publications/imp_wp4gordon.asp

Granville, W. "Bestriding the World." *Campaign for Press and Broadcasting Freedom*, Mediachannel.org, 2001.

Hardisty, J. *Mobilizing Resentment: Conservative Resurgence from the John Birch Society to the Promise Keepers.* Boston: Beacon Press, 1999.

Horwitt, S. D. *Let Them Call Me Rebel: Saul Alinsky, His Life and Legacy.* New York: Knopf, 1989.

Ignatiev, N. *How the Irish Became White.* New York: Routledge, 1995.

Kelley, R.D.G. "Identity Politics and Class Struggle." *New Politics,* 1997, *6* (2, whole no. 22). Available at www.wpunj.edu/~newpol/issue22/lalley22.htm

Klein, K. *Fundraising for Social Change.* San Francisco: Jossey-Bass, 2000.

LaBotz, D. *The Troublemakers' Handbook.* Detroit: Labor Notes, 1991.

Louie, M. C. *Sweatshop Warriors: Immigrant Women Workers Take on the Global Factory.* Boston: South End Press, 2001.

Lytle, T., and Horvitz, L. "Praise for the Bush Policy Questioned." *South Florida Sun Sentinel,* Mar. 2, 2002. Available at www.sun-sentinel.com/news/local/florida/sfl-fjeb02mar02.story?coll=sfla%2Dnews%2Dflorida

Madigan, T. "Who Is Killing the Women of Juarez?" *Fort Worth Star-Telegram,* Mar. 16, 1999. Available at http://takenbythesky.net//juarez//march16_1999.html

Maggio, R. *The New Beacon Book of Quotations by Women.* Boston: Beacon Press, 1998.

Milbank, D. "Religious Right Finds Its Center in Oval Office: Bush Emerges as Movement's Leader After Robertson Leaves Christian Coalition." *Washington Post,* Dec. 24, 2001, p. A2.

Miller, M. *Critique of Gary Delgado, Beyond the Politics of Place.* San Francisco: Organize! Training Center, 1996. Available at comm.org.utoledo.edu/papers96/miller.html#major

Moberg, D. "Why Women Still Don't Get Equal Pay." *In These Times* (Chicago), Jan. 8, 2001.

Murray, B. "Living Wage Comes of Age: An Increasingly Sophisticated Movement Has Put Opponents on the Defensive." *The Nation,* July 23, 2001. Available at www.acorn.org/acorn10/livingwagepressclips/comes.htm

9to5, National Association of Working Women. *Illegal and Unfair: Milwaukee Temp Agencies Fail Employment Testing.* Milwaukee: 9to5, National Association of Working Women, 2000.

North American Alliance for Fair Employment. *Contingent Workers Fight for Fairness.* Boston: North American Alliance for Fair Employment, 2000.

Pearce, D. "The Feminization of Poverty: Women, Work and Family." *Urban and Social Change Review* (Special Issue on Women and Work), 1978, *11*, 28–36. Republished in vol. 4, *Women's Studies Yearbook: Working Women and Families.* Thousand Oaks, Calif.: Sage, 1979.

Roberts, D. *Killing the Black Body: Race, Reproduction and the Meaning of Liberty.* New York: Pantheon Books, 1997.

Robinson, A. *Grassroots Grants: An Activist's Guide to Proposal Writing.* San Francisco: Jossey-Bass, 1996.

Robinson, A. *Selling Social Change (Without Selling Out): Earned Income Strategies for Nonprofits.* San Francisco: Jossey-Bass, 2002.

Romero, M. *Maid in the U.S.A.* New York: Routledge, 1992.

Segrest, M. *Memoirs of a Race Traitor.* Boston: South End Press, 1994.

Santa Monicans Allied for Responsible Tourism. "Background on Misleading Anti-Measure Voter Guides." Santa Monica, Nov. 2002.

Shaw, R. *The Activists' Handbook: A Primer for the 1990s and Beyond.* Berkeley: University of California Press, 1996.

Steinbeck, J. *The Grapes of Wrath*. New York: Viking, 1939.

Stoecker, R., and Stall, S. *Community Organizing or Organizing Community? Gender and the Crafts of Empowerment*. Revised Nov. 1997; available at comm.org.utoledo.edu

Tomasky, M. *Left for Dead: The Life, Death and Possible Resurrection of Progressive Politics in America*. New York: Free Press, 1996.

Toney, M. "Identity and Formation Among Korean Immigrants in Los Angeles." Paper presented at the North American Labor History Conference, Detroit, Oct. 2000.

Walsh, M. W. "The Biggest Company Secret: Workers Challenge Employer Policies on Pay Confidentiality." *New York Times,* July 28, 2000, late edition, p. C1.

Working Partnerships. *Growing Together or Drifting Apart? Working Families and Business in the New Economy*. San Jose, Calif.: Working Partnerships, 1998a.

Working Partnerships. *Living Wage—An Opportunity for San Jose*. San Jose, Calif.: Working Partnerships, 1998b.

Yang, A. S. *The 2000 National Election Study and Gay and Lesbian Rights: Support for Equality Grows*. New York: National Gay and Lesbian Task Force Policy Institute, 2001.

INDEX

S

Sabbatical policies, 113
Salt Lake City, xxxi, 88–89
Same-boat argument, lx, 16
Sampson, T., 139
San Francisco, xxvi, xlix, 58, 63
San Jose, 66–67, 108, 130
Santa Monicans Allied for Responsible Tourism (SMART), LAANE, xxxiii, 65, 129–130
Scale, identity politics and achieving, lxiii
School system issues, public, 74, 119
Scientific management, 13–14
Seed, D., xxxi, 82, 84–85, 96
Segrest, M., 180
Self-interest of partner groups, 141
Self-Sufficiency Standard (WOW): development of by counties, 128–129; uses of the, 121; and welfare policy, xxxvi–xxxvii, 71–72, 121, 128–129
"Send a Message with Your Vote" campaign, 180
September 11th tragedy, xxx, 154; education and decision-making after, 172–173, 182; layoffs after, xxxiii, xl
Service Employees International Union (SEIU), lvii, 72; local 925, xxxiv, 31–32; nontraditional workers joining the, xxxvii, lviii
Service provision, limiting organization, 44–47
Service workers, lowest-paid, 119–120
Sexism: centrality and strength of, 13–14; challenging, 53, 181–182; and leadership development, 109; in unions, xxxviii
Sexual liberation issues, 63, 181; reproductive freedom, lxii, 14, 15
Sexuality: and gay rights, lxi, lxii, 123; the politics of, 169
Silicon Valley, xxxix–xl, 106, 130, 133
Single mothers, lxiii, 30, 112
Sites of community organizing: changes in, l, 9; conservative,

84–85, 96; geographically based versus community of interest, l; and political education, 168–174; public and private spheres as, liv, lx. *See also* Cultural contexts of organizing
Slavery, economic, 11
Small-group-activity learning methods, 105–106
Smith, M., xxx
Social change: approaches and organizing, 25, 47; and calculated risk, 184; is the goal of action education, 176
Social construction of biological characteristics, lx, 10
Social movements: 1960s, 2, 22; 1980s, 22; and building organizations, 2, 22–23; compared to community organizations, 22–23; new twenty-first century, 23, 47; and self-organization, 25–26; supporting large, 21–23
Social services caseworkers, xxxii, 154
Social work graduate schools, xlix
Southeast Regional Economic Justice Network (REJN): address, 186; illustrations from, 111, 114, 139, 169–171; profile of, xxxiv–xxxv
The Southern Empowerment Project, 188
Southerners on New Ground, 169
Southwest Network for Environmental and Economic Justice, 190
Spanish language, 147, 152, 153
Staffs of community organizations: former members joining, 29, 112; political education of, 169; white and male, xlix–l. *See also* Leadership development
Stall, S., liv
Standards and measures: childcare work, 120; of community benefits from contract tax subsidy or economic-development, 138; contingent work, 143–144; Self-Sufficiency Standard of welfare, xxxvi–xxxvii, 71–72, 128–129; universal, 17

Statements, group consensus, lxi, 173
Statistics,, keeping, 46
Steeg, M., 50, 55–56, 58, 66, 167
Steinbeck, J., 180
Stewart, B., 86
Stier, A., 39, 42, 180
Stoecker, R., liv
Stories: media coverage of victory, 147; mining ongoing organizational work for, 152; for the press, guidelines for, 160–162; societal problem family personification, 77
Strategic planning process: direct action, 88; and political education, 166, 179. *See also* Planning
Strategy and tactics: of collaboration or alliances, 137, 139, 147; inside-outside, 93; multiple, 92; of people of color, li–lii; planning Worksheet, 90–91; in Utah, 84–85; visual effects, 88–89. *See also* Direct action
Structural adjustment policies, neoliberal, 8
Structureless organizations, 27
Student Nonviolent Coordinating Committee (SNCC), lii
Students, marginalized groups of, 50
Students and Parents Taking Action for a Real Tomorrow (START), DARE, xxxi
Subsidy accountability, 70
Substantive demands, defined, 46
Survey form, for political education, 174, 175
Sweatshop system, xxix–xxx, 46, 59–60
Sweeney, J., lviii
Swift, J., 150–151

T

Tactics of organizers: challenging cultural domination, 54; conflict or cooperation, lv
Talking to people: by members as spokespeople, 161–163; and personal visits to targets, 40–41; reporters, 160–162; as research sources, 126–127, 152. *See also* Networks and coalitions

RESOURCES FOR SOCIAL CHANGE
AVAILABLE FROM JOSSEY-BASS AND CHARDON PRESS

Raise More Money:
The Best of the Grassroots Fundraising Journal
Kim Klein, Stephanie Roth, Editors

"When I want to know the answer to a fundraising question or a way to motivate and teach others, I go to some of the best fundraisers in the business-whose writing appears in this amazing collection of articles from the *Grassroots Fundraising Journal*."

—*Joan Garner, Southern Partners Fund*

Whether you are a new or seasoned fundraiser, this collection of the best articles from the *Grassroots Fundraising Journal* will provide you with new inspiration to help bring in more money for your organization. Filled with strategies and guidance, this unprecedented anthology shows you how small nonprofits can raise money from their communities and develop long-term financial stability.

Paperback ISBN: 0-7879-6175-2

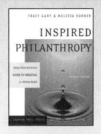

Inspired Philanthropy:
Your Step-by-Step Guide to Creating a Giving Plan
SECOND EDITION
Tracy Gary and Melissa Kohner

If you want to change the world, you'll want to read *Inspired Philanthropy*. No matter how much or little you have to give, you'll learn how to create a giving plan that will make your charitable giving catalytic and align your giving with your deepest values-to help bring about the very changes you want.

"*Inspired Philanthropy* lets us in on the secret that giving money for social change is the most rewarding form of investment. Whether you have a few hundred or a few million dollars, this workbook will help you give it effectively."

—*Gloria Steinem, consulting editor,* Ms. Magazine, *writer, activist*

Paperback ISBN: 0-7879-6410-7

Fundraising for Social Change
4TH EDITION
Kim Klein

This classic how-to fundraising text teaches you what you need to know to raise money from individuals. Learn how to set fundraising goals based on realistic budgets; write successful direct mail appeals; produce special events; and raise money from major gifts, planned giving, capital campaigns, and more.

Paperback ISBN: 0-7879-6174-4

Making Policy, Making Change
How Communities are Taking Law into Their Own Hands
Makani N. Themba

"A much-needed life jacket for those committed to progressive social change. In a straightforward, full-blast recitation from one who knows, Makani Themba weaves powerful stories of grassroots struggles to shape and construct policy. This book is a requiem for apathy and inaction."

—*Clarence Lusane, assistant professor, School of International Service, American University*

Paperback ISBN: 0-7879-6179-5

TO ORDER, CALL **(800) 956-7739** OR VISIT US AT **www.josseybass.com/go/chardonpress**

Ask and You Shall Receive:

A Fundraising Training Program for Religious Organizations and Projects

Kim Klein

Fundraising expert Kim Klein has trained thousands of groups and individuals to cultivate assets that make good works possible. *The Ask and You Shall Receive* training package is a do-it-yourself, start-to-finish program on jumpstarting fundraising efforts. Realistic time allowances keep the training within reach of busy volunteers.

Paperback   ISBN: 0-7879-5563-9
(Includes 1 Leader's Guide and 1 Workbook)

Selling Social Change (Without Selling Out):

Earned Income Strategies for Nonprofits

Andy Robinson

Expert fundraising trainer and consultant Andy Robinson shows you how to initiate and sustain successful earned income ventures that not only provide you with greater financial security but also advance your organization's mission. Robinson's accessible and lively style guides you through the step-by-step process of organizing a team, selecting a venture, drafting a business plan, finding start-up funding, and successfully marketing goods and services.

Chapters include critical information on the tax implications of earned income and the pros and cons of corporate partnerships and when to consider outsourcing, collaborating with competitors, and securing second-stage financing.

Paperback   ISBN: 0-7879-6216-3

Fundraising for the Long Haul

New companion to Fundraising for Social Change

Kim Klein

"An extraordinarily useful book. Kim Klein deserves much of the credit for having defined and developed the field of contemporary grassroots fundraising."

—*Fred Goff, president, The DataCenter*

In this companion to her classic, Fundraising for Social Change, Kim Klein distills her 25 years of experience and wisdom to provide the practical guidance for sustaining a long-term commitment to social change for organizations that are understaffed and under-resourced.

Paperback   ISBN: 0-7879-6173-6

Grassroots Grants:

An Activist's Guide to Proposal Writing

FIRST EDITION

Andy Robinson

Andy Robinson describes just what it takes to win grants, including how grants fit into your complete fund raising program. He covers using your grant proposal as an organizing plan, designing fundable projects, building your proposal piece by piece, and more.

Paperback   ISBN: 0-7879-6177-9

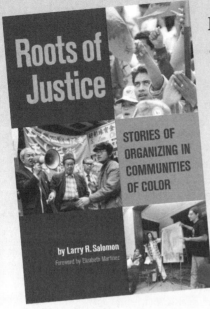

Roots of Justice:

Stories of Organizing in Communities of Color

Larry R. Salomon

Roots of Justice recaptures some of the nearly forgotten histories of communities of color. These are the stories of people who fought back against exploitation and injustice—and won. From the Zoot Suiters who refused to put up with abuse at the hands of the Navy to the women who organized the welfare rights movement of the 1970s, this book shows how ordinary people have made extraordinary contributions to change society.

Paperback   ISBN: 0-7879-6178-7

"I Never Run Off the Track"
Organizing the Underground Railroad

"Ang Laka Ay Nasa Pagkakaisa"
Strength is in the Union": Filipino Farmworkers Organize in the1930s

The "Zoot Suit Riots"
Pachucos vs. the Navy

"It's Our Union Too"
Chicanas Rescue the "Salt of the Earth" Strike

Affirmative Action from the Grassroots
Black Americans Demand Jobs in San Francisco

"Stand on a Street and Bounce a Ball"
Organizing the Mississippi Freedom Democratic Party

Unafraid and Dignified
Welfare Recipients Organize for their Rights

"No Evictions: We Won't Move!"
The Struggle to Save the I-Hotel

"You Are Now on Indian Land"
Native Americans Occupy Alcatraz

Participation with Power
Parents Fight for Community Control of New York City Schools

Back to the Blanket
The Trail of Broken Treaties Marches on Washington

"Justice, Not Sympathy"
Japanese Americans Fight for Dignity and Reparations